REPUTATIONS

LOUIS XVI
The Silent King

John Hardman

A member of the Hodder Headline Group
LONDON
Co-published in the United States of America by
Oxford University Press Inc., New York

To my sister Jane
and to Harry, David and
John Procter

First published in Great Britain in 2000 by
Arnold, a member of the Hodder Headline Group,
338 Euston Road, London NW1 3BH

http://www.arnoldpublishers.com

Co-published in the United States of America by
Oxford University Press Inc.,
198 Madison Avenue, New York, NY10016

© 2000 John Hardman

British Library Cataloguing in Publication Data
A catalogue record for this book is available from the British Library

Library of Congress Cataloging-in-Publication Data
A catalog record for this book is available from the Library of Congress

ISBN 0 340 70649 X (hb)
ISBN 0 340 70650 3 (pb)

1 2 3 4 5 6 7 8 9 10

Production Editor: Anke Ueberberg
Production Controller: Fiona Byrne
Cover Design: Terry Griffiths

Typeset in 10 on 12 pt Sabon by Phoenix Photosetting, Chatham, Kent
Printed and bound in Great Britain by MPG Books, Bodmin, Cornwall

What do you think about this book? Or any other Arnold title?
Please send your comments to feedback.arnold@hodder.co.uk

Contents

'A hundred people have attempted to define Louis XVI and a hundred have failed.'

M. Mortimer-Ternaux, 1863

General editorial preface

Hero or villain? Charlatan or true prophet? Sinner or saint? The volumes in the Reputations series examine the reputations of some of history's most conspicuous, powerful and influential individuals, considering a range of representations, some of striking incompatibility. The aim is not merely to demonstrate that history is indeed, in Pieter Geyl's phrase, 'argument without end' but that the study even of contradictory conceptions can be fruitful: that the jettisoning of one thesis or presentation leaves behind something of value.

In Iago's self-serving denunciation of it, reputation is 'an idle and most false imposition; oft got without merit, and lost without deserving', but a more generous definition would allow its use as one of the principal currencies of historical understanding. In seeking to analyse the cultivation, creation, and deconstruction of reputation we can understand better the well-springs of action, the workings out of competing claims to power, the different purposes of rival ideologies – in short, see more clearly ways in which the past becomes History.

There is a commitment in each volume to showing how understanding of an individual develops (sometimes in uneven and divergent ways), whether in response to fresh evidence, the emergence or waning of dominant ideologies, changing attitudes and preoccupations of the age in which an author writes, or the creation of new historical paradigms. Will Hitler ever seem *quite* the same after the evidence of a recent study revealing the extent of his Jewish connections during the Vienna years? Reassessment of Lenin and Stalin has been given fresh impetus by the collapse of the Soviet Union and the opening of many of its archives; and the end of the Cold War and of its attendant assumptions must alter our views of Eisenhower and Kennedy. How will our

perceptions of Elizabeth I change in the presence of a new aware-
ness of 'gendered history'?

There is more to the series than illumination of ways in which
recent discoveries or trends have refashioned identities or given
actions new meaning – though that is an important part. The
corresponding aim is to provide readers with a strong sense of the
channels and course of debate from the outset: not a Cook's Tour
of the historiography, but identification of the key interpretative
issues and guidance as to how commentators of different eras
and persuasions have tackled them.

Preface

The major problem in writing a book on the reputation of Louis XVI is the near consensus of historians concerning the king. He was inert, mentally and physically, acutely and chronically indecisive and he preferred mechanical pursuits such as locksmithing and hunting to affairs of state. But he was kindly, a good family man – in short, he was ideally suited to a private station in life. The Revolution, which he neither comprehended nor accepted, revealed a new, and surprising, characteristic: duplicity. He went through the motions of being a constitutional monarch but all the time planned the forcible restoration of the *ancien régime*, first with his own troops, and then, when the storming of the Bastille ended that possibility, with the aid of the foreign troops of his brother-in-law the Holy Roman Emperor and the king of Prussia. Thus a final element was added to the indictment: treason. All this morally justified his execution in January 1793, even if his trial did not srictly conform to the rule of law. Despite a disastrous life, however, he made a good death, fortified by the very religion which had made it impossible for him to come to terms with the Revolution.

A tale briefly told, and with very little variety, by the major historians of the French Marxist/neo-Jacobin school which dominated the first half of the twentieth century: Albert Mathiez, Georges Lefebvre, Albert Soboul. Their revisionist critic François Furet is at one with them at least on this point. English 'revisionist' historians, such as W. Doyle and T. C. W. Blanning, come to similar conclusions. They may all be right, though I differ from them on several major issues, notably the interpretation of the king's escape from Paris in 1791, the so-called 'flight to Varennes'. That is not, however, the immediate point, which is that a book following the mainstream would, if representative, be short, unvaried and dull.

I have therefore decided to make my selection mainly with a view to variety. And to give each stage of Louis's story to those historians who offer the most insights. So his youth and education are told by Mme Girault de Coursac, who has conducted pioneering work in this field. She goes furthest in seeking to rehabilitate Louis's reputation, arguing at times that he was a genius and a saint! For the early part of the reign, the baton is taken up by two historians: J.-L. Soulavie, writing in 1800, and Peter Burley, writing in 1981. Soulavie had the unique advantage of access to Louis's papers before they were dispersed. He also had a highly original mind, if one tainted by the conspiracy theories common to those who had lived through the Revolution. Burley looks at the personal input of the young king into the early reforms and speaks of a distinctive Louis-seizième monarchy. For foreign policy, the chief task of kings, the story is told by Soulavie again, who praises Louis for standing up to Austria, the country of his wife's family, and by the great nineteenth-century diplomatic historian Albert Sorel, who offers the thesis that Louis's foreign policy was effective because there was a consensus about its guidelines so that Louis's common sense was not here vitiated by his weakness of will.

At his trial, Louis was held responsible for his conduct during but not before the Revolution. As such, Louis's role in summoning troops in 1789, fleeing Paris in 1791 and the declaration of war against Austria in 1792 are doubly controversial. Paul and Pierrette Girault de Coursac in their comprehensive *Enquête* (Investigation) systematically examine each of the accusations made against Louis. Naturally the king is triumphantly vindicated. Whether or not one agrees with their conclusions (some of which are eccentric to say the least) they provide a corpus of new evidence to discuss.

The great republican, anti-clerical historian Jules Michelet is used extensively throughout because his final condemnation of Louis is reluctant and his insights seem as it were generated by his magnificent prose.

Apart from assuming the general role of referee, I have myself taken up the baton at key points in Louis's history which have remained obscure: notably his role in the war of American Independence and the 1787 Assembly of Notables, where new evidence has become available, and the flight to Varennes. I have also made a systematic analysis of the marginal notes Louis wrote on various memoranda submitted to him and published by Soulavie, in an attempt to reconstruct the king's political thought for the light it throws on the crisis of 1788–89.

I should like to thank Mrs Esther Procter and Dr Doris Sauermann-Westwood for their help.

John Hardman

French kings from Louis XIV

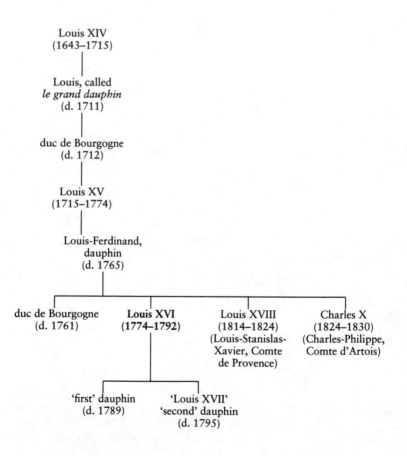

Louis XIV
(1643–1715)

Louis, called
le grand dauphin
(d. 1711)

duc de Bourgogne
(d. 1712)

Louis XV
(1715–1774)

Louis-Ferdinand,
dauphin
(d. 1765)

duc de Bourgogne
(d. 1761)

**Louis XVI
(1774–1792)**

Louis XVIII
(1814–1824)
(Louis-Stanislas-
Xavier, Comte
de Provence)

Charles X
(1824–1830)
(Charles-Philippe,
Comte d'Artois)

'first' dauphin
(d. 1789)

'Louis XVII'
'second' dauphin
(d. 1795)

Introduction

The many faces of Louis XVI

J.-L. Soulavie, Louis XVI's early historian, lists eight different titles, official or unofficial, by which his subject was known at the various stages of his 39-year life:

> Louis XVI had heard himself successively called by various names, the first of which in his infancy, was that of *duc de Berry*.
> On the (premature) death of his father, *dauphin of France*.
> On the death of Louis XV (his grandfather) *King of France and Navarre*.
> Before the Revolution, *Louis the beneficent*.
> In the month of August 1789, by the decree of the constituent assembly, *Restorer of French liberty*.
> By the constitution of 1791, *King of the French*.
> By the minority of the legislative assembly in the month of June 1792, *Monsieur Veto*.
> in the month of August of the same year, *Louis Capet, Louis the traitor*, and *Louis the last*.[1]

We can narrow the selection down to two or three. The first was Louis XVI, by the grace of God, King of France and Navarre and by the gift of the Pope, Rex Christianissimus, the most Christian king – a theoretically 'absolute' monarch. This Louis ascended the throne in 1774 at the age of 19 in succession to his grandfather, Louis XV. The second Louis was King of the French in virtue of the constitution, though that document wished, incongruously, to retain the hereditary succession also. The constitution was known as the Constitution of 1791, the date when it had been completed by the National Assembly and accepted by the king. However, in practice, the king had ceased to be an absolute monarch sometime before, arguably as early as 1787 when his reform programme was rejected by the Assembly of Notables and his freedom to appoint and dismiss ministers was challenged.

There was also, briefly, a third Louis who had no title at all, being merely addressed mockingly as Louis Capet. Louis objected to this: 'I am not called Capet,' he told the mayor of Paris, 'it is the name of one of my ancestors' – Hughes Capet, elected King of France in 987.[2] This third Louis existed between the fall of the monarchy on 10 August 1792 and his execution on 21 January 1793. The shortest period, it has nevertheless left the most abiding impression on the national psyche of France, even though Louis's role was mostly passive, in prison, on trial and on the scaffold. And this final phase has contributed the most to Louis's posthumous reputation, both positive and negative. Louis's defenders point to his courage and the Christ-like qualities which to their minds he displayed. And they see his trial as rather that of the French Revolution than of the king; as the prototype of the political trials which were to stain its republican phase. His detractors, even when accepting the limitations of the political trial, argue that however silly the actual charges against Louis, 'conspiring against liberty' and the like, nevertheless he did betray France and the constitution which he had sworn to uphold.

The impact of this final phase on Louis's reputation is the harder to explain because he spent most of it in almost total seclusion in prison in the Temple, leaving it only three times: twice to appear at his own trial (which was thus largely conducted *in absentia*) and the third time to the place of execution. He reached this not in a tumbril but in a closed carriage, which denied David the opportunity to draw a thumbnail sketch as he did for Marie-Antoinette later that year. Thousands watched his execution, including almost the entire armed force of Paris, but his last words were mostly muffled by a drum roll which explains the total variance between the many versions of them.

In respect of its seclusion, Louis's life as Louis Capet or *Louis-le-dernier*, was similar to his life as an absolute monarch at Versailles. At Versailles Louis was surrounded by a numerous court but access to him was strictly regulated and many topics of conversation, notably politics, were taboo. Until 1780 Louis's chief minister, Maurepas, would not even allow the other ministers to talk to the king except in Maurepas's presence. Such control became the hallmark of a prime minister. So very few people 'knew' Louis, which gave rise, since he was necessarily the centre of attention, to much speculation, many myths and apocryphal sayings, which have formed the basis of many books about him. To some extent all monarchs are inaccessible but they usually reach their historians through their surviving letters. Indeed some of them wrote so much that the exercise may be said to be a compensation for their seclusion. Frederick the Great, Napoleon and Queen Victoria spring to mind as voluminous correspondents.

However, very few letters indeed survive from Louis XVI, at least for the period before the Revolution – until very recently fewer than 50 were known and many of these of dubious authenticity. That, his detractors proclaimed, is because he spent his time hunting, locksmithing and watching arrivals and departures from Versailles through the telescope he installed in a turret above his private apartments. Affairs of state bored him, when he could understand them. Then in the 1990s the descendant of Louis's foreign secretary, the comte de Vergennes, made available to a few scholars 171 letters from Louis to his ancestor and in 1998 authorized their publication;[3] 171 letters is not a lot by which to judge a man and it is clear from their pattern that they are merely the tip of an iceberg consisting of some 1000. Moreover their subject matter is restricted – largely but not entirely to foreign policy as one would expect from the duties of the recipient; but foreign policy was also the *métier* of a king, the matter which occupied most of his time, and above all the letters allow us to grasp the general contours of the king's mind and character, his sense of humour, his turn of phrase.

It will be objected that these contours were already perfectly clear from the post-Versailles period of Louis's existence. During the period of the Revolution, Louis wrote hundreds of letters, made dozens of speeches and doubtless patted innumerable babies on the head at this dawning of modern politics. But there are two problems here. Louis did not regard himself as 'free' during this period. In the physical sense this is obvious: he had been forcibly removed from Versailles and installed in the Tuileries, so that he called his palace his prison. But at a deeper level Louis did not feel free to express himself about the burning issues of the day: the role of the monarchy and of the clergy; the abolition of feudalism and of the nobility; foreign policy and finance, his two fields of special expertise. He hedged his words and this was at the heart of the reputation for duplicity which he rapidly acquired.

The second problem in projecting the Louis of the Revolution back on to the screen of the *ancien régime* is that the two were not the same. It is not just that one was a constitutional and the other an absolute monarch but that Louis's character changed at the same time as and in consequence of the destruction of his authority. The turning point was the defeat of Calonne's reform programme by the Notables. Louis gave his personal backing to this programme and, as the Austrian ambassador wrote, Calonne's plans had been 'so openly approved by the king, that he had scarcely left himself any way of disowning him'.[4] Yet he was forced to dismiss the man who still retained his confidence and this led I believe to what we would call today a 'nervous breakdown' from which he never fully recovered.

It is notoriously difficult to make medical diagnoses of historical personages: physical ones are hard enough, mental ones well nigh impossible. However, Louis would seem to exhibit several features of clinical depression, such as apathy – 'talking about his own affairs as if they were those of the Emperor of China', as one minister put it.[5] After Calonne's fall, Louis increased his hunting dramatically and consumed such immoderate amounts of food and drink on his return that, according to the Austrian amabassador, 'there were occasional lapses of reason and a kind of brusque thoughtlessness which is very hard for those who have to endure it'.[6] In the summer of 1792 the governess of the royal children noted that he did not speak to anyone for 10 whole days except to articulate the moves of backgammon, which he played with his sister, Elisabeth. And on seeing his son he asked who the boy was.

So many characteristics, good and bad, which it has been assumed Louis possessed from the start – dependence on Marie-Antoinette, apathy, kindness, sentimentality – probably date from 1787 onwards. It is easy to demonstrate, for example, that Louis rigidly excluded Marie-Antoinette from all aspects of policy-making in the earlier period. The earlier Louis is crisp, trenchant, assured, judgemental, at times brusque.

PART
I

LOUIS XVI AND THE
ANCIEN RÉGIME

|1|

Inheritance

The crust of the *ancien régime* was thin: the kings walked on a volcano; sometimes it erupted as in the civil war known as the Fronde (1648–53) when the boy-king Louis XIV was forced to flee Paris, as Louis XVI attempted in 1791; sometimes it smouldered and smoked as during Louis XV's struggles with the *parlements* from the 1730s, until his chancellor, Maupeou, put a cap on it in 1771 by replacing the Parlement of Paris. The problem was one of consent, and in particular consent to taxation. Not democratic consent to the acts of government but the consent of those asked to contribute to financing them, the consent of those in a position to refuse – either by tax evasion, overawing the king's local agents or concerting opposition through the *parlements*. Such people formed the nobility since anyone with a certain level of wealth could purchase nobility and, such was the social climate, everyone who could, did.

I define the *ancien régime* as a political rather than a social system and, unlike the feudal society it ruled, a relatively recent one – roughly coterminous with the Bourbon branch of the Capetian dynasty, founded by Henri IV in 1589. Its hallmark was the abeyance of the central representative institution of France, the Estates-General, which did not meet between 1614 and 1789. This meant that the Bourbon kings were 'absolute' in the sense of possessing legislative self-sufficiency (their own definition of the term), and a number of political thinkers from Bodin to Bossuet gave a theoretical basis to this royal *souveraineté*, as they termed it, grounded on practical and theological arguments. In this ideal world, the kings were free to sit at their magnificent ormolu-mounted desks and concentrate their attention on eradicating heresy at home and developing their *gloire* abroad through a successful foreign policy. Politics, as we conceive it, did not in theory exist and *la politique* is translated as 'foreign policy' – the principal *métier* of the kings.

In practice politics was very much alive, except perhaps during the majority of Louis XIV (1653–1715), and was located in the 13 appeal courts known as *parlements*, of which that of Paris, *the* Parlement, was easily the most important. Apart from their appellate functions, the *parlements* registered the king's legislation but there was a difference of opinion as to what that involved. Crown lawyers argued that registration was necessary only to show that the king was speaking *ex cathedra*, a formal promulgation. *Parlementaires* argued that registration involved 'verifying' whether the proposed legislation was in conformity with natural justice and the unwritten constitution or Fundamental Laws of the kingdom. If they thought it was not they could 'remonstrate' and though the king could override this by enforcing his legislation personally in a *lit de justice* this created a bad impression and made it more difficult to implement the legislation, particularly if it was for a loan or a tax. A *lit de justice* seemed to legitimate tax evasion.

At first sight it might seem that the kings' two preoccupations – religious uniformity and the conduct of foreign policy – were outside the scope of *parlementaire* interference. However, the Jansenists, a Catholic sect which believed in predestination, and which the Pope had condemned as heretical in the Bull *Unigenitus* of 1711, had many adherents in the Parlement. They put so much pressure on Louis XV that in 1764 he was forced, reluctantly, to expel from France the Jesuits, regarded as the spearhead of the assault on the Jansenists. The Jansenists are sometimes dubbed 'Catholic Calvinists' and the connection between Calvinist and republican thought was not lost on contemporaries or on historians – Louis XV called the *parlements* republicans.

The *parlements* did not go so far as to criticize the king's conduct of foreign policy or military strategy – defective though this often was – in the wars with which the Bourbon era was strewn. But they undermined the sinews of war by questioning the level of taxation the king thought necessary to finance them. Continuous warfare was a function of an aristocratic society which was trained for nothing else. However, it was not land wars which strained the financial system of the *ancien régime* to breaking point but naval wars. These required not only the recurrent expenditure on men but the capital outlay on ships; indeed since ships only lasted 12 years and had to be extensively overhauled after a year's campaigning, this can be viewed as additional current expenditure. A strong navy was not really a luxury, since France had a coastline longer than her land frontiers and was engaged in a competition for empire with England throughout the reigns of Louis XV and Louis XVI.

However, there was not general support in the country for naval expansion. It seemed to lead to a two-speed economy with the great mercantile centres such as Bordeaux and Marseille thriving and the rest of the country stagnating. And yet the economically more developed areas, such as Bordeaux, often offered greater resistance to the central government. The military aristocracy, for whom a naval career was a minority taste confined to those from coastal regions, lamented the fact that there was no land war between 1763 and the end of the *ancien régime*. And in the past such periods had also been ones of internal unrest – Louis XVI's minister Malesherbes even wrote a pamphlet suggesting ways in which the nobility could occupy themselves in peacetime. In particular the *parlements*, whose members were lawyers not soldiers, though noble, did not identify with colonial expansion in the way that the English parliament did, in which the merchant interest was strong. In England the beneficiaries of war were asked to finance it. In France it was administratively and, given current physiocratic economic ideas, ideologically difficult to make the towns pay for the wars from which they benefited.

And this was the cardinal weakness of absolutism: that it did not yield sufficient funds to carry out successfully its principal task – the conduct of foreign policy and its continuation by war. So that defeat in the Seven Years' War (1756–63), when France surrendered control of North America and India to England, amounted to defeat in the monarchy's own terms. On the other hand the English kings, through surrendering the power of the purse to Parliament, were showered with guineas from that same purse. Also, and perhaps even more important, because the debt was national not just royal, the rate of interest they had to pay on it was 2 per cent less than the Bourbons had to pay. This was the problem which faced Louis XVI. He did not want, at least until 1788, to surrender his absolute power and yet he wanted a more efficient and fairer system of taxation to finance his foreign policy. His attempt to square the circle involved what he called in 1787 'simulated consent' to taxation through regional assemblies.[1]

The often successful resistance of the *parlements* to the kings' demands cannot be explained in terms of legitimacy. They had nothing in common with their English namesake; they were not elected and they represented only the king who appointed them (though in practice their offices had become hereditary). Their power derived partly from the king's choice to preserve them as a screen to cloak accusations of 'despotism', accusations which were levelled when he replaced the Parlement in 1771. Also they became a surrogate democracy for the disenfranchised – that is all Frenchmen save the king: the moment the Estates-General met in 1789 their power evaporated. They also had practical weapons at their disposal: they could refuse to carry out their primary, judicial functions, a strike which quickly brought such a litigious society as eighteenth-century France to its knees. They could also arrest royal officials for implementing legislation which they considered had not been properly registered.

The royal government alternated between bullying the *parlements* (by arrest, internal exile, replacement) – which risked the accusation of despotism, and caving into them – which led to paralysis. The personal inclinations of the Bourbons – Louis XV (reigned 1715–74), his son the dauphin (1728–65) and his son Louis XVI (reigned 1774–92) – were to take a hard line with the *parlements*: Louis XVI detested them so much that his facial muscles moved in strange directions when they were mentioned. However, the governments of Louis XV often appeased them, particularly during the dominance of the duc de Choiseul, 1758–70, minister for war and foreign affairs. As we have seen, the Jesuits were sacrificed to the *parlements'* rage in 1764.

The expulsion of the Jesuits caused not just a rift between the dauphin, father of Louis XVI, and Choiseul, but a coolness between the dauphin and his father the king. It was not just the sacrifice of the Jesuits to heretical elements in the Parlement which offended the dauphin, but the sacrifice of royal authority also. Indeed the two were linked: traditional kingship derived its sanction from traditional religion, and the regime suffered ideological damage from the expulsion of the Jesuits.

There was also disagreement about the conduct of foreign policy. Not just the ridiculous claim of the dauphin – fat, lethargic, determined hater of all exercise – to lead the French armies in person, but the dauphin's belief that the Austrian alliance, the cornerstone of Choiseul's diplomatic system, was misguided. The Austrian Habsburgs had been for over two hundred years the hereditary enemies of France. But it was argued that this rivalry was superannuated given that both France and Austria now had more deadly enemies than each other in the shape of England and Prussia respectively.

This led to the 'diplomatic revolution' of 1756 which carried France and Austria as allies into the Seven Years' War. However, it was felt that France had made a disproportionate contribution, both in terms of men and money, to the war effort and that this had led to the losses overseas and also the crushing defeat at Rossbach which was comparable to the defeat at Agincourt. These defeats, which clouded Louis XVI's adolescence, determined him never to risk a war on two fronts again. This objective was complicated by his marriage to the Austrian archduchess Maria Antonia in 1770, arranged by Choiseul as the fruit of the new diplomatic system. For her Austrian relatives, her mother Maria Theresa and her brother Joseph II, ruthlessly exploited her as a tool and extension of their foreign policy.

Choiseul used the period of *entente* with the Parlement – symbolized by the appointment of the *parlementaire* Jansenist L'Averdy as controller-general of finances – to expand the navy in readiness for a war of revenge against England. The Parlement let the king have money provided it was on their terms. Whenever a controller-general sought to introduce a land survey (*cadastre*) to end tax evasion by the nobility, they made a dead-set at him with the full armoury at their disposal, especially the judicial strike. In this way Bertin had been driven out of office and replaced by L'Averdy in 1763. So in the short term, peace with the *parlements* facilitated a forward foreign policy, as tinkering with the bore of an existing engine will yield a little extra power. The *parlementaires* would grant additional taxation, provided it was collected according to the old rolls, which treated them lightly as individuals.

Louis XV ground his teeth in silence until the end of 1770 when he suddenly dismissed Choiseul for seeking to involve France in war with England over its dispute with France's ally Spain concerning possession of the Falkland Islands. Louis XV would be termed today a pacifist. He also realized that war would still further increase his dependence on the *parlements*. Indeed the dismissal of Choiseul led directly to Maupeou's first disciplining the Parlement and then in April 1771 replacing it by a puppet body, dubbed the 'Parlement Maupeou'. On the former occasion, the future Louis XVI, then aged 16 and the new dauphin after his father's death in 1765, publicly congratulated the chancellor on 'having put the crown back on the king's head'. He wrote on his copy of the disciplinary edict, 'that is the correct public law; I am absolutely delighted with M. le chancelier'.[2]

The Parlement had been suppressed with an ease – it was a bloodless coup – which made some tremble for French liberties, though others such as Voltaire welcomed the demise of obscurantist oligarchs, the persecutors of the Protestant merchant Calas, broken on the wheel on suspicion that he had murdered his own son to prevent him from converting to Catholicism. At first litigants boycotted the new Parlement but mainly one suspects because they feared reprisals if the king weakened and the notoriously vengeful old Parlement were restored. By the time of Louis XV's sudden death in 1774 the new system seemed to be bedding down. It had allowed the new controller-general, the abbé Terray, forcibly to reduce the rate of interest on the royal debt (a process which was termed a 'bankruptcy') and to institute a parish by parish investigation of tax evasion of the *vingtième* tax by the nobility. Though this raised revenue by 50 per cent, it was slow work and by the time the process was abandoned in 1781 only a quarter of the country had been covered.

With so much on his plate at home, Louis XV pursued a negative foreign policy. In particular he had to stand by whilst Russia, Prussia and his nominal ally Austria accomplished the first partition of France's historic ally Poland in 1772. This was a bitter personal blow to the king since he had constructed around Poland a secret (that is secret from his ministers) foreign policy designed to limit France's dependence on Austria. Also, to save money, France's navy was run down to the point that on Louis XVI's accession there was only a single French battleship at sea! By 1774 Terray had increased annual revenue by about 80,000,000 livres and reduced the annual deficit to 25,000,000 or less (there were 24 livres to the pound sterling). Marcel Marion, the historian of *ancien régime* finances, considered that Terray prolonged the life of the *ancien régime* by a generation – but at the price of abandoning the foreign policy which was the *raison d'être* of the kings.

|2|

The education of a king

Louis XVI was born in 1754, the third but eldest surviving son of
the dauphin Louis-Ferdinand, only son of Louis XV (1715–74)
and Marie-Josèphe, daughter of Augustus III, Elector of Saxony
and King of Poland. Both Louis's parents died young, his father
in 1765 and his mother in 1767, both of tuberculosis. They lived
long enough, however, to instil in their son a respect for
traditional values and orthodox Catholicism, distrust of the new
intellectual currents of the Enlightenment (which stressed reason
at the expense of revealed religion) and belief in the absolute
monarchy transmitted by Louis XIV – values summed up by the
phrase *le parti dévot* for the court faction they headed: the French
word having a suggestion of bigotry as well as devoutness.
Louis's parents were able to exercise their influence on their
children even beyond the grave through their choice of the *dévot*
duc de la Vauguyon to be their governor, and through the various
preceptors and tutors who performed the actual educative task
under his supervision.

We know a fair amount about the education of Louis XVI
thanks to a pioneering study by Mme P. Girault de Coursac,
L'Education d'un roi: Louis XVI, published in 1972. This was
the first in an ambitious series of works in which she sought to
rehabilitate the king; works which cover his trial, his relations
with Marie-Antoinette, the flight to Varennes, La Pérouse's
expedition to the South Seas and *Auto-portrait*, a selection of his
writings. We shall have occasion to return to some of these in our
assessment of Louis's reputation since they constitute the most
systematic scholarly attempt at rehabilitation. We will start however with François Furet's revision of Mme de Coursac's radically
revising account of Louis's education. La Vauguyon's, according
to Furet:

was a serious programme, with an industrious pupil, but perhaps neither deserves the excessive praise which white-washing historiography has sought to shower on them. There were few innovations in the subject matter: the basis of the lessons and 'discussions' drawn up for the instruction of the future king remained a mixture of religion, morality and the humanities . . . .

As far as the pupil is concerned, his work manifests a docile and unimaginative way of thinking, reflecting only what he was being taught. His style, sometimes elegant, is more interesting than his thoughts, which are always banal; in these pastorals on paternal monarchy, superficial commentaries on Fénelon . . . and Bossuet, the future king learned neither to conduct a reasoned argument nor to govern a state.[1]

Furet's general verdict on Louis's reign is in keeping:

It is easy to see how historians have been able to turn this really very average man into a hero, an incompetent, a martyr or a culprit: this honourable king with his simple nature, ill-adapted to the role he had to assume and the history which awaited him, can equally well inspire emotion at the unfairness of fate or an indictment against his lack of foresight as a sovereign. Where personal qualities were concerned, Louis was not the ideal monarch to personify the twilight of royalty in the history of France; he was too serious, too faithful to his duties, too thrifty, too chaste and, in his final hour, too courageous.[2]

Furet, the debunker of Marxist or as he calls them neo-Jacobin myths about the Revolution, nevertheless insists on restoring the traditional picture of Louis. But there are specific errors in his analysis. Louis's style was not elegant, it was clumsy; for example he avoids constructions using the word 'dont' and ties himself in knots with substitutes. He was also perfectly capable of conduct-ing 'a reasoned argument', as we shall see. Louis may have been cheese-paring – quartering his notepaper to save money – but he was not 'thrifty'. In 1783, when he knew the finances to be desperate at the end of the American war, Louis bought the chateau of Rambouillet and in 1784 that of Saint-Cloud, being already in possession, apart from Versailles, of the residences of Compiègne, Fontainebleau, Choisy, La Muette and Marly.

For Mme de Coursac, on the other hand, Louis was not just a hard-working but a gifted child. She seeks the evidence for her assertions in her attempt to reconstruct the lad's homework from the publications of two of his tutors, *L'Arithmétique et la géométrie de l'officier* (1767) and *Eléments d'algèbre* (1768) by his mathematics tutor, Le Blonde, and *L'Art des expériences* (1770) by the abbé Nollet, who taught experimental physics at the Collège de Navarre. Both books are fulsomely dedicated to Louis. Le Blonde wrote in the preface to *Eléments*, 'the pleasure you found in the solution of the majority of problems contained in this book and the ease with which you grasped the key to their solution are new proofs of your intelligence and the excellence of your judgement'. Nollet claims a similar degee of understanding from the royal dedicatee. Since Le Blonde's book, published when Louis was 14, contains linear simultaneous equations, quadratic equations, the concept of real and imaginary numbers and progressions and series, and since Nollet's work, published when Louis was 16, was the textbook for his university course, Mme de Coursac's case would seem to be unanswerable: not only was Louis not dull and lazy (the generally accepted view) but he was indeed 'an exceptionally gifted and brilliant pupil, consumed by curiosity and a thirst for knowledge, for whom time spent in study flew by'.[3]

Mme de Coursac, however, does not discount the degree of flattery necessarily involved in addressing a prince. Most people like flattery, especially the young. Louis XVI's foreign secretary, Vergennes, subjected him to systematic flattery over a 13-year period, without ever being made to feel he had overstepped the mark. On one occasion Vergennes solemnly declared that if justice were banished from the earth, it would seek refuge in the king's breast. On the other hand one would have to be extraordinarily vain to be taken in by flattery which bore no relation whatsoever to the truth. One detail from Nollet's preface tallies with Louis's known practice as king: his account of how Louis during the 10 years he was taught physics (1760–70) 'liked to take the apparatus to bits and reassemble it to understand better how it worked'.[4] We also know that his brother Provence abandoned his physics lessons whilst Louis continued his.

Some objective confirmation for his ability in mathematics comes from his skill in cartography, which has always been generally acknowledged. His tutor in geography was Philippe

Buache, the leading cartographer of the day, who specialized in oceanic exploration. Louis was an adept and enthusiastic pupil: there was always a map-in-progress on Louis's table throughout his reign. As dauphin he made a splendid map of the environs of Versailles now in the Bibliothèque Nationale.[5] To make this Louis would have had to understand the mathematics behind scale and projections. Likewise some of the problems Le Blonde claimed Louis had solved concerned compound interest on loans. We know from his reign that Louis, unlike Philip II of Spain who confessed that loans and interest rates baffled him, understood these things. And was at least aware of the effects of inflation. So if Mme de Coursac's contention that Louis was 'a gifted pupil' displaying 'a stupefying precosity'[6] is not proven, he was no dunce either.

Yet the general impression at the time was that he was a dunce and it has remained that of the vast majority of Louis's historians. The major source for this impression comes from Marie-Antoinette's circle: the dauphine herself, her mother the Empress Maria Theresa and above all the Austrian ambassador to France, Mercy-Argenteau, who was charged with taking a special care over the young girl and reported regularly on her progress to her royal and imperial mother. No childish escapade is beneath the guardian's notice and Marie-Antoinette emerges as an angel trying to tame a bear, her royal husband. At the end of July 1770, we are told, Louis, then coming up to his sixteenth birthday, had suffered from indigestion after overindulging in *pâtisserie*. At supper on 2 August Marie-Antoinette 'caused all the *pâtisserie* to be removed from the table and ordered that no more be served until further orders. The dauphin [Louis] smiled and took this considerateness very well.'[7]

Two years later Marie-Antoinette heroically intervened in two quarrels between Louis and his brother the comte de Provence, one year his junior. Provence, who loved to collect bibelots, was very much attached to a porcelain figure 'very artistically modelled' which stood on his mantlepiece. Louis also liked this object which he was accustomed to handle. This made Provence nervous, fearing his clumsy brother would drop it, and on this occasion, with Marie-Antoinette chiding Provence for his fears, on cue Louis proceeded to drop it and it 'smashed into smithereens'. Provence flew at his brother and a lively scuffle ensued. Fortunately Marie-Antoinette 'had the presence of mind to separate the combatants' though she received a 'scratch on the hand' for her pains. 'A perfect reconciliation followed the quarrel which fortunately no one else had witnessed.' Marie-Antoinette told Mercy that she had nearly called for help but Mercy reassured her that she had done the right thing, since it would have damaged Provence to be seen fighting with the heir to the throne.[8]

The following August occurred the *affaire de la baguette*. Marie-Antoinette, having spent the morning 'in reading and other serious occupations' was playing piquet with her brother-in-law Provence, then 17. Louis was also present but having nothing better to do (he disliked card games) he started hitting his brother with a baguette (the form of the French loaf has not altered over the centuries). After a while Provence became angry 'and grabbed the baguette and tried to snatch it from the hands of M. le dauphin'. 'The quarrel was becoming heated but Mme la dauphine seized the baguette and broke it into pieces, thus terminating the dispute.' When Marie-Antoinette related this incident to Mercy, he advised her to 'make serious representations' to her husband and 'give him to understand the regrettable consequences which such horseplay could occasion'. Louis was contrite and promised to abstain from such conduct in future. Mercy's comment on the episode was: 'M. le dauphin has against him only the results of an excessively bad education'.[9]

Mercy's conclusion would seem to fly in the face of the evidence. Had not Louis's tutors included two university professors, an eminent geographer, and a pioneering philologist and academician, the abbé de Radonvilliers, to teach him languages? One might argue that the *dévot* circle in which Louis's father moved and which inspired his choice of tutors left Louis with an old-fashioned sense of the royal authority, with a tendency to religious bigotry and a scorn for current intellectual currents, epitomized by the *encyclopédistes*. (Though Louis actually purchased the *Encyclopédie* out of his allowance.) One might also argue that the old dauphin, La Vauguyon and the rest inspired in their royal charge a distrust of the house of Austria, as Marie-Antoinette with some justice came to believe.[10] But it would be hard to fault the intellectual calibre of the education Louis received, whether one thinks that he profited from it or not.

However, according to Mercy, it fell to Marie-Antoinette's lot to supplement by her example the deficiencies of her husband's education, a tall order given the rudimentary state of her own. In

1768, two years before she left for France, she was given a French 'reader', the abbé Vermond, to devote 'an hour a day' instructing the future dauphine about her adopted country: 'religion, the history of France ... knowledge of the great families and especially of those occupying places at court' and 'French language and orthography'. Despite his efforts, he confessed privately to Mercy in October 1769 that she still wrote 'inexpressibly slowly' and the following year she made two spelling mistakes in writing her own Christian names on her marriage contract![11]

Perhaps the Gallic air sharpened her faculties for by 1773 Mercy reported back to Maria Theresa that not only was her daughter studying hard but that by so doing she was shaming her husband the dauphin into 'emulating' her: 'he is accustoming himself to read at least for a few moments in each day, and he likes to find occasions to work in the bits of knowledge he picks up through his reading'.[12] A month later, in April 1773, Mercy writes:

> M. le dauphin ... is showing an interest in public events; he has the gazettes read to him and a few journals, and he spares a few moments in reading other works of an historical nature. This beginning of application is without contradiction down to hints from Mme la dauphine and she is rightly proud of it.[13]

Maria Theresa was not impressed, replying: 'I hope that my daughter may succeed more and more in instilling the dauphin with a taste for solid application but having none herself there is little to be hoped for from that quarter.'[14]

The Austrian material is also the source for the legend of Louis's spending all his time in hunting and mechanical pursuits, notably locksmithing. In July 1771 Mercy has Marie-Antoinette chiding him over these pastimes:

> On Monday, in the presence of ... [Provence and his wife, Marie-Antoinette] gave the dauphin a lecture on his immoderate taste for hunting, which was wrecking his health, and on the boorishness which this exercise was developing in him. M. le dauphin sought to cut short the reprimand by retiring to his apartments but the dauphine followed him and continued to berate him for his conduct. This language distressed the dauphin so much that he began to cry.[15]

Two years later, with Louis coming up to his nineteenth birthday, Mercy relates:

> All the dauphine's ascendancy over the dauphin has not yet
> sufficed to turn him from his extraordinary love of every-
> thing to do with building, such as masonry, carpentry,
> cabinet-making and related trades. He always has some
> adjustment to be made to his apartments and he joins in
> himself with the workmen to shift building materials,
> girders and pavings, devoting whole hours to this heavy
> exercise. Sometimes he comes away more exhausted than a
> workman would who was obliged to carry out this work. I
> saw the dauphine finally exasperated with such conduct.[16]

The material emanating from Marie-Antoinette and her circle
was biased and is still influential. In writing a book about Louis
XVI there is a great temptation to write one about Marie-
Antoinette instead, and many have succumbed to it. She was
livelier and better looking than her husband and her tragedy
more dramatic: compare for example the portrait painted by
Mme Vigée-Lebrun in 1784 of the blossoming mother and her
children with David's cruel sketch of her in the tumbril, hair cut
for guillotining, haggard but proud as Lucifer, her Habsburg
chin dominating her face. Then again material from her circle is
both more voluminous and more accessible than that from
Louis's: most of it was published in scholarly editions during the
second half of the nineteenth century and is readily available.
Much of the material is anecdotal and about personalities and
the sex life of Louis and Marie-Antoinette. This was non-
existent until 1777 when his brother-in-law the Emperor Joseph
II persuaded Louis to have a small operation to cut a tight
ligament which prevented him from having a proper erection.
This sort of material can be incorporated neat into popular
biographies of the royal couple which, so to speak, almost write
themselves.

But why should the Austrian information be at the expense
of Louis? Mme de Coursac falls back on the conspiracy
theories which have so plagued Revolutionary studies, as they
plagued the Revolution itself. For her the villains of the piece
are what she calls the 'Lorraine faction', that is the duc de
Choiseul, who was a Lorrainer, and Marie-Antoinette herself,
whose father had been duke of Lorraine. We have noted the
bad blood between Louis's father and Choiseul, and Louis

himself was never reconciled to Choiseul, despite Marie-Antoinette's efforts. However, Mme de Coursac goes further and asserts that Choiseul disparaged Louis 'as the heir presumptive to the Crown',[17] thus entering the realm of fantasy. Choiseul probably did favour an aristocratic and decentralized monarchy rather than the absolute one theoretically in place but there is no evidence of his having sought to undermine the institution of monarchy itself.

The reason why the Austrian material is biased is at one level simply because Mercy and Marie-Antoinette are both concerned to make a good impression on Maria Theresa, he by stressing that he is giving the dauphine good advice, she that she is taking it. At a higher level, the Austrian 'project' for Marie-Antoinette was to use her to forward the international cause of the Habsburgs. The project was put most succinctly in a letter from Mercy to Maria Theresa as Louis XV lay dying of smallpox in 1774:

> If the king should die it would be very advantageous to the 'service' [that is to the Habsburg dynasty] if Your Majesty would deign to write to Mme la dauphine that she 'should be so good as to listen to me on major matters concerning the dynastic union and the diplomatic system of the two courts'. This notice from Your Majesty, giving all the necessary weight to what I have to say, will concentrate the mind of [Marie-Antoinette], who has always been a little distanced from serious affairs. It is necessary, however, for future happiness, that she begin to seize the authority that M. le dauphin will never exercise in more than a precarious fashion. And, given the character of the people who make up this court . . . it would be highly dangerous both for the state and for the alliance should anyone whatsoever have a hold over the dauphin and that he be led by anyone but the dauphine.[18]

Unfortunately, and this is the point of the Austrians' disparagement of Louis's abilities and education, the whole bent of that education was to make him distrustful of Austria and forearmed against the attempts that would be made to make him a tool of Austria's ambition. So, in a nutshell, the Austrian circle regarded Louis's education as bad because it was anti-Austrian. Ten years after she had become queen, Marie-Antoinette still harked back to this, writing to Joseph:

M. de la Vauguyon had frightened him about the empire his wife would want to exercise over him and his black mind took a pleasure in scaring him with all the bogies invented about the house of Austria.[19]

Marie-Antoinette's circle, though the major source, was not the only one for a belief in the dauphin's inadequacies. Just after Louis XVI's accession in 1774, a fictitious Russian baron in a satire published in London recounts:

When I was in Paris, there wasn't a gentleman who spoke of M. le dauphin to his advantage: indeed everyone in France thought the same . . . a prince so sombre, so limited, promised a reign of severity in his reply to his preceptor: *I will be a severe king* – a reply which is known throughout Europe'.[20]

The uniformity of the denigration of Louis is addressed by one of the earliest defenders of his reputation, the abbé Proyart, writing in the reign of Napoleon. Louis's detractors, he relates:

spoke of the dauphin's amusements in his workshop and remained silent about his occupations in his cabinet. They said *he is making locks*: this one ill-intentioned phrase gained currency to the prejudice of the Dauphin's reputation.[21]

But why did the phrase 'gain currency'? To answer this question one has to look at Louis himself. Unlike his witty brother Provence, Louis was not blessed with verbal felicity. *Pace* Furet, his prose style is awkward. This was exacerbated by his timidity in public. Addressing the Parlement in 1775 it took him four attempts to begin his speech and his timidity stayed with him to the end of his life. He could not rouse his troops before the assault on the Tuileries on 10 August 1792 for, as Marie-Antoinette observed, 'he fears above all speaking to assembled men'.[22] He could seldom find the gracious words with which to cheer his adherents and win over his enemies. In 1782 his *valet de chambre* advised the minister for marine:

I am convinced that when you ask him [Louis] to speak to naval officers, to those you want him to praise, he does nothing of the sort . . . he is seized by timidity and when he wants to say something obliging, the words stick in his throat and with the best will in the world, nothing comes out. Try to give him a phrase ready made, he won't be offended and he'll use it'.[23]

Vergennes employed the same technique: when the commercial treaty with England was about to be signed in September 1786, Vergennes asked the king:

> to be so good as to treat Mr Eden with consideration and to let him know that he lends himself with pleasure and interest to everything which can establish friendly links and good relations between himself and the King of England and between their respective peoples.[24]

Louis's timidity was partly personal and partly institutional; Louis XV had been the same and so, to a lesser degree, had Louis XIV. The hereditary characteristics of a dynasty become a system. Mercy talks of 'the dreadful effects produced by this taciturnity, this making no effort to please, which hitherto has characterized all the actions of the royal family'.[25] One of those involved in Louis's education, the abbé Berthier, went so far as to argue that timidity is a necessary royal characteristic. Louis's confessor, the abbé Soldini, advised him in 1770: 'never let people read your mind'. And he seems to have taken this advice to heart. On 14 July of that year, Mercy-Argenteau wrote: 'His sombre and reserved character have so far rendered him impenetrable'; and on 17 December: 'one cannot predict the impressions that are made on so taciturn and evasive a prince'. This evasiveness was summed up by Provence's *bon mot* that trying to pin Louis down was like trying to hold oiled billiard balls together. If Louis XV and Louis XVI were asked an embarrassing question, they greeted the questioner with total silence – a silence which the courtiers or ministers then sought to interpret. So a defect of character in the kings was elevated into a system of government. But those who did not understand the system could come away with the impression that they were ruled by an idiot.[26]

This impression seems to be confirmed for historians by the famous diary which Louis started in 1766 and continued until the fall of the monarchy. Until the publication of his letters to Vergennes, it was the only sizeable corpus of his writings before 1789. Its format, a cross between an engagement diary and a hunting record, partly explains the banality of some of the entries in this numbing catalogue of trivial achievement, such as that for

23 December 1780 after the death of Maria Theresa: 'respects of 319 men in the morning and 256 women at six o'clock'. The format partly explains the banality, but Louis stuck to it. Over half the space is devoted to the achievements of his hunt, a minute record not just of every deer or boar but of every swallow killed, and this follows the pattern of the hunting diaries traditionally kept by the kings.

However, he also decided that it was worth making a fair copy of the list of his engagements, which explains the celebrated entry of *'rien'* for 14 July 1789, corresponding to a blank in his original schedule as the storming of the Bastille was not an official engagement.[27] Moreover he does sometimes depart from his chosen format to record personal details such as taking a bath or taking yogurt for constipation, but these are always strictly factual, and although the number of entries increases with the years – the first use of *'rien'* implying that something usually happened is 10 July 1770 – the quality of entry when he is 38 is the same as when he is 12. This meticulous record not just of every animal slaughtered but journeys made, masses celebrated, medicine taken, reveals an obsession with facts and figures, the mind of an accountant. Over a period of 20 years the diary contains only one display of feeling, or rather pique, the entry for 9 July 1786: 'The queen gave birth to my second daughter . . . there were no congratulations, no firework display and no Te Deum.'

Whatever his reflections on the events of his times, Louis does not choose to confide them to his diary. However, the abbé Proyart had sight of another 'repertory' of Louis's 'started at the very beginning of his reign' in which he recorded 'his observations on the principal events of his reign'. This 'record of his conscience, his opinions, his projects and his motives in everything he had done' would form a counterparty to the banality of the known diary. Proyart believed that the revolutionary authorities who assiduously published everything to the king's discredit, deliberately suppressed the reflective diary which, 'would have restored the monarch to the love of his subjects and the veneration of the world'. It has not resurfaced and probably never will.[28]

Maurepas, England and the sea

Jean Frédéric Phélypeaux, comte de Maurepas, was appointed minister for the marine in 1723 but in 1749 had been dismissed and exiled to his estates. Nevertheless he enjoyed the confidence of the young court centred on Louis's father. Maurepas was also a personal friend of La Vauguyon, the young princes' governor, who turned to him to provide tutors for his charges. This turned out to be a stroke of fortune for Maurepas who by placing his protégés about the future king was able to mitigate the loss of influence and contacts that internal exile was designed to bring about. This explains why Louis, on his accession to the throne in May 1774, recalled Maurepas to be his personal adviser and unofficial prime minister. Maurepas recommended tutors who would give the future king a scientific and in particular a nautical bent. Particularly influential in developing Louis's tastes were Philippe Buache and the chevalier de Fleurieu.

Maurepas had appointed Buache hydrographer in his newly formed map bureau at the ministry for the marine and, as Louis's geography tutor, he developed his interest in oceanography. Fleurieu, as *directeur-général des ports et arsenaux*, drafted the instructions for naval campaigns and Louis appointed him minister for the marine in 1791. The fruit of Louis's interest in things naval and of Maurepas's return in 1774 was, as we shall see, to be naval rearmament and a resumption of war with England which Louis XV had put behind him.

Maurepas also supplied the abbé de Radonvilliers, *de l'Académie française*, who instilled in Louis an abiding love of Latin. Radonvilliers was a philologist and he wanted to teach the princes the common features of languages but was prevented from doing this by Louis's parents. Louis was proficient in Latin and Italian, knew a little German and had a good reading knowledge of English, 'sufficient to read the London news-papers'.[29] Maurepas also occupied some of his enforced leisure in learning English.[30] Louis's mother, who censored all the princes' books, stopped the lessons in English after Provence had been caught using Anglicisms: Marie-Josèphe characterized English as 'a hateful language full of dangers'.[31] The young princes could learn Italian instead.

After his mother's death in 1767 Louis taught himself English, employing Radonvilliers's preferred method of translating passages from English into French, without bothering with the grammar. He used passages from David Hume's *History of England*, from the *Spectator* and the first five volumes of Gibbon's *Decline and Fall of the Roman Empire*, but his major enterprise was a translation of Horace Walpole's *Historic Doubts on the Life and Reign of King Richard III*, which had been published in 1768, when Louis was 14. Curiously, he returned to this translation when he was imprisoned in the Temple in 1792 and his work was published posthumously in 1800. It has been said of this production that Louis 'appears to have entered so thoroughly into the English mind that his turns of phrase have been severely criticized by French purists'.[32] He employed such Anglicisms as 'improbable' and 'inquestionable'. He also, during his reign, referred to (French) cabinet 'committés' rather than '*comités*'.

Louis became fascinated not only by the English langauge but by its history and political institutions. He took Hansard and continued during his reign to read the debates in both Houses of Parliament. During the Revolution he would read English journals during sessions of the council of ministers and if the ministers wanted any English material translated, they turned to the king. Was this anything more than a party trick? It is hard to be sure, but I would suggest two things. First, that Louis had a love-hate relationship with England: despite his fascination with England and its naval traditions – James Cook was an early hero and he based his instructions to La Pérouse on Cook's remit – England was nevertheless, as he told his uncle Charles III of Spain, 'the natural and hereditary enemy of our House'.[33] Second, Louis's interest in English history and politics may have stemmed from a realization that the institutions of the two regimes were converging – the use of 'committé' may be a small indication of this. According to his finance minister, Necker, Louis was hostile to introducing elements of the English political system into France, only changing his mind 'when it was too late'.[34] Louis's interest in English history also had a certain morbidity since his favourite passage was Hume's account of the reign of Charles I, Louis's direct ancestor, which he read and reread to avoid the mistakes committed by that unfortunate monarch.

Such was the youth who on 10 May 1774 succeeded his grand-father, Louis XV, who had died of smallpox, unlamented and in great pain, which many thought was deserved. Soulavie remembered a king sequestered in a harem with no grip on government. Michelet considered that the damage Louis XV had done the monarchy was irreparable. The monarchy he bequeathed is sometimes called the administrative monarchy.

And France was well administered thanks to the efforts of the service nobility which the Bourbons had raised from the bourgeosie and in which Louis XVI was to glory.

If no more than directing an administration was required of a king, then Louis XVI was well qualified to perform the task. His cast of mind was suited to regulating the complex but also concrete financial and judicial matters which lay at the heart of the administrative monarchy. That the abbé de la Ville had turned him into an expert diplomatist is also clear from the very first letters of his reign to his personally selected foreign secretary, the comte de Vergennes.

However, there were new ideas, intellectual and political, infecting old wounds opened by Louis XV's destruction of the Parlement. As the philosopher-minister Malesherbes observed, if Louis XVI and Charles I of England had reigned at a time when the respective rights of monarch and nation had been fixed they would both have had glorious reigns but neither was equipped for managing the transition.

|3|

1774

A *new monarch – and a new monarchy?*

Louis: 'the Cassandra of the nation'

Jean-Louis Soulavie, 1752–1813, was something of a polymath. He was a pioneer in the field of geology, writing about the unusual rock formations in his native Ardèche mountains; having embraced holy orders during the *ancien régime*, he unfrocked himself and married during the Revolution, and in the republic he pursued a diplomatic career culminating in the post of French resident at Geneva 1793–94; he was an ardent Robespierrist and four of his letters to the 'incorruptible' were found in the latter's papers. At all times and in all regimes, however, he pursued his principal interest as an historian.

Soulavie, who published his six-volume *Mémoires historiques et politiques du règne de Louis XVI* in 1801, was better placed than any historian before or since to write about Louis XVI. For, as the semi-official historian of the Revolution, on the fall of the monarchy on 10 August 1792 he was authorized to go through the king's papers, both those in the Tuileries and those left behind at Versailles when Louis had been forced to abandon the chateau on 6 October 1789. Arguing his case to be admitted to the papers to the Jacobin leader Chabot, Soulavie claimed:

> since authors first began to write history, they have never had an opportunity of drawing their information from so authentic source as is now open. The king's papers must develop every secret cause of the events of his reign.[1]

Chabot replied that if he wanted his request to be granted he must stop calling Louis the king and start calling him 'the tyrant'. Notwithstanding, in December, supervised by two officials and guided by the king's former locksmith Gamain, Soulavie was admitted to Louis's private apartments in a turret of the chateau of Versailles. Versailles stood in a time warp, abandoned but not yet looted, and Soulavie was able to peruse Louis's papers at his leisure. Here he found private dynastic memoranda stretching back centuries and, hidden 'under the stand for the anvils' of the smithy, the foreign secretary Vergennes's copious warnings that Marie-Antoinette was an Austrian fifth columnist.[2] He saw the whole of Louis's correspondence with Vergennes, some thousand letters, of which only 171 have survived. Moreover Soulavie was writing at a time and in a place, France of the Consulate, when a certain objectivity was possible.

A major infuence on Soulavie's historical writings was his association with the House of Richelieu-Aiguillon, whose memoirs he published. There were two planks to their policy. First a staunch defence of the royal authority against encroachments by the Parlement: d'Aiguillon's trial by the Parlement of Paris had precipitated Maupeou's *coup d'état* and d'Aiguillon served as both foreign secretary and minister for war in Louis XV's last administration. Second the defence of traditional foreign policy as enunciated by the founder of the fortunes of the house, the Cardinal-Duke de Richelieu. This stressed the traditional importance of alliance with the secondary Powers of Europe, such as Sweden and Turkey, at the expense of the new (1756) alliance with Austria, the traditional enemy. Soulavie accepted the validity of these two policies without question. Soulavie had his hobby horses, of course, notably a paranoid hatred of Austria, and a belief that England was trying to subvert the French state. As French agent in Switzerland he had fed Robespierre's even greater paranoia, and not just in the field of foreign policy. But this paranoia of Soulavie's was the unhealthy excrescence of an original, analytical mind which makes his memoirs more than the usual mishmash of hagiography or hatred. Given the range of Soulavie's intellect and sources, he will be our principal guide for the period of Louis's reign up to the Revolution.

Soulavie's main thesis was that the *ancien régime* was destroyed by a series of destructive contradictions and role reversals infecting every aspect of government. The most important contradiction resided in the king himself:

> Louis XVI was distinguished by such a peculiarity of character, that it may, in some measure be said, there were in him two men; a man who *knows* and a man who *wills*.[3]

Louis 'was endowed with an understanding methodical and analytical'. He corrected the speeches his ministers wrote for him to use on great occasions:

In the execution of this business, it may be seen that he sought for a proper word and that he found it. The word employed by the minister, and erased by the king, was sometimes unsuitable, proceeding from the passion of the minister; but that which was substituted by the king was always apposite. The word indeed was so well adapted to express the sentiment with precision, that it would scarcely be hyperbolical to say it was necessary to be a king to find it.

Furthermore, 'he was endowed with a spirit of foresight' and 'alone beheld from a distance the destiny and ruin of France'; so that he became 'the Cassandra of the Nation'.[4]

But these admirable qualities were of no avail because, 'such was his natural disposition that nothing could beget resolution in the mind of this indolent prince'.[5] For, Soulavie observes:

in the great affairs of state, the king who *wills*, who *commands*, was not to be found in this monarch. Louis XVI was, upon the throne, nothing superior to those private persons whom we meet with in society, so weak in intellectual faculties, that nature has rendered them incapable of forming an opinion. In the midst of his pusillanimity, he placed his confidence entirely in a particular minister; and though among the variety of opinions delivered in his cabinet-council, he well knew which was the best, he never once had the resolution to say, 'I prefer the advice of such a one'. Here lay the copious source of national misfortune.[6]

Soulavie speculates on why Louis lacked will power. Perhaps it stemmed from his repressed childhood, to put it in a modern way. Soulavie relates that his aunt Adélaïde, daughter of Louis XV:

who tenderly loved him, said to him jocosely, with the view to dissipating his timidity, 'Speak at your ease, Berry; exclaim, bawl out, make a noise like your brother Artois: dash and break my china to pieces, and make yourself be talked of.' The young duke of Berry, however, was every day more silent, and could never correct the tendency of his natural disposition.[7]

This disposition, Soulavie considers, was reinforced by the deaths in his childhood of so many of his immediate family: father, mother, two elder brothers etc. – poisoned for the most part, according to Soulavie's conspiratorial mind. Partly, he speculates, it derived from the inbreeding of his family: the Protestant Reformation halved the number of suitable matches for the dynasty so that marriages were contracted mainly with the Catholic dynasties of Habsburg, Savoy and Medici. Louis was five times descended from Henri IV and five times from Marie Medici. This also had the effect of making the members of the dynasty resemble each other more than those of ordinary families – in character as well as in physique. So that Louis's want of resolution was not unique to him but was shared by most of the members of his dynasty: only Henri IV and Louis XIV, in the middle portion of his reign, displayed any independence of their ministers. 'The prevailing defect in the princes of the house of Bourbon', Soulavie concludes, 'arose not from the faculty of the mind which *conceives and judges*, but from that which *wills and either commands or executes*'.[8]

In fact, new blood was introduced into the dynasty in the eighteenth century with the marriage of Louis XV to Maria Lesczinska, who had no royal blood, and of his son the dauphin to a Saxon princess, a dynasty which had not previously figured in the Bourbon bloodline since it had only recently reconverted to Catholicism. And from the Saxon Wettins Louis XVI derived his enormous physical strength, his great-grandfather being Augustus the Strong, Elector of Saxony and King of Poland. Michelet considered that the Saxon element in Louis's make-up was preponderant.

The Bourbons all possessed 'courage in danger'. Louis XVI, however, alone of them never appeared on the field of battle, so that 'the only instances of courage we are acquainted with in Louis XVI are those he showed on the 20th of June [1792, when his palace was invaded] and the 21st of January [1793], at sight of the instruments of death'. However, 'This kind of courage', Soulavie adds, 'was compatible in the latter kings, with the most extravagant weakness of character'[9] – another contradiction. Soulavie considers that Louis XV was dominated in the first half of the reign by Cardinal Fleury and in the second by a string of mistresses. Similarly with Louis XVI: Maurepas and Vergennes dominated the first part of the reign, and Marie-Antoinette the second.

In one respect, however, Louis XVI did show resolution: his determination not to allow Marie-Antoinette to exploit her marriage to further the interests of her House. This was enough to win Soulavie's sympathy, whose work is an extended diatribe against the Habsburgs. Louis's resolution, however, led to a further contradiction, for 'there were two princes in Louis XVI, the husband of Marie-Antoinette, and the secret enemy of the court of Vienna'.[10] One might add that there were three for Louis never took a mistress and after his operation in 1777 Marie-Antoinette served in that role too. Louis possessed an open-eyed devotion to his wife and determined to protect her and France from her folly. In foreign policy he succeeded totally, but in domestic policy (after 1787) he failed lamentably.

Each of the 'two princes' was represented at court by a different faction: that of the government was represented by Maurepas and Vergennes, that of the queen was represented by herself, Choiseul and the *choiseulistes*, some of whom entered the government after 1780. Soulavie says of this unusual situation:

> What is extremely remarkable in the two hostile factions at court is that the king, who was thoroughly acquainted with the contests and the reciprocal accusations of the parties, never once remitted his attachment either to the queen or his minister [Vergennes]; but reposed in the latter his confidence, and adopted such measures with regard to the former as might preserve his cabinet vigilant against the enterprises of the court of Vienna.[11]

The recall of Maurepas

Soulavie divides the reign of Louis XVI into ten 'epochs', eight before 1789 and two after, which each represent a stage in the decline and fall of the monarchy. The first act of Louis as king constituted an epoch in itself, the recall of the comte de Maurepas. Soulavie relates the anecdote relating to Maurepas's choice: how the king's aunt Adélaïde guided Louis through a list of recommendations bequeathed to him by her brother, Louis's father, the 'old' dauphin. The element of chance, often emphasized by early historians of the reign, both to depict Louis as a 'shuttlecock', to use Soulavie's phrase, and his tragic fate, also played its part. For Louis having written the letter to the former

finance minister Machault, his Latin tutor Radonvilliers induced
him to alter the name on the envelope to his patron Maurepas
instead. (Louis's letters never mention his correspondent by
name, just 'monsieur', so there was no need for him to waste his
efforts and his precious paper on a second draft.)

This change in destination was also, for Soulavie, a change in
destiny. For the stern, unbending, authoritarian Machault, the
scourge of the *parlements*, would have successfully defended the
traditional monarchy, whereas the frivolous Maurepas, now 74,
was only interested in short-term popularity. Under him,

> It was not . . . the court of Versailles that governed the exist-
> ing generation, but the existing generation that governed
> the court; an infallible symptom that revolution
> impended.[12]

Sénac de Meilhan, a former *intendant* writing in 1795, makes
the same observation about Maurepas that Soulavie makes about
Louis:

> there were two men in him, the one who saw and the one
> who willed. One was penetrating and enlightened, the
> other changeable and irresolute.[13]

And it was indeed to be characteristic of Louis to choose
ministers of complementary rather than opposite character to his
own, thereby reinforcing rather than counterbalancing his
defects.

Maurepas's influence on Louis, however, was not, Soulavie
considered, all bad; or rather he strengthened him where he was
strong (in seeking a 'patriotic', that is anti-Austrian foreign
policy) even if he weakened him where he was weak (in seeking
to follow rather than guide opinion). The Austrian alliance could
not be ended since Louis XVI had married a Habsburg, but that
only heightened the need for vigilance in keeping her out of
foreign policy making. Soulavie gives Louis, Maurepas and
Vergennes full credit for realizing this and sticking to their guns.

With Maurepas and Vergennes there was a selfish motive to
buttress their principled opposition to Marie-Antoinette: she
aimed to implement the Austrian policy by replacing them with
the former foreign secretary, the duc de Choiseul, the broker of
her marriage. Their success cost them nothing. For Louis, however, it represented a constant strain, for increasingly he loved his
wife, even if, increasingly he detested her brother Joseph II. At

moments of international tension, particularly in 1778 and 1784–85, he had to endure tantrums from his wife and 'mother-in-law' letters from Maria Theresa.

Both Maurepas and Vergennes also realized that it was necessary to conceal Louis's weakness from the nation:

> When [Maurepas] thoroughly discovered the character of the king ... he endeavoured constantly to prevent the weakness of that prince from being known; and this was one of the greatest advantages he procured to the state. He represented the king as a good and just prince, a lover of order and the friend of the people. He thought that for the character of a king, weak and destitute of resolution, to be known was the greatest misfortune that could happen to the French.[14]

Which is why Louis's weakness was not much discussed by the uninitiated before 1789.

The recall of the Parlement

Soulavie's 'second epoch' in the reign of Louis XVI was, again, constituted by a single act, but a momentous one: the restoration of the exiled Parlement on 12 November 1774. The Maupeou coup and Louis XVI's reversal of it were considered at the time to have been decisive turning points. Modern historiography has tended if anything further to play up their significance. Since Louis XVI brought about the recall he staked his reputation (and arguably his life) on it. But opinion is sharply divided on the implications both of the coup and its reversal. The 'patriot' opposition to the coup, among the exiled *parlementaires* and the pamphleteers who supported them, argued that the coup revealed that the country no longer had a viable constitution, since the king could do as he pleased; since the unwritten constitution had failed, perhaps it should be replaced with a written one; since the Parlement had proved an insufficient bulwark against royal despotism, perhaps it should be supplemented by the Estates-General. The coup, on this reading, directly led to the calling of the Estates in 1789, if not to the Revolution itself. This view has been taken up in modern times by the Franco-American discourse school – which is unsurprising since they base their conclusions on these same pamphlets.[15]

Another French tradition, again going back to the reign of
Louis XV and exemplified by Antoine's recent biography of that
king, argues that the reassertion of royal authority in 1771 was
necessary because it had been captured by an oligarchy of
magistrates, the *parlements*, to the detriment of the country as a
whole.[16] In particular, the coup made possible a restoration of
royal finances, a more equitable distribution of taxation and the
provision of free justice. If Louis XVI had not reversed the policy,
it would have culminated in the codification of French laws,
upon which Maupeou was working and which his secretary
Lebrun implemented as the Code Napoléon, when he was Second
Consul. With the return of the Parlement major reform became
impossible and since Louis was accessible to reform plans –
unlike Maurepas and the keeper of the seals, Miromesnil, who
merely wanted to preserve the status quo, or rather the status quo
ante-1750 – the restoration was a major blunder. I incline to
this view.

A rather more subtle approach is adopted by Doyle and by
Burley. It is that the restrictions of Miromesnil (who replaced
Maupeou) on the Parlement – notably that they could not
suspend the giving of justice – worked. Or rather that the
parlements were, if not chastened by their four years of exile,
so shaken by the coup that they did not consider that unaided
they had the strength to resist the encroachments of royal
despotism and, when serious quarrels with the crown re-
emerged from 1785, began to call for the Estates-General, even
though they knew it would eclipse their political power.[17]
Burley even argues that right from the moment of their
restoration, or even of Maupeou's coup, they envisaged the
Estates as the palladium that would replace the sum of the 13
parlements, invoked by the *théorie des classes,* as the guarantee
against royal despotism.[18] Malesherbes called for the Estates-
General in the *grandes remontrances* of the Cour des Aides
in 1771.

The implication of both Doyle's and Burley's line is that Louis
XVI did not err in recalling the Parlement: if it was weak, it could
not block reforms. Burley even argues that not only did the recall
not preclude reform, it was its precondition, since the manner of
Maupeou's coup, the 'process', was so vicious that it vitiated the
reforms it apparently facilitated. The reforms introduced by
Maupeou and Terray were poisoned at the source, given the
immorality of these ministers, who had clung to the coat-tails of

Mme du Barry. This was certainly Maurepas's main argument in persuading Louis XVI to undo his grandfather's work. This view should be contrasted with the strikingly modern view of Soulavie, that the morals of the 'triumvirate' and of Louis XV himself were execrable but their private lives did not affect the quality of their public policy.

The recall of the Parlement represented the antithesis of the Richelieu-Aiguillon thesis to which Soulavie subscribed and whose twin planks met on this issue. The demise of the old Parlement had been linked to the dismissal of the pro-Austrian Choiseul and Marie-Antoinette was the champion of the recall of both of them in 1774. It also meant a surrender by what Soulavie terms the 'military monarchy' and was preceded by the actual fall and exile of d'Aiguillon. Soulavie concludes his synopsis of this section with the words:

> The king was a silent spectator during the debates which tore to pieces the royal authority and analysed it before the eyes of the people.[19]

He continues:

> In the progress of this transaction, the king was not destitute either of information or advice; he carefully collected the opinions and memoirs on the subject; he classed them in his cabinet with particular attention, and he wrote on the covers of the memoirs of the two parties the words: 'opinions favourable to the return of the old *parlements*'; 'opinions favourable to the existing *parlements*'; and he embraced that which was to him the most fatal.

Why, given his support as dauphin of Maupeou's coup, which was the embodiment of the *dévot* tradition in which he had been reared?

Primarily because Maurepas whom Louis had summoned as an adviser, advised it, which came as a shock to Louis and a betrayal to his aunt Adélaïde. But though Maurepas came with the recommendation of the old dauphin, his advice could have been anticipated for, as Soulavie notes, during his first administration he had ever been the friend of the *parlements* and of the Jansenists. But Soulavie does not exclude the motive of malice. Maurepas 'hated the late king who had left him in exile for thirty years' and

He wished to indulge his revenge in destroying the principal measure of the reign of the late king, and these motives overturned the magistracy of M. de Maupeou.[20]

Soulavie considers that one of the fundamental weaknesses of all the Bourbon kings, with the exception of the first, Henri IV, had been their inability to impose what he calls *the coalition system* on France. In England, after the religious and civil conflict of the seventeenth century, a pacifying synthesis of the warring elements had led to stability and glory in the eighteenth. Henri IV had imposed a similar synthesis after the wars of the League, but the knack had been forgotten by his successors. So the plan of Soulavie's hero d'Aiguillon, 'who wished to form one parliament [from elements] of the two, was treated with sarcasms and ridicule'. Louis XVI was so weak that he could not impose conditions on the old Parlement even whilst in exile nor stop it from giving full vent to its legendary vengefulness.[21]

This is a little unfair. Louis, as we have seen, imposed some conditions on the restored Parlement and these it did observe. Moreover there was no wholesale return to favour of the Parlement's partisans at court: notably Louis resisted all Marie-Antoinette's pressure to restore Choiseul to office or even favour, and he returned to Chanteloup, his country seat. But Soulavie is right in saying that in his first year Louis constructed a cabinet of malcontents: Maurepas, who had been exiled, Miromesnil and Malesherbes, the exiled heads of the *parlement* of Rouen and the Cour des Aides respectively, and Saint-Germain, the minister for war, who had exiled himself after quarrelling with his superior officers. All these men had a grudge to work off against the 'military monarchy'; all introduced measures which undermined it. This meant that the natural order was reversed by the introduction of the opposition into the government at the outset of the reign, whence it was never absent, for 'from 1774 the government contained within its very bosom the principle of its decline'.[22] For Soulavie, opposition was seldom absent in a liberty-loving country like France. There was nothing wrong with this providing the opposition opposed and the government governed.

Soulavie sums up his appraisal of Louis's conduct during the debates leading up to the recall of the Parlement as follows:

> the king a mere spectator of these disputes, gave sanction to both parties by the want of decision in his character. This

prince, however, was not destitute either of sagacity or foresight. Strength of mind to execute what he judged to be
most expedient for his interests was the great defect he
laboured under.[23]

This was also Soulavie's general conclusion to the reign. But it
is somewhat inconsistent with another general conclusion he
applies both to the recall and to the reign:

> The king, who had a sound judgement, acknowledged
> afterwards to Madame Adélaïde that the side which she
> had taken in these debates was the safest and that it would
> have been more prudent to suffer things to remain in the
> state in which his grandfather had left them; but he owed it
> that the love of his people, who seemed to desire the re-
> establishment of the old magistracy, had prevailed on him
> more than the love of power, and that he had resolved to
> recall the *parlements* chiefly for the purpose of restraining
> the abuses of the royal authority ... a revolution is
> imminent and the government turned out of its natural
> course when the state calls exclusively into its admini-
> stration jansenistical opinions and parties. ... We shall see
> the king, in many circumstances of his reign, support this
> revolution, which he had begun in 1774, and favour
> incessantly the popular interests of dawning liberty, in pref-
> erence to the interests of power.[24]

An important but neglected aspect of the recall of the
Parlement is the ingratitude displayed by the new king to those
who had seconded his grandfather in his struggle against the
parlements. This was put most forcefully at the time by
Monsieur, comte de Provence, in a memorandum presented to his
brother the king:

> Will the king confiscate the places of an obedient
> parlement, which has re-established the crown on the king's
> head, to give them to a parlement which had attempted to
> dethrone him? Will he abandon the members of a faithful
> parlement to the public scorn, to the outrages of a
> parlement vindictive and flushed with victory on its
> return?[25]

Soulavie also castigates Louis for his ingratitude to the
royalists: 'Louis XVI, indulgent towards the exiled Parlement,

appeared unjust, severe and scornful to that which was sub-
missive'. Hearing rumours of its impending dissolution, the
'Parlement Maupeou' petitioned Louis, but received the crushing
reply, 'that he was suprised that ... [it] should make any
remonstrances to him upon mere public reports'.[26] But it was not
just a question of ingratitude (to which Louis himself was
abnormally sensitive when he perceived that he was its object). In
his moving conclusion to his study of the conflicts between Louis
XV and his *parlements*, Julian Swann has eloquently depicted the
psychological damage done to the loyalists by the recall of the
parlements. Of these loyalists, known as 'the king's good
servants', Swann writes:

> Whilst undoubtedly a minority ... [they] were still
> sufficiently numerous to provide a functioning judicial
> system between 1771 and 1774. Had Louis XVI given them
> the opportunity they would have continued to do so.[27]

But the new king broke their heart or at least their spirit and
they were unavailable to help him when he was fighting for his
life and that of the regime in 1787–89. And it was not just the
members of the Parlement Maupeou who were spurned but the
ministers, military commandants and *intendants* who had
assisted the late king to recover his authority. When there was
talk of Terray's recall to office in 1777, he told a confidant, 'do
you seriously believe that having been insulted by the people,
having been forced to rely on the protection of soldiers, I would
return [to office] again?'[28] Similarly, d'Aiguillon's son, in whose
family loyalty to the absolute monarchy was seemingly
absolute, was the man whose speech led to the dismantling of
the society of the *ancien régime* in the National Assembly on the
night of 4 August 1789.

Louis XVI and a new monarchy?

The conventional view of Louis being bamboozled by the wily
Maurepas into recalling the Parlement, as the police minister put
it, 'despite the principles of his education'[29] is challenged by the
work of Peter Burley, in an unpublished thesis of 1981 with the
provocative title, 'Louis XVI and a new monarchy'. Burley
argues that so far from being duped into dismissing Maupeou,
Louis could not wait to be rid of him: 'He had been bullied into

accepting Maupeou as the saviour of the monarchy, and to reject the chancellor was Louis's revenge against his dreadful childhood and adolescence.'[30] This view conflicts with that of Mme de Coursac who argued that despite the numerous deaths within his immediate family, Louis at least had an intellectually fulfilling adolescence and was close to La Vauguyon who became almost a second father.

In considering Louis's education I have emphasized the dauphin's aptitudes and personal predilections, skill in geography, oceanography, mathematics, languages, a strong interest in history, both to offer a limited refutation of his reputation for stupidity and laziness and to indicate how his interests may have influenced his reign – for example his interest in the navy and England as prefiguring his participation in the war of American Independence. These were Louis's personal interests, often pursued, as with his study of English, on his own. I have concurred, however, with Furet, in the view that his ideological development was entirely conventional for a member of his dynasty: a throne-and-altar conservatism, anti-*philosophe*, with a narrow interpretation of the role of the *parlements*. The label for the political manifestation of such orthodox Catholicism, detesting the *parlements* as much for their tincture of Jansenist heresy as for opposition to the crown, was the *dévot* party – that word connoting an element of bigotry absent from the English 'devout': Louis is said to have replied to a plea to grant French Protestants civil rights, that they had only to convert to enjoy them! Louis's firm grounding in the *dévot* tradition resulted in his first known political acts: his public congratulation of Maupeou for his attack on the Parlement and his private endorsement on his copy of Maupeou's disciplinary edict.

Peter Burley, however, questions whether Louis was a *dévot* in the conventional sense of the word. Burley, whose work covers the period of Louis's education and the first years of his reign (1768–78) and seeks to rehabilitate Louis's reputation at least for these years, makes a distinction between the 'authoritarian *dévots*', such as Maupeou and La Vauguyon, and what he calls the '*philosophe dévots*', represented pre-eminently by J.-N. Moreau, the historiographer royal, and Louis himself. Louis, according to Burley and in contradistinction with de Coursac, detested La Vauguyon, 'who had determined to create a king no matter what the cost in human terms'. In July 1770 Louis had caught him listening at a keyhole; and in 1772 La Vauguyon had surprised his charge reading 'patriot', that is anti-Maupeou, pamphlets, and rebuked him for it. Louis, according to this account, was so angry that he dismissed La Vauguyon on the spot for exceeding his authority.[31] (In fact La Vauguyon's formal duties ended automatically with Louis's marriage in 1770.) For Burley, La Vauguyon's main influence on his charge was through his collaboration with Moreau, which led to Louis's *Réflexions sur mes entretiens avec M. le duc de la Vauguyon*, a paraphrase on their work dating from 1767–69. The work of Moreau's which most influenced Louis was *Les Devoirs d'un prince*.

A '*philosophe dévot*', according to Burley, was a man of deep religious beliefs, as Louis undoubtedly was, but not one addicted to extravagant religious observances, perpetually clutching a crucifix or indulging in esoteric Spanish-style mortifications of the flesh. This particular qualification of Louis's 'devotedness' is correct and the widespread prediction that he would be in the hands of priests was indeed quickly shown to have been misplaced. But Louis the *philosophe*? Louis the child of the Enlightenment? Did he not rule out the ministerial candidacy of the *philosophe-parlementaire* Malesherbes on the grounds that he was 'too dangerous an *Encyclopédiste*'?[32] Did he not tell his valet in prison that 'those two men [Voltaire and Rousseau] have ruined France'?[33] On the other hand Louis, as dauphin, bought the *Encyclopédie* out of his pocket money and he made a point of meeting David Hume when he visited Versailles in 1763, though one suspects it was to Hume the historian of England rather than to Hume the philosopher that the 9-year-old was attracted.

'*Philosophe dévot*' seems a contradiction in terms. However, Burley argues, Louis was drawn to reformers who were personally 'spiritual' if not conventional Catholics – notably to Turgot and Necker, finance ministers 1774–76 and 1776–81 respectively, the latter a Protestant. If '*philosophe dévot*' is a contradiction in terms so is the more conventional label 'enlightened despot' – the appellation accorded to Louis's brother-in-law the Emperor Joseph II. This accolade is sometimes tentatively extended to Louis himself but Burley would forcibly decline it on the king's behalf on the grounds that Louis was no despot.

The tincture of despotism, according to Burley, marred the revival in 1771 of Bourbon kingship which in the 1760s had degenerated into a 'moribund pornocracy'. Not only did

Maupeou's *coup d'état* cross the dividing line between absolute monarchy and despotism but Louis XV himself was a pawn in the hands of his ministers: hence the accusatory slogan of 'ministerial despotism'.

The start of Louis XVI's reign was an improvement on both these fronts. Louis, in accordance with the precepts of Moreau and Curban de Réal, sought enlightened submission rather than blind obedience from what were increasingly thought of as citizens rather than subjects. So censorship of the press was totally lifted in 1774–76 and partially in 1777–89 and all Louis's major edicts were prefaced by preambles explaining his good intentions to the people. Sénac de Meilhan, however, considered this a weakness: 'explanations rather than a simple and precise enunciation of the sovereign's intention . . . encouraged scribblers to enter into discussion of administrative controversies'.[34]

At the same time, Burley argues, by developing a system of cabinet committees, Louis forced through reforming measures such as the recall of the exiled Parlement, the abolition of the *corvée* (forced labour on the roads) and the freeing of the grain trade from internal customs, which did not command a majority in the *conseil d'état*. Thereby Louis succeeded in 'raising both the quality of public life and the expectation of the public spirited among the elite'.[35] Burley's claim that Louis dominated his cabinets from the outset is controversial. Decision-making was transferred from the council to *ad hoc* committees shortly after the start of the new reign. However, the force behind this was Maurepas, ostensibly to enable him to teach the young king his *métier* more efficiently, in fact as the only way in which he could outmanoeuvre Louis XV's old ministers who still dominated the council, in which decisions were taken by majority voting. And the policy reason why Maurepas instituted this change was precisely to remove from influencing the king those, such as Vergennes as well as the old ministers, who would have strengthened him in his resolve to maintain the 'Parlement Maupeou'.

Furthermore, after the dismissal of Maupeou and Terray, Maurepas used a small committee to 'indoctrinate' Louis on the new thinking on the Parlement so that he would come to believe it had been his own decision and enforce the new system effectively. Something of the mental confusion with which Louis emerged from this traumatizing process comes across in the diary entry of Maurepas's confidant, the abbé de Véri:

As this decision is different from the ideas [Louis] had before ascending the throne, he has himself confessed his astonishment: 'Who would have said, a few years back when I went to the *lit de justice* with my grandfather [installing the Parlement Maupeou], that I would be holding the one I am to hold [restoring the old Parlement].[36]

The demoralizing effect of this process on the young king is hard to over-estimate. It is true, however, that by the 1780s, Louis had learned to use the cabinet committee system and in 1786 he did 'force through reforming measures . . . which did not command a majority in the *conseil d'état*', in the shape of the programme to be presented to the Assembly of Notables.

Louis at the outset of his reign was confident of success. As he told Noailles: 'With good intentions, justice, firmness, religion, I fear neither Jesuits, nor Jansensists, neither *Encyclopédistes* nor physiocrats.'[37] He would indeed, *pace* Soulavie, create a coalition of the men of goodwill. He would create a new sense of community, and that was why de Tocqueville could say that he was the only one of France's kings who had not pursued a policy of divide and rule. His specific policies, according to Burley, favoured 'legal and penal reform, an easing of the *corvée* . . . and of slavery, a complete review of *lettres de cachet*, the abolition of legal torture and the abolition of serfdom'.[38] Burley concludes his synopsis of Louis's programme:

What is suprising, considering . . . [intertia] and Louis's personal limitations, is how much . . . was implemented. It must never be overlooked, for example, that Louis had the courage to appoint and for a time support, *philosophe* ministers, something which delighted public opinion, was beyond the reformers' wildest dreams, and was distinct to the *Louis-seizième* monarchy.[39]

Louis XVI and public opinion

Against the picture of Louis forming an enlightened citizenry through the preambles to his reforming edicts, we must set that of the man who slavishly followed public opinion. Louis had written as dauphin, 'I must always follow public opinion, it is never wrong'[40] and de Tocqueville maintained that Louis followed this advice throughout his reign. Louis himself made a telling comment about the recall of the Parlement: 'It may be considered politically unwise, but it seems to me to be the general wish and I want to be loved.'[41] There is no doubt that the recall was popular and with it its author. Louis's reputation soared at the start of the reign. The unflattering stories which had circulated when he was dauphin – that he was morose, stupid, short-sighted – were eclipsed by the glow of the new reign and the young court centred on the good king and his radiant consort. The word *'resurrexit'* was daubed on the equestrian statue of Henri IV on the Pont Neuf, the most popular, indeed the only popular, Bourbon king.

The *philosophe* d'Holbach enthused, in his *Ethocracie, ou le gouvernement fondé sur la morale*, published in 1776 and dedicated to Louis:

> The first moments of the reign of Louis XVI ... seemed to promise to a kingdom crushed by two very long and very catastrophic reigns, a totally unexpected return to happiness. There is no kind of happiness that the French nation is not entitled to expect from a prince filled with goodness, justice, love and peace, of contempt for luxury, surrounded by enlightened and virtuous ministers.[42]

But how vapid, how stylised these words are, even from the pen of a radical thinker such as d'Holbach! Such a flimsy caricature could not survive subjection to much disappointment or hard information. Particularly as the body of d'Holbach's work goes on to advocate the return of the Estates-General, the disestablishment of the Church and the abolition of hereditary titles. The search for popularity always ends in failure. Stormont, the English ambassador, had observed that the king's popularity at his accession would evaporate unless he restored the Parlement; and this sop only increased the public's desire for more. As Burley observes: 'Louis XV sacrificed popularity to power in 1771, Louis XVI was to sacrifice power to the fickle will-o'-the-wisp of popularity from the first act of his reign to the Revolution.'[43]

Soulavie also drew a distinction between Henri's kind of popularity and Louis's. Henri IV who 'alone knew how to reconcile popularity with the exercise of absolute power', knew also 'that kings were entirely ignorant of the art of accommodating themselves to the people'. That, however, was precisely what Louis XVI attempted to do:

Under the kings who preceded Louis XVI the monarch was universally the idol of the nation. Under Louis XVI, on the contrarary, the nation was the object almost of adoration to the king.[44]

It was one of the many role reversals which Soulavie noted in the government of Louis XVI which he considered contributed to the fall of the regime.

And though Louis cared desperately about his popularity, he did very little to manage it. In considering Louis's diary, I mentioned his pique that there was no Te Deum or fireworks to mark the birth of his second daughter in 1786. Louis expected the celebrations to occur spontaneously but in previous reigns Te Deums had been more frequent precisely because they were celebrated on the personal initiative of the king: if the king's illness accompanied a victory, a Te Deum could not be ordered because a ministerial letter would be insufficient. If Louis wanted his daughter's birth to be celebrated in this way (which he clearly did), it was up to him to organize a Te Deum. However, a letter to Vergennes of 21 January 1783, the day after peace preliminaries with England had been signed at the end of the war of American Independence, suggests that Louis was not sure what the form was: 'there was not meant to have been a Te Deum tomorrow; I've heard it said that there would be one just as you did, but it's just palace gossip'.[45] It is significant that the American war, which furnished its share of French victories, gave rise to only three Te Deums, compared to eight in the Seven Years' War, which afforded few opportunities for rejoicing, and 12 in the single year 1745.[46]

The abbé Proyart relates how the aldermen of Paris wanted to mark the victorious peace in 1783 with days of festivities. Louis replied to their deputation:

> Don't you think, gentlemen, that instead of these expensive celebrations which nearly always end in tears [he was think- ing of his wedding celebrations when a stand collapsed killing hundreds] it would be better to mark this occasion with some useful public work. A bridge to link the new Chaussée d'Antin district with that of Les Invalides is becom- ing increasingly necessary. You could call it *le pont de la paix*.

The aldermen took up the suggestion, but called it Pont de Louis XVI.[47] One is reminded of Octavius Caesar's rebuke to his sister for creeping into Rome unannounced:

You ... have prevented
The ostentation of our love, which, left unshown,
Is often left unloved.[48]

Proyart also gives examples of Louis ordering fulsome
dedications to him to be deleted. There are scarcely any statues to
Louis XVI, nothing remotely resembling Louis XIV's Place des
victoires, and the quality of the coinage continued to decline
(both technically and artistically, though the first bust of Louis
made him look quite handsome). Louis checked the court
circular, the *Gazette de France*, before publication, but he only
made minor changes, such as deleting a reference to his brother
Provence's hunting at Brunoy as being of little interest, or
correcting a genealogical error, or someone's rank in one of the
military orders.

|4|

Louis XVI and Turgot

Soulavie's fourth epoch of the reign of Louis XVI covers the reforming ministries of Turgot, controller-general of finances, Malesherbes at the Household and Saint-Germain at the war ministry. This phase begins with the appointment of Turgot to the finance ministry in August 1774 and ends with his dismissal, preceded by the resignation of Malesherbes in May 1776. Many historians and many contemporaries believed that this was the last best chance to reform the regime. Soulavie, however, believed that this ministry of *philosophes* was a Trojan horse inside the citadel of 'the military monarchy' at Versailles. Moreover when the *philosophe* ministers were expelled that made their sectaries the enemies of the monarchy, which had uniquely managed to alienate its natural friends in 1774 (by the recall of the Parlement) and its natural enemies in 1776. Soulavie illustrates the contradictions which he believed led the monarchy to its ruin with the case of Malesherbes, a man who 'subjected to a *lettre de cachet* in 1771, became the minister of *lettres de cachet* in 1775 and accepted the place only on the condition that he never should sign any more'.[1]

We shall concern ourselves with what has always been regarded as the most important of these three appointments, that of Turgot; his was also the crucial dismissal, on 12 May 1776. Both were regarded as turning points at the time and thereafter. Véri characterized the period 1774–76 as 'les deux belles années de Louis XVI' – a sort of *quinquennium Neronis*. Edgar Faure in 1961 wrote *La Disgrace de Turgot* as a volume in a series 'Thirty days which made France' – another in the series was the fall of the Bastille and a third the fall of the monarchy on 10 August 1792. For Burley, Turgot's appointment was perfectly natural for Louis, the *'philosophe dévot'*. By the same token Louis's dismissal of Turgot, on the pretext that his 'familiarity was an affront to the monarchy', showed his inability to withstand long-term pressures from the court.[2] Soulavie's analysis is similar; Louis shared Turgot's ideals, and in his reign 'philosophy was seated on the throne';[3] only for Soulavie Turgot's appointment and dismissal were both equally damaging to the regime.

Too much has been made of Louis's indentification with Turgot. His was not a personal appointment by Louis, as those of Vergennes and du Muy, to the war office, were – it was mediated through a common friend of Turgot and Maurepas, the abbé de Véri, and imposed on the king, who had reservations about Turgot as a 'systems man'.[4] He was worried that Turgot did not attend mass, an anxiety not wholly allayed by Maurepas's characteristic quip that the abbé Terray attended every day. The relationship between Louis and Turgot was largely based on a vague fund of sentimentality which was established at their first encounter. Turgot wrote how

> the affecting kindness with which your majesty conde-
> scended to press my hand between your own . . . will never
> be effaced from my memory

whilst Louis proclaimed, 'I know in France but two men who sincerely love the people, M. Turgot and myself'.[5]

Nor was this sentimentality unique to Louis and Turgot; *sensibilité* was the common currency of the day. Necker spoke this language, as did Robespierre. Men of the older generation, such as Louis XV, Vergennes and Maurepas, did not. And the moral sentiments that Louis expressed at the outset of the reign were vague to the point of platitude, as sentimental credos usually are.

True, Turgot made three concrete demands of Louis in his first audience: no bankruptcy,* no new peacetime taxation, no new loans – and the first of these Louis adhered to rigidly to the end of his reign, with disastrous consequences. And in September 1774 Turgot removed restrictions on the circulation of grain within the country – though peasants hated to see grain leaving

---

* By bankruptcy the French did not understand total or partial repudiation of the capital owed but rather a reduction of the rate of interest paid – what would be called a 'forced conversion' in England, such as occurred in 1931. Terray had operated one of these 'bankruptcies' in 1770.

their locality. Turgot's measures, following on a bad harvest, led to serious riots in May 1775 when the government temporarily lost control of the Ile-de-France and several adjoining provinces.

The so-called 'flour war' was brutally suppressed, with exemplary executions from a 40-foot gibbet. Accounts are at total variance about Louis's role in this early crisis. Soulavie has him appearing on the balcony of Versailles and weakly capitulating to the demands of the rioters to fix the price of grain themselves. Véri more plausibly has him censuring the local military for ceding to these same demands; and of weathering the storm whilst Maurepas skulked in Paris. His firm conduct here is to be contrasted with that during the insurrection in 1789.

Louis also comes out of the flour war well in the correspondence between the *philosophe* d'Alembert, who refers to Louis' 'calm and courageous conduct', and the *roi-philosophe*, Frederick the Great of Prussia, who enthuses:

> I admire the conduct of your young king who has not been shaken by the conspiracies of evil-intentioned men . . . this quality of firmness will bolster his administration in the years to come: those who are keen on change have been trying him out.[6]

Of course Turgot was at this time the *philosophes'* darling and Louis benefits from the association.

The flour war led to rifts in the government and even in the regime. Turgot persuaded Louis to replace Lenoir, Maurepas's appointment as *lieutenant de police*, for negligence – a stab in the back which Maurepas never forgot. Turgot also, believing that the recently restored Parlement had a hand in the riots, got Louis to remove its jurisdiction in grain matters by *lit de justice*. This was the point at which the Parlement, whose recall Turgot had advocated or accepted, parted company with the minister. This meant that a *lit de justice* had also to be employed for the next tranche of Turgot's reforms, the famous 'six edicts', registered in March 1776. Four of these concerned the grain trade but the most controversial were the ones replacing the *corvée* (forced peasant labour on the roads) with a tax and abolishing the Parisian craft guilds. Exactly two months after Louis enforced the registration of Turgot's edicts, he dismissed him from office.

The implications of these two edicts were considerable. The *corvée* was performed only by the peasantry, but the tax was to be paid by everyone, including the nobility, who felt insulted to be asked to pay what had been a *roturier* (plebeian) tax. This represented a moral dilemma for Louis as it had for his father the old dauphin, and one which was to become more acute as the reign progressed. On the one hand Louis's father believed that the nobility should be preserved in their property and status, on the other he believed that fiscal privilege 'makes the whole burden fall on the poor people'.[7] Louis attempted to square the circle on this occasion by telling the Parlement that there was no shame involved, since he would be paying the tax himself in virtue of his royal domain.[8] Similarly the abolition of the guilds struck at the heart of the corporate organization of the *ancien régime*, that is, a system in which the government has dealings not with individuals but with 'corps' such as a guild, a municipality, a village or a province. For this reason, the deeply conservative Miromesnil undermined his own ministerial colleague in the Parlement. Miromesnil told Malesherbes that Turgot was 'destroying the privileges of corps' and though some were 'unjust in origin', nevertheless 'they must be respected because they are tied to all the rest'.[9]

Miromesnil's instinct was right to advance the 'thin end of the wedge' argument because what Turgot had proposed was only, to use another homely figure, the tip of the iceberg. Turgot planned to sell off the crownlands, take over the Church's assets and liabilities in return for paying the salary of the clergy, institute a doomsday survey or *cadastre* of landed wealth to end tax evasion and, most important of all, to institute a hierarchy of assemblies, or 'municipalities' based on the possession of landed wealth and culminating in a national municipality. Behind these practical measures there was a theoretical link, about which a little must now be said.

Turgot was one of the leading economists of his day, the worthy rival of Adam Smith. At the risk of oversimplification, his doctrine can be summed up by the belief that land was the primary basis of wealth and that other forms of wealth, industrial or commercial, were merely derivative. Such beliefs were held by the school of physiocrats, or *économistes* as they were usually called at the time, though there is debate as to whether Turgot was a mainstream physiocrat. But if Turgot's economic ideas were complicated, his application of them to the polity was simplicity itself. Political power should not be organized according to the traditional division of society into three orders (clergy, nobility and Third Estate) such as applied in the provinces which retained their local estates (*pays d'état*) and the national Estates-General when they met. Rather, it should belong exclusively to those who possessed sufficient landed wealth to support themselves and their families. If a man possessed some land but not enough to support his family, he could combine with others similarly placed to form a collective citizen. Birth and occupation were alike irrelevant. Turgot proclaimed that 'the man who owns no land can be bound to no country' – peasants from the Auvergne sweep the chimneys in Spain, labourers from the Limousin engage in the building trade in Paris etc.; 'they are as mobile as the legs that carry them'. 'A landed property', however, 'instantly places a man in the class of those who pay instead of the class of those who receive a wage from the community.' They alone should have a political voice.[10]

The landowners should be represented in three tiers of administration at municipal, provincial and national level. The king would treat with these for the allocation of taxes and the implication was that the role of both the *parlements* and *intendants* and ultimately the *pays d'état* and the Estates-General would wither away. Turgot, then, is rejecting both the traditional political and administrative articulation of society and the classical agents of the administrative or, in Soulavie's phrase, the 'military' monarchy.

Burley argues that Louis agreed with many of these objectives but weakly acceded to pressure to dismiss him on the grounds that he was endangering the monarchy.[11] Véri, on the other hand, argued that Turgot's ideas were above Louis's comprehension – 'ideas above a certain level are beyond him'.[12] Neither view is correct. Very often we do not know precisely what Louis thought about the various reform projects which were presented to him and enacted in his name, but in the case of Turgot's most important project, the 'municipal assemblies', we have a clear picture because he wrote extensive marginal annotations on the proposals, which Soulavie managed to transcribe. There was a heated scholarly debate at the turn of the twentieth century about the authenticity of Soulavie's material in general and these marginal comments in particular. Recent scholars increasingly tend to accept that Soulavie is generally reliable as more of the originals he transcribed come to light in private archives.[13]

Louis goes to the heart of Turgot's proposals:

I know not whether France, administered by the representatives of the people and by her richest inhabitants would be more virtuous than she is, being administered by those who derive their claim from their birth, or the nomination of their sovereign. I find in the series of administrators nominated by my ancestors, and in the principal families of the law, and even of *la finance*, Frenchmen who would have done honour to any nation of the known world.

Power then, according to Louis, depended on just two things, birth or royal appointment. 'All monarchies, ancient and modern,' he argued, 'and most republics', depended on a hierarchy of birth. The kings alone had the power to modify society. This they had done by creating a service nobility (the *noblesse de robe*), to which Turgot himself (son and grandson of *intendants*) belonged. Turgot's system would undermine one of its chief positions, that of the *intendant*. Louis, however, believed that the administration 'of the *intendants*, with the exception of certain abuses, is the best administered branch of the national government'. Turgot was replacing both birth and royal appointment by landed wealth as the criterion for power. But, Louis argued, 'this is the very way to introduce discontent into the class of non-proprietors'. Louis also explicitly rejects the notion of 'collective citizens'. He then goes on to consider the proposed 'national municipality' which would become in effect 'a perpetual Estates-General' which would be 'subversive of the monarchy which is only absolute because its authority does not admit of a partner' – he refers to the 'indivisibility' of legislative power on which the Bourbons had always prided themselves. This crucial aspect will be considered in greater detail when we examine Louis's handling of the Estates in 1789.

Turgot next addresses a problem which had exercised all governments for a century: the impossibility of enacting general legislation (including taxation) for the whole of France. Instead it had to be negotiated with and modified by the 12 provincial *parlements*, the *pays d'états* etc. This, according to Turgot, 'multiplies by 10 the workload' of government. The municipalities would facilitate general legislation. Louis's reaction is curious:

if the organization of my provinces were everywhere similar, ... it would be more difficult to move at the same moment a complicated mass than to move it through the medium of the *intendants* and the *pays d'état*, as my ancestors did.

The king's attitude is curious because Turgot's was an objective which lay within the mainstream of royal administrative reform; it was to be fully realized and implemented during the French Revolution.

Louis makes a final practical and cynical observation about Turgot's proposed assemblies: that self-assessment leads to fraud: 'The abbé Terray clearly found that one is never sure of carrying a tax into effect unless it be imposed by the party which pays no part of it, or that pays a very small part of it.' He gives the example of the Parlement

> which has been in the habit of yielding to everything that is demanded of them when it bears only on the people at large. They are in the habit of refusing everything and of submitting to hardship and exile, when any revenue is required to their individual detriment.

Louis's marginal comments, therefore, would seem to indicate a sufficiently fundamental divergence between him and his minister to explain his dismissal of Turgot without having recourse to explanations centring on the king's lack of resolution or comprehension, though this conclusion must be qualified because of the date when Louis wrote his comments. Turgot wrote his memorandum in 1775 but Louis dates his comments 15 February 1788, in the period of acute crisis preceding the Revolution.

Two further reasons may be adduced for Louis's decision to dismiss Turgot. First, by seeking to intervene in the running of the other ministerial departments, Turgot was usurping the role of a premier or the king. Hence Louis's outburst: 'M. Turgot wants to be me and I don't want him to be me.'[14] The second relates to foreign and military policy. By 1776 England's relations with her American colonies were at a difficult stage (the Declaration of Independence was issued on 4 July of that year). In April Vergennes invited all the ministers to give their written opinion on the line France should take, whether to take advantage of England's difficulties to intervene in the conflict or to abstain. Turgot's pacific memorandum is usually cited as a reason for his dimissal. It was, but Turgot's line is often misunderstood, as is Louis's.

Turgot certainly argued that the best course of action for France was total abstention; otherwise the chance to reform the financial structure of the regime would be lost 'for a long time perhaps forever'.[15] Nevertheless, he argued, France could sustain war if a successful and therefore short one could be guaranteed. What the finances could not stand, however, was rearmament without war because then there would be no excuse to raise taxes and adopt other time-hallowed wartime expedients. This middle course, however, is precisely what Louis and Maurepas wanted: to take the unique opportunity to rebuild the navy which England's present weakness presented. But for these difficulties, they believed, England would go to war to prevent French rearmament. Louis did not decide to enter the war until 1778 but in the meantime, and quite independently, he rebuilt the navy at some cost. Turgot stood in the way of rearmament rather than war and had to go.

|5|

Necker, 1776–1781

Charlatan or saviour?

Necker was Louis XVI's most controversial minister, both at the time and in historiography. Uniquely for the Bourbon period, he had not just one but three ministries: 1776–81, 1788–12 July 1789 and 16 July 1789–90. His first ministry is the subject of the present chapter. In this ministry, Necker was closely associated with Louis. He was Louis's personal appointment and, according to Burley, 'the apogee of the abortive *Louis-seizième* monarchy'.[1]

The manner of Necker's appointment sheds light on a controversial aspect of Louis XVI's kingship: his addiction to unofficial channels of information. Louis's tutors had stressed that a king was at a disadvantage in that his exalted position cut him off from information coming from the world outside Versailles and that he should strive to rectify this. Louis needed little prompting, and he was keen to chat to those menials and peasants who were thrown in his way. He also read the contemporary journals widely, and the English-language ones everyday, to see what people thought of him. In 1780 Vergennes tactfully alluded to this practice apropos of a series of pamphlet attacks on Necker:

> Your Majesty is able to judge of the evident effect of such a number of writings, since you have had the goodness to show me, several times, that your majesty was employed in reading them.[2]

But there was a darker side to this habit. Louis continued Louis XV's practice of reading private mail. This was furnished through the *cabinet noir* of the postal inspector, d'Ogny, who provided him with a selection of titbits in his weekly *travail* with the king. Soulavie considered this a perfectly natural extension of the king's systematic and necessary interception of foreign dispatches. Véri, on the other hand, considered that opening mail was a breach of faith with his subjects and, he added, one which intensified Louis's tendency to indecisiveness. The latter point is a truism: escape from the control of information by a prime minister is bound to lead to an independence of view from that minister, which can be portrayed as indecisiveness. When d'Ogny died, Pezay performed a similar service.

Jean Masson, marquis de Pezay, was a charlatan whose marquisate was bogus. In the words of Véri, 'he created for himself a kind of ministry by writing letters to the king and receiving replies'.[3] Pezay attracted to himself another charlatan – at least according to Sénac de Meilhan, Soulavie, Calonne and some later historians – who also ruined the monarchy, though according to himself and recent historians such as Burley, Bosher and Harris, the man most likely to save it: Necker.[4] Jacques Necker (1732–1817) was the son of a professor of German law at Geneva who had come to France 'poor as Job' as a youth, starting as a bank clerk. He made a fortune out of privileged information, buying English stock just before the signing of the Peace of Paris in 1763. By the 1770s, according to Soulavie, his avarice was being displaced by his vanity and, pushed by his wife, a literary social climber and salon hostess, he sought a public position.

This was not easy as high office was the preserve of the legal service nobility, and (a recent trend which Necker favoured) the odd member of the military aristocracy. A further disqualification was Necker's Protestant religion. Nevertheless he acquired a certain celebrity from his *Eloge de Colbert* which attacked Turgot's grain policy – Turgot referred to him privately as 'that joker' (*ce drôle-là*). And, reputedly for the sum of 100,000 livres, Pezay forwarded financial projects of Necker's to Louis, who found them interesting. Necker then bounced Maurepas into sanctioning his appointment as 'director-general of finance' by brazenly informing him of 'the analysis of the financial situation which I have made and of which the king approves'.[5]

A year later Maurepas and Vergennes had their revenge on Pezay, whose hubris soon played into their hands. He was exiled and died of a broken heart. Louis did nothing to save him and for this was criticized by Soulavie, who thought that it was essential for the king to have unofficial sources of information. He believed, for example, that Louis was wrong to dismiss the agents of Louis XV's secret diplomacy, *le secret du roi*, because it had

protected him from the wiles of Austria and had been a bulwark
of traditional diplomacy. Similarly with Pezay. Soulavie writes:

> Thus did Louis XVI deliver up his favourite and his
> correspondence to the secret resentment and malice of ...
> [his ministers]. This trait began to develop the weakness of
> the prince. Pezay's letters, frequently composed or revised
> by Necker, had been his chief delight; he sacrificed these
> letters and their author to the restless jealousy of two
> ministers, who had for some time past concerted the ruin of
> Pezay. ...
>
> Louis XV, who was also weak and easily persuaded,
> would never have abandoned his favourite correspondence
> to the discretion of his mistresses or ministers. The conduct
> of his successor was a lesson for Vergennes and Maurepas.
> They endeavoured assiduously to conceal this weakness of
> the monarch, well aware that it might become the radical
> defect of the state which they had to govern and support.[6]

I stress the unconventional and personal nature of Louis's
appointment of Necker because of its consequences. This was the
great age of the charlatan. Cagliostro and Mesmer (the latter
with adherents in the French cabinet) were the most famous of
them but there were many others. It was the age of the 'project':
the scheme for getting something for nothing, the quest for the
philosopher's stone. As in the late twentieth century, the rapid
decline of formal religion gave rise to an increase in superstition.
As de Tocqueville observed, the French Revolution itself was a
displacement activity of this kind. Louis was interested in
projects and therefore susceptible to their authors. And in public
finance he was particularly vulnerable to them because he too
needed to square a circle, to turn dross into gold. How else could
he pursue naval rearmament let alone fight a war without
increasing taxation or declaring a bankruptcy? Turgot had said it
could not be done and Turgot was right.

Necker argued that it was permissible to raise loans provided
that sufficient to service them was saved by economies. Good
husbandry, individual economies appealed to Louis who
practised them himself, sometimes to a ludicrous extent, such as
when he told Marie-Antoinette, who remarked on his shabby
coat, 'nevertheless, Madame, it will have to last the summer'.[7]
Burley demonstrates why Necker appealed to Louis. He was a
reformer but, unlike Turgot, not *systématique* (an ideologue).

Louis had specifically charged Turgot with being *systématique* and Necker specifically said he himself was not. Necker, whose principles were eclectic, had read and absorbed the writings of men such as Moreau, Le Trosne and Réal who had influenced Louis's intellectual development. Both Louis and Necker wanted to explain the objectives of government to the people but through paternal absolutism rather than enlightened despotism. Both were adepts of the sentimental style of the day. Consider the words that Necker put into Louis's mouth in a public declaration of 1788: 'For several years I have known only moments of happiness ... What does spending money do for one's happiness?'[8]

Necker's gradualist approach was similar to the 'economical reform' advocated by the Opposition in England. As such it gained for Louis this extravagant encomium from Edmund Burke in the Commons in 1780:

By economy Lewis XVI has found sufficient resources to sustain the war [against England, begun in 1778]. In the first two years of it he has laid no burden whatever on his people. The third year is arrived; still no talk of imposts; and I believe that even those which are common in time of war have not been laid on. I conceive that in the end France must have recourse to imposts but those three years saved will extend their benign influence through a whole age. The French people feel the happiness of having an economical master; economy has induced that monarch rather to retrench his own splendours than the subsistence of his people. In the suppression of great numbers of places he has found a resource to continue the war, without adding to his expenses. He has despoiled himself of the magnificence and purple of royalty; but he has established a navy; he has reduced the number of his household servants but he has augmented the number of his sailors; he has given France such a navy as she never before possessed, and which will immortalize his reign; and he has established it without laying on a penny of imposts. The people under his reign are great, glorious and formidable; they do not groan under the burden of expenses to which our nation must submit to acquire greatness and inspire fear. This is true glory; this is a reign which must raise the name of Lewis XVI above the boasted reign of Henry IV.

Lewis XVI, like a patriot king, has exhibited great firmness in protecting Mr Necker, a foreigner without support and without connexion at court, alone indebted for his elevation to merit and the discernment of his sovereign, who has been able to discover and appreciate his talents. Here is a good example to follow; and, if we wish to conquer France, it is with her own weapons that we must attack her here; it is with econcomy and reformation.[9]

This, as far as I know, is the highest praise Louis XVI has ever received. Louis translated Burke's speech into French, and showed it to Necker, ostensibly to ask whether his translation was correct, in fact as a graceful way of letting Necker know of Burke's praise for his ministry.

Necker got away with reducing court pensions, which so impressed Burke, because the pill was sweetened by the simultaneous increase in the political power of the military aristocracy. This occurred both at the centre – where Necker introduced two soldiers, the marquis de Castries and the marquis de Ségur into the ministry over Maurepas's dying body – and in the provinces, where he set up two pilot 'provincial administrations' at Bourges and Montauban. In the Bourges assembly, set up in 1778, the original 16 members were appointed by the king and these co-opted a further 32 colleagues: Turgot's planned assemblies were to have been directly elected. Moreover whereas in Turgot's scheme the members were to be chosen from and by landowners irrespective of birth, in Necker's membership was allocated, a third each, to the three juridical orders of *ancien régime* society: clergy, nobility and Third Estate. Necker also decided that the noble members should be restricted to those who had owned a fief for over 100 years. This discriminated heavily in favour of the old military nobility, since more recent ennoblements were largely through the purchase of legal appointments, with no obligation to acquire a fief.

This attack on the service nobility, the *noblesse de robe*, lay at the philosophical heart of Necker's project but there is evidence that it did not find favour with the king. Necker believed that France was governed by some hundred families of the administrative *noblesse de robe* who were promoted according to seniority, but that it was patently absurd to consider that such families had a monopoly of the administrative talent in the kingdom. His particular *bête noire* was the *intendant*, of whom he wrote in a celebrated passage:

One can hardly give the name administration to this arbitrary volition of a single man who, whether present or absent, informed or incompetent, is obliged to run the most important aspects of the public service, for which he is necessarily unsuited, having devoted his entire life previously to the appellate functions of the council.[10]

Even then, Necker claimed, *intendants* spent most of their time intriguing to get back to Versailles as a *conseiller d'état* or a minister. Necker, like Turgot, envisaged his assemblies as ultimately replacing both the *intendants* and the provincial *parlements* as well as giving the regime a wider basis of support, though in practical terms that meant transferring the basis of support from the administrative nobility to the military one and to the clergy (Necker placed bishops as presidents of his assemblies).

Not surprisingly one of the most virulent opponents of Necker (both in an anonymous pamphlet in 1781 and in his memoirs) was an *intendant*, Sénac de Meilhan. Sénac makes the modern distinction between what he calls the 'causes' of the French Revolution and its 'occasion'. He reduces the causes to three:

The writings and conduct of M. Necker, which stirred up the *noblesse* and the people; the king's too easy-going kindness; and the Assembly of Notables [of 1787].[11]

Calonne, another *intendant*, criticized Necker for introducing the military aristocracy, ignorant of everything and therefore equally equipped to run anything, into the government.

Necker's contention that France was run by 100 administrative families was not controversial. Soulavie thought indeed that it was only 50, whom he 'religiously preserves' by naming them in a footnote. These men by their very caution preserved the systems which had been installed by Richelieu and Colbert, the founding fathers of Bourbon absolutism. 'Such', he concludes, 'was the form and regularity of the customs that one vigorous mind might preserve inviolate our ancient institutions.'[12] Vergennes also reminded Louis that the kings have

confided to illustrious families in the magistracy the care of presiding in the courts of justice and in the offices of the superior administration. It is from these families, distinguished by long services, that your majesty's ancestors have generally chosen persons, celebrated for their virtue and talents, to make them ministers of state.[13]

But Louis needed no reminding of this, though he revealed his thoughts, as we have seen, in marginal comments not on Necker's assemblies, where his observations are laconic and cryptic, but on Turgot's project:

> I find in the series of administrators, nominated by my ancestors, and in the principal families of the robe [law] and even of *la finance* of my kingdom, Frenchmen who would have done honour to any nation of the known world.[14]

These families, coeval with the Bourbon absolutism, had created it and would die for it. As Malesherbes of the Lamoignon family did. His freedom of intellect led him to criticize the regime but when the time came he was to be found defending the Tuileries on 10 August 1792, wearing a sword for the first time in his life. He contributed to Louis's defence when he was on trial before the National Convention and was guillotined in 1794. Miromesnil, from another of these families, also offered his services for Louis's trial.

The attack on *la finance*

Louis's unsolicited if backhanded praise for *la finance* is of relevance because its members, even more than the administrative robe, bore the brunt of Necker's attacks. *La finance* was one of the most characteristic institutions of the *ancien régime*. Like other office holders, such as *parlementaires*, its members bought their offices which represented a loan to the state on which they received 5 per cent interest. The most important were the *intendants des finances* who formed a permanent council for the usually transient finance ministers and the receivers-general of the direct and farmers-general of the indirect taxes. The *intendants des finances* were unpopular because they decided the tax affairs of individuals in secrecy and without appeal. They also acted as a break on a reforming finance minister and Necker abolished them. Members of '*la haute finance*', such as the receivers and farmers-general, employed their own people to collect the taxes and advanced money to the crown against future receipts whose level was contractually guaranteed. The distinction between public and private was blurred. Necker moved from these early modern arrangements towards the modern system of paying officials a salary to collect taxes, though with an element of bonus if the expected receipts were exceeded. As such he receives praise from the modern historians Bosher and Harris.

Soulavie, however, and Louis, defended the traditional financiers as a bulwark of the regime. They paid the crown less than they collected but it was an advance against taxes which in the case of the *taille* took two years to collect. Moreover the financiers would also lend unsecured sums to the king through thick and thin because they were 'tied to the maintenance of the machine'.[15] They lent to the crown because that was their *raison d'être*. They also provided a self-correcting mechanism, providing for the king's legitimate needs and more, but recoiling if his policies seemed to be going off the rails, as during Louis XIV's minority and dotage. Because they were tied to the regime, they defended it against all comers. How else than by their being 'tied to the maintenance of the machine' could one explain the willingness of the old financiers to lend to the Breteuil government days before the fall of the Bastille or to the king had the flight to Varennes succeeded?[16] As Malesherbes, for the administrative robe, paid the price on the scaffold, so, for *la finance*, did Magon de la Balue and the Farmers–General *en bloc*. That is why Louis said that '*even* the financiers . . . would have done honour to any nation of the known world'. Yet, perceiving their utility, he nevertheless permitted the attack on them.

Soulavie contrasts the willingness of the old financiers to lend to their native government with the footloose international capital favoured by Necker, eager to seek out the maximum advantage wherever it was to be found. The former system he dubs 'French' and the latter 'Anglo-Genevan'. The French system, which had prevailed until Louis XVI's accession, also required that extraordinary wartime expenditure should be 'derived only from taxes or loans founded upon them'. The Anglo-Genevan system countenanced financing war from loans without the collateral of additional taxation. Soulavie argued that Louis was buffeted like a 'shuttlecock' between these two systems, just as he was buffeted between pro- and anti-*philosophe* and pro- and anti-Austrian factions. The two financial systems alternated during the period 1774–94: when the 'French' system was installed in government, the Anglo-Genevan formed the opposition, until it was at length replaced by it. So Turgot (1774–76) told Louis on his appointment that in peacetime there should neither be new loans nor new taxes but considered that war must be financed by new taxation. He was followed by Necker who in his first ministry (1776–81) financed the American war by unsecured loans; Joly de Fleury (1781–83) instituted loans secured by increased taxation; that was also the aim of Calonne (1783–87) though his pursuit of the taxation side of the equation was unsuccessful. The alternating cycle continued into the Revolution with the Genevan Clavière versus the native Cambon.[17]

Necker's resignation

Louis parted from Necker in 1781 on different terms from the ones on which he had parted from Turgot in 1776: Necker resigned and Turgot was dismissed. Louis would not see Turgot in the days before his fall; his door was open to Necker and so was Marie-Antoinette's. Louis considered that Necker had deserted him in the middle of the American war (1778–83). When Necker's ally, the naval minister Castries, asked Louis to reappoint Necker in 1783, Louis wrote to him: 'I must tell you plainly that *from the manner in which I treated him and from his leaving me as he did*, I cannot think of taking him again into my service, in any situation.'[18] Soulavie considered that Necker's letter of resignation to the king was 'truly republican' and insulting, being written 'carelessly on a scrap of paper three and a half inches long by two and a half wide'.[19]

Necker had been under pressure following the leaking of his memorandum on provincial assemblies, which achieved the rare distinction of uniting both the *parlements* and the *intendants* against him. To counter this opposition he launched a propaganda coup by publishing his *Compte rendu au roi* in February 1781. In this celebrated work, he sought to demonstrate that despite three years of war and with little increase in taxation, there was a surplus of 10 million livres on the 'ordinary' account for 1781. Ever since there has been controversy about the veracity of these figures and/or the terminology employed by Necker. Necker, vigorously defended recently by Robert Harris, maintained that 'the ordinary revenues and expenditure are as well known at the beginning of the year as at the end of the fiscal year'.[20] Therefore these could be published in February as he had done. But it was impossible to know the 'extraordinary' expenditure in advance. Unfortunately this distinction meant omitting the entire expenditure on the war!

If Necker's intention had not been to obfuscate, he could have provided fairly accurate figures for both 'ordinary' and 'extra-ordinary' expenditure for the previous year, 1780. Or, he could have employed the formula provided by Louis himself at the end of his first year, 1774, to the departmental ministers:

> Send me as quickly as possible two detailed statements of expenditure for your department for the year 1775, one containing the fixed expenditure, the other the variable expenditure. By the first I mean what is bound to be incurred, by the second that which, being uncertain, nevertheless recurs every year and which can be measured by taking the average of the last ten years.[21]

Louis's approach suggests not only that Necker could easily have provided an 'average' figure but also that Louis probably saw through the *Compte rendu*. This suggests that he sanctioned a lie to facilitate the loans which were becoming more difficult to fill despite the generous terms Necker was forced to offer. But it would also suggest that he would be less ready to fight to retain Necker's services.

Necker resigned over Louis's refusal, on Maurepas's advice, to grant him entry to the *conseil d'état*. Necker wanted this as a mark of approval to buttress his position but also so that he could defend his measures in the council against his enemies, 'who', Soulavie relates, 'pretended not to understand his ideas, which the king had the goodness to explain and develop'.[22] One way of explaining the ultimate failure of both Turgot's and Necker's ministries is to say that each had had to make a Faustian bargain to achieve office: Turgot had to countenance the recall of the Parlement which fought his grain policy and six edicts tooth and nail; Necker had to finance war without taxes, which swamped his painstaking 'economical reforms' and drove him from office before he had time to set up the nationwide network of provincial assemblies with which, according to the duc de Lévis, 'the monarchy would have been indestructible and the prosperity of the state would have increased indefinitely'.[23]

Burley regards the appointment of Necker as giving Louis an unexpected second chance to redeem his dismissal of Turgot. Necker's departure 'left the regime with no new options and on the path to disintegration'.[24] For Burley, the turning point in

Louis's decline had been earlier, in 1778, with France's entry into the American war. This led to plans for further provincial assemblies being shelved and to a financial crisis so serious that Louis could not comprehend it. Nor, with his veto on bankruptcy, would he allow his ministers to tackle it.

Burley also asserts that from this time Louis became both bored with politics and dependent on Marie-Antoinette. We find no evidence for either of these propositions until 1787 when the king becomes not so much bored as depressed by politics after the rejection of his reform plan by the Assembly of Notables. It is true that from 1777, following his operation, Louis was able to enjoy full sexual relations with Marie-Antoinette and that he undoubtedly became fond of her. A daughter was born in 1778 and the long-hoped-for dauphin in 1781. Nevertheless Louis still managed to exclude her influence on major policy decisions, particularly, as we shall see in the next chapter, in foreign policy. The appointments of the naval and war ministers, Castries and Ségur, in 1780 are sometimes ascribed to her influence. But I have concluded that Necker's was the determinant force in these, though Castries and Ségur quickly adopted the queen as their patron. Furthermore the queen was unable to secure for Necker, who was highly regarded by her brother Joseph II, the marks of royal confidence which would have prevented his resignation.

|6|

Foreign policy, 1774–1789

Biographers tend to deal with what their readers want to know about their subject rather than what their subject cared about. Judging by his surviving correspondence Louis XVI, in common with his fellow sovereigns, spent the vast majority of his time dealing with foreign policy. That was *le métier du roi*; in a theoretically absolute monarchy politics was deemed not to exist; *la politique* is translated as 'foreign policy'. With the benefit of hindsight, we tend to think that such concerns were almost frivolous, given the problems of the regime; tend to agree with Turgot that if France entered the American war, the chance to reform the financial structure of the regime would be lost 'for a long time perhaps forever'.[1] But his was a minority view and we should at least be aware that in devoting just this one chapter to foreign policy, Louis's main preoccupation, I am guilty of distortion.

Our guide through the diplomatic minefield will be the great French nineteenth-century diplomatic historian, Albert Sorel, who published his *L'Europe et la Révolution française* in eight volumes between 1885 and 1904. For Sorel, as for Soulavie, Louis XVI 'had intelligence without will power, common sense without strength of character'.[2] At the start of his reign the French monarchy was even sicker in reputation abroad than at home, given the catastrophic defeats in the Seven Years' War, subservience to Austrian interests and the partition of her ancient ally Poland in 1772. In 1780 Vergennes reminded the king that at his accession, France, naturally the premier European power, barely ranked in the second division. Because there was no Richelieu to hand to cure ills both foreign and domestic in a coordinated policy, Louis appointed Turgot to cure the internal ills and Vergennes the external – though the one undermined the work of the other. Turgot failed and Vergennes succeeded.

There were, according to Sorel, two reasons for this. The first:

> The king understood the affairs of Europe infinitely better
> than those of France, because he had received instruction in
> the former, whilst the latter had been neglected. In any case,
> by whom could he have been taught? If such a tutor had
> existed he would have been the great minister of whom
> France had need.

The second reason for Vergennes's success and Turgot's failure was 'the extreme complication of the internal situation and the comparative simplicity of external affairs'. Consequently whereas the nation was divided on Turgot's policies – not just because he threatened vested interests but because many thought his grain policies were misguided – it was united in supporting Vergennes's objectives. These were: turn the Austrian alliance to France's advantage and take revenge on England for the humiliating peace of 1763. Nearly everyone in France, before and during the Revolution, on whatever side, *émigrés* or republicans, detested Austria. Moreover, since the nation was united, it did not require any will power on Louis's part to support Vergennes, since 'all that was needed was an honest intention and a knowledge of the permanent interests of France in Europe, both of which Louis XVI had'. Consequently, 'he could accept good counsels and give good advice'.[3]

An ethical foreign policy?

Sorel makes great play of Louis's 'honest intention', as does the king himself. As dauphin, Louis had received not only technical instruction in diplomacy from his *lecteur*, the veteran diplomatist the abbé de la Ville, also Vergennes's mentor, but instruction on international morality from Moreau who in 1773 published with the imprimatur of the foreign office a summation of his work, *Leçons de morale, de politique [foreign policy] et de droit public, tirées de l'Histoire de France et rédigées par l'ordre et d'après les vues de feu M. Le Dauphin pour l'éducation des princes ses enfants*, ('Lessons of morality, foreign policy and public law drawn from the history of France etc.').[4] When the abbé de la Ville died that year after a banquet to celebrate his elevation to the episcopacy, Moreau sought his job of *lecteur* to the dauphin, but Louis decided not to fill the vacancy.

In a policy statement at the start of his reign, Louis told
Vergennes that 'honesty and restraint must be our watchwords'.[5]
By 'honesty' he meant primarily observance of international
treaties. He told a diplomatic envoy: 'the first duty of sovereigns
is the observance of treaties; I will set an example and justice will
always be the basis of my conduct'.[6] The principal treaty was that
of Westphalia of 1648, the defence of which he claimed 'was
inherent in the crown'.[7] This treaty had instituted France as the
protector of the Holy Roman German Empire. Louis took this to
be the protection of the smaller German states against incursions
by the Austrian emperor. So when his brother-in-law, the
Emperor Joseph II, tried to get his hands on Bavaria in 1778 and
in 1785, Louis offered no help despite the nominal continuation
of the alliance and despite the tantrums of Marie-Antoinette
who, on one occasion, bawled at Vergennes like a fishwife.

Indeed Louis secretly encouraged the successful resistance of
Frederick the Great to Joseph's ambitions and Frederick's
creation of a league of German princes, the *Fürstenbund*, for that
purpose. Frederick would have been the principal loser from the
extension of his rival's power into the heart of Germany, but
France would also have found Alsace open to an Austrian
invasion and the Austrian hold on Italy consolidated by the
increased access of its armies to the peninsula via Bavaria. In the
same spirit, Louis refused to countenance Joseph's opening of the
Scheldt for the benefit of the Austrian Netherlands (modern
Belgium). The Scheldt had been closed to prevent Antwerp from
competing with Amsterdam. This may have been unfair, but it
was enshrined in the Westphalia treaties.

Louis believed that there had been a total collapse of international morality in the previous generation. This was
symbolized by the partition of the vast but weakly governed
Poland by Russia, Prussia and Austria in 1772. Louis had
nothing but contempt for the robbers who, he predicted, would
quickly fall out over their spoils. He detested Joseph, whom he
did not thank for persuading him, during his visit to France in
1777, to have his operation. He believed that the emperor should
learn to exploit his own territories fully before annexing new
ones. Thus in 1775 he told Vergennes that instead of annexing
Moldavia from the Turks, Joseph should have supported his own
efforts to secure freedom of commerce in the Black Sea from the
Ottomans.[8] Thus also he declined to support Joseph in his
Bavarian ambitions, even with the offer of a slice of Belgium or

Luxembourg or to countenance the dismemberment of the Ottoman Empire with Egypt as his share of the spoils.

In the same spirit he instructed Vergennes in October 1776:

> If we are forced to make war on England, it must be for the defence of our possessions and the abasement of her power, without any idea of territorial aggrandizement on our part, aiming solely to ruin English commerce and sap her strength by supporting the revolt and secession of the colonies, despite the axiom of M. de Grimaldi [Spanish foreign secretary] that one only fights wars for aggrandizement.[9]

And true to his word, French gains when peace was signed in 1783 were largely confined to trading advantages in India and fishing rights off Newfoundland. All France's diplomatic energy was expended in securing gains for her allies Spain and Holland, whose demands were as excessive as France's were modest. This was what Louis meant by saying 'restraint' should be the watchword. According to Sorel, Louis's policies anticipated the renunciation of foreign conquests proclaimed by the National Assembly at the start of the French Revolution, a policy blatantly violated by later assemblies.

Intervention in the American war

The moral dimension

I think that one has to qualify Sorel's view of both Louis's morality and his expertise, even accepting Sorel's point that Louis and Vergennes were operating in a world inhabited by sharks. It may seem churlish to criticize an ethical foreign policy, but when a man proclaims it rather than doing good by stealth, one's suspicions are raised and, despite Louis XVI's good intentions, his behaviour towards England at least was duplicitous. It also reveals, at the outset of his reign, the kind of subterfuges and casuistry for which this basically honourable man would acquire a reputation for duplicity among his own subjects during the Revolution.

The temptation to exploit England's difficulties with her colonies was too good a chance to miss. The colonies proclaimed their independence in 1776 but France was in no position to intervene since her rearmament was incomplete. Louis therefore authorized the clandestine payment of 1 million livres to the colonists (and facilitated the 'laundering' of a further million from Spain) and allowed them to trade in French ports and purchase arms and munitions. According to one account, he later, during the Revolution, expressed some remorse for this underhand dealing.[10] At the time, however, he wrote the following highly casuistical interpretation of his conduct to his cousin Charles III of Spain in 1778:

> We both agreed not to intervene in the American war and, regarding both parties as English, we have made trade with our countries free to whichever can turn it to their account. In this way America has furnished herself with the arms and munitions it was lacking. I make no mention of the monetary and other help we have given them, the whole having taken the form of a commercial transaction.[11]

Louis's last sentence refers to the fact that the 1 million livres was sent to America through a fictitious trading company organized by Beaumarchais.

Louis was much more honest in the marginal comments he made on the French manifesto which sought to justify French entry into the American war. Soulavie, who published these comments, concludes:

> It appears . . . that Louis XVI was secretly ashamed of the part he was playing and that he wished, in his manifestos, to reduce the number of opportunities for reproach, which England might find in replying to his memorials.[12]

The manifesto proclaimed that Louis had 'remained a tranquil spectator' in the dispute between England and her colonies, avoiding 'the slightest suspicion' of 'entering into correspondences of any sort with the insurgents'. Louis noted that it would be 'difficult to persuade' the French let alone the English that France had remained aloof; 'it would therefore be better not to utter a syllable on this subject since true or false our asseveration will not be believed'.[13]

The manifesto skated on thin ice for a monarchist, arguing as it did that revolts of provinces or whole nations against their rulers were a fact of life which international relations should recognize, the examples of Charles I and Mary Queen of Scots being adduced. Louis, embarrassed by Louis XIV's alliance with

Cromwell, wanted to omit these references, as also that to Elizabeth I helping the Low Countries shake off the Spanish yoke: 'The conduct of Elizabeth is neither a rule nor a precedent in the code of the law of nations.'

Nor, Louis argued, was it fair to argue that a section of English opinion favoured the colonists, since this section formed the Opposition. To support factions opposed to government was a violation of the law of nations and would set a precedent for English intrigues with the *parlements* or the independent-minded province of Brittany. Earlier, Louis had specifically rejected a proposal by Beaumarchais to subsidize the English Opposition as 'unjust'.[14] Beaumarchais, who organized the supply of guns to the colonists, had advanced the argument of *raison d'état* used by Machiavelli and Richelieu that actions which might be wrong in a private individual could be justified in a ruler. Louis repudiated this notion. Soulavie, who maintained that Louis was and remained an honourable man, transcribed some reflections of Louis's on authorizing 'certain [unspecified] unjust measures against the tranquillity of England':

> What a situation is mine! Why should I be obliged, by reasons of state, and the pretext of a great military operation, already entered upon [the planned Franco-Spanish invasion of England in 1779?], to sign orders which my heart condemns, and to which my opinions are adverse.[15]

Louis also vetoed any hostile references to George III in the French manifesto on the grounds that under the English constitution the king acted only on advice from his ministers. The English manifesto adopted a similar stance:

> It is sad that the ministers of His Most Christian Majesty have surprised the religion of their sovereign to cover their baseless assertions with so respectable a name.[16]

Louis's obvious discomfort on these matters lends weight to Burley's contention that the ideological confusion of a monarch supporting the rebellious subjects of a fellow monarch sapped his morale – a secondary reason, on top of the financial, for Burley's view that France's declaration of war marked the decline of Louis's reign. This moral confusion also suggests that Louis's foreign policy did not have the cogent simplicity Sorel suggests.

Realpolitik

The French manifesto argued that England had clearly been unable to hold down her colonies, so that they had achieved a *de facto* independence which should be recognized (a guideline applied in British diplomacy to this day). Louis XVI, however, countered: 'What if England should reply to this that she should have been able to suppress the rebellion if France had not lent her aid to the insurgents?' This counterfactual note may serve to introduce a second possible criticism of Louis XVI's foreign policy: was the decision to intervene mistaken even in terms of *realpolitik*? In October 1776, the king told Vergennes that the recent English recapture of New York was good news. First because it would commit George III more deeply to a war which he could not win, since even if he reasserted his control, the colonies would be ruined and England too. Second it would strengthen the North administration which was well disposed to France or, put another way, turned a blind eye both to French rearmament and to French clandestine help to the colonists for fear of bringing about full-scale war.[17]

So why, having made this lucid and correct analysis, did Louis not stick to it instead of entering the war some 18 months later? England's preoccupations in America permitted France to carry out a rearmament which it would otherwise have put a stop to – and France *ipso facto* increased its prestige, as Louis realized, without the risk and expense of war. The issues are complicated. The American historian Jonathan Dull, in his account of the navy under Louis XVI, argued that 'hawks' like Vergennes and Sartine, the naval minister, were determined on war from the outset and the delay in entering the war was precisely as long as it took for rearmament to be completed. They bamboozled the inexperienced and pacific Louis XVI into a rearmament which, as naval races usually do, carried with it its own momentum towards war. In persuading the king they deployed an argument in which they did not believe, namely that once the struggle with its colonies was over then, whether they had won or lost, the English troops then in the American hemisphere would be turned on the French sugar islands and the Spanish Main. France, then, should waste no time in entering the war whilst she could have the colonists as an ally. Another American historian, C.H. Van Tyne, argues that Vergennes' fears, whether grounded or not, were sincere.[18]

Both these historians depict the king as a pawn in the hands of his ministers. He thought it wrong to support the rebellious subjects of a fellow sovereign and he believed the financial situation would be irremediably damaged by a war. Beaumarchais put it in so many words to Maurepas that just as Maurepas had overcome the king's basic instincts in persuading him to recall the *parlements* in 1774, so now he should overcome similar resistance on the part of his sovereign.[19] Dull and Van Tyne's line implies a criticism of the ministers for overpersuading the king and of the king for being seduced. The modern French historian of Vergennes, Labourdette, believes that his subject constantly behaved in this way and that the mountainous correspondence to which Vergennes subjected Louis XVI consisted of a specious presentation of alternatives angled towards the desired conclusion.[20]

It is indeed a common view among historians that Louis XVI's ministers 'took advantage of his youth' to embroil him in the American war.[21] The quotation actually comes from some words attributed to the king by his naval minister in 1792 when, with hindsight, the deficit caused by the war had played a part in the outbreak of the French Revolution. Whether these words are apocryphal or not, the fact remains that though he was only 19 on his accession, Louis XVI came to his tasks as a diplomat fully armed. Whatever skills he possessed, he possessed them then; there is no development in the 13 years of his correspondence with Vergennes. We have seen his analysis of the consequences of the English victory off Long Island in 1776. Equally impressive was his analysis of Ottoman affairs made in 1774 and his detailed instructions for the French ambassador to Constantinople.[22] The view of the king as a pawn in his ministers' hands also contrasts with the earlier view of Soulavie and Sorel which assumed both greater diplomatic skill on his part and a basic agreement between him and his ministers (and public opinion) on objectives.

My own view of Louis XVI's crucial decision to enter the American war is as follows. Louis did not initially want to enter the war but he did want to rearm: this was why Turgot had to go. Louis was obsessed with the sea: even as a boy he 'knew as much as one can know about naval affairs without having gone to sea' – this from Mercy-Argenteau who belittled his abilities.[23] He may well have appointed Maurepas, a successful naval minister under Louis XV, in order to rebuild the navy. Dull's contention that

Sartine, in pursuit of bureaucratic empire building as much as bellicosity, rebuilt the navy by tricking Louis progressively to increase the naval estimates is not convincing. Louis constantly kept Sartine, a lawyer by training, on his toes as regards naval matters. Louis was just as anxious as Vergennes to restore French prestige in the world and was aware that by 1776 the rearmament had already achieved much of this without war.

Then in December 1777 news arrived that a British army of 5000 men had capitulated to American irregulars at Saratoga Springs. Vergennes and Sartine pressed for war. (Whether they believed that the capitulation showed that the Americans were a force to be relied upon or whether they believed that the endgame had been reached and English troops were about to be unleashed on Franco-Spanish possessions does not matter.) Vergennes then persuaded Louis to authorize him to negotiate with the American envoys then in France. This Louis did in instructions he dictated to Vergennes in December 1777. Vergennes wrote them on the king's own blue quartered paper and the king minuted them, *approuvé le 6 decembre 1777*. H. Doniol, writing in 1886, considered that the moment here preserved marked the renaissance of French foreign policy. In fact Louis's instructions are very restrictive, insisting on maximum secrecy and above all stipulating that nothing be decided until the views of Charles III had been obtained: Charles was notoriously unwilling to enter the war lest he set an example to his own American colonists (North and South).[24]

What determined Louis to enter the fray was an event nearer at home than Saratoga Springs: the death of the elector of Bavaria, news of which reached Versailles on 6 January 1778. Louis knew that Joseph II would be putting pressure on him to support his claim to the duchy as a lapsed imperial fief. His entry into the American war gave him the pretext to refuse backing for a claim which Louis believed to be worthless. Further to box himself in, Louis made Charles III the unsolicited pledge that he would not be involved in the German dispute further than supplying his good offices. When Joseph reproached Louis for his lack of assistance in Bavaria, Louis rhetorically asked what help he had received in America.

Sorel considered that Louis possessed neither the genius of the first Bourbon, Henri IV, nor the discerning self-effacement of the second, Louis XIII, in delegating power to another genius, Richelieu. What would Richelieu have done at this juncture? He

would have accepted Belgium from Joseph as the price of his
support for the latter's annexation of Bavaria. And he would
have accepted it because this was the one moment in history
when England was in no position to stop the transaction. In
return for George III's recognition of the cession, he would have
abstained from all further help for the colonists: that would have
tied England up for the foreseeable future, as Louis had predicted
in 1776. This may have been behaving a little dishonourably
towards the colonists but they behaved dishonourably towards
France: in 1782 they broke the one condition France placed on
them in the 1778 treaty, that they would not negotiate a separate
peace with England. But it would have been more honourable
conduct towards England. Belgium was French-speaking and in
the middle ages had been part of France. Its assimilation and
retention would have been easier than that of Alsace and
Lorraine. Louis XVI would have gained far more prestige than he
gained through war and without the expense.

The early historian of Louis XVI, the abbé Proyart, writing in
the hagiographical tradition, offers an interesting perspective on
his hero's decision to enter the American war. Louis had been
'imbued since his childhood with the sad truth that even the most
successful war was still a calamity'. He would have done anything to spare his people from the misfortune of war. However,
'the American war was the work of the whole nation', as well as
the unanimous wish of the *conseil d'état*.[25] Two fundamental
principles clashed in Louis' mind: his pacifism and belief in the
observance of treaties and his even stronger belief that he should
follow public opinion. Proyart and Sorel are right in saying that
the American war was a popular one: after the French defeat at
the battle of The Saints in 1782, many corporate bodies opened
subscriptions to replace the destroyed ships. Indeed, given the
vogue for this particular war, Louis was perhaps unwise not to
have raised taxation earlier (though, as we have seen, Edmund
Burke applauded his abstinence) because of the effects of
financial embarrassments on future foreign policy.

Dutch débâcle

The war caused the deficit which caused the Revolution is a
commonly accepted causal sequence. Recently T.C.W. Blanning
has suggested another link in the chain: the war caused the deficit

which caused a humiliating diplomatic climbdown in 1787 which led to the Revolution.[26] During the American war, the Dutch Republic had been weaned away from her traditional dependence on England and had entered the war on the French side. In 1785 this alliance was cemented in peacetime also by the Treaty of Fontainebleau, arguably the highwater mark of Louis XVI's reign. Apart from key ports held by Holland, particularly on the Cape of Good Hope and in Ceylon, in the post-Necker era, Holland had replaced Geneva as the main source for royal loans. However, the Dutch Republic was unstable internally, indeed on the verge of civil war between the stadtholder (who represented the monarchical element in the complicated constitution) and the Patriots, a revolutionary group which had taken over from the traditional opposition party in the States General. France supported the Patriots. This was part and parcel with the ideologically ambiguous policy Louis XVI had pursued in America. But it also stemmed from the fact that England traditionally supported the stadtholder's family, the House of Orange, with whom it had dynastic links. The closest dynastic link, however, was with the Hohenzollerns: the stadtholder had married the sister of Frederick William II of Prussia, who succeeded his uncle Frederick II in 1786.

This being the case, it was very silly of the Patriots to interrupt a journey of Frederick William's sister in 1787. Prussia and England intervened militarily to restore power to the stadtholder, who abrogated the Treaty of Fontainebleau. Louis XVI, weakened by Calonne's revelation of the size of the deficit to the Assembly of Notables, stood helplessly aside. The naval and army ministers protested and resigned. The former plausibly argued that the French, who put national pride before all else, would tolerate increased taxation for intervention in Holland and for that alone. The shame sealed the fate of the monarchy. The Peace of Paris of 1783 had, Vergennes rightly believed, removed the stain of the Peace of Paris of 1763, when India and Canada had been lost. Now it was back.

|7|

1781–1787

Personal rule?

In November 1781 as the dying premier Maurepas slipped in and out of consciousness, news reached Versailles of the decisive victory of Yorktown when 8000 British troops under Cornwallis surrendered to the Franco-American forces. Thoughtfully, Louis XVI sent the duc de Lauzun to give the old man the news. As Lauzun detailed the 214 cannon seized and the 22 standards, Maurepas seemed to be taking it all in, ticking off each item with a crisp '*bon*', but then he confessed that 'he was dying and did not even know whom he had the honour of addressing'.[1] He would not have been able to comprehend that though the war might yet continue some time, its outcome had been decided.

A month before, on 22 October, three days after Cornwallis's capitulation, Louis secured a victory of equal worth: Marie-Antoinette at last gave birth to a dauphin. Soulavie drew a conclusion from the near simultaneous birth of a dauphin and death of a premier: Marie-Antoinette, 'a woman deficient in capacity' became the premier, thanks to 'the too easy disposition of Louis XVI'.[2] The process may indeed have begun then, or even in 1780 when the queen began to influence ministerial appointments, but it was not really significant until 1787 when the king, demoralized by his defeat at the hands of the Assembly of Notables, turned towards her, politically, for the first time.

Instead, the period 1781–87 can arguably be called the period of Louis XVI's personal rule. Castries, the naval minister, noted in his diary that the day after Maurepas's death, 'The king summoned a *comité* where he spoke more than usual, as one who was saying to himself, "I intend to reign." '.[3] The truth is that in this period Louis slips from view, except for foreign policy. Louis's correspondence with Vergennes reveals the anguish felt by both men as the French war machine begins to crumble with the naval defeat at The Saints in April 1782. Yet for months her Spanish ally will not allow her to conclude peace with England without the cession of Gibraltar, which they are incapable of recapturing. When in December Spain finally gives way and peace preliminaries are signed the following January, the relief is palpable. But all this is behind closed doors. No one outside the council chamber realized how near to ruin the reign, indeed the regime, had come.

Next year Louis strenuously resists Joseph II's attempts to bully France's new ally the Dutch Republic into granting territorial and commercial concessions and, that failing, Joseph's attempts to revive the Bavarian exchange. In this Louis is aided by a united cabinet, not excluding ministers who were the protégés of Joseph's sister, Marie-Antoinette. Yet the secrecy of foreign policy gave rise to malicious speculation. Much effort in diplomacy is expended on saving the face of the vanquished: on this occasion Joseph's face was saved by a payment of 2 million florins from the Dutch, which in fact was provided by France. With nothing but malice to go on, the public jumped to the conclusion that Marie-Antoinette was siphoning off funds to give to her brother – *de là le déficit*, as de Tocqueville encapsulates the popular logic. An argument perhaps for more open government. De Tocqueville also relates as evidence of Marie-Antoinette's dangerous and increasing unpopularity that when she visited the church of Sainte-Geneviève in 1785 to give thanks for the birth of her second son, the duc de Normandie, 'she was greeted by the people with a coolness which bordered on impertinence'.[4]

The doors were closed on home affairs too. Those gilded doors which Necker, in his *Compte rendu*, had opened *à deux battants* to the sovereign public opinion, if only to admit a flattering light, were now slammed in the same public's face as the *arcana imperii* returned to their former arcane state. The authorities I have used so far scarcely mention these years. Soulavie, who devotes five volumes to the period up to Maurepas's death, devotes only one, admittedly plump, volume to the rest of the reign to the king's death in 1793. He does, however, consider the years following Necker's dismissal as propitious ones:

All these ministers, endowed with what M. Necker's public opinion called confined ideas, procured the only quiet time which the reign of Louis XVI had enjoyed, and which lasted for five years. It would have remained unalterably so, if the queen had not succeeded in dismissing the virtuous d'Ormesson [controller-general of finances, March–November 1783], and putting M. de Calonne in his place.[5]

Soulavie believed that all ministers were divided into those who believed in human perfectibility and reform and those who wished to maintain the status quo.

He was, however, mistaken in placing 'the virtuous d'Ormesson', who attempted to end tax-farming, in the latter camp. In 1783 important reforms were undertaken as part of the stock-taking often made at the end of a war. In the past these had included a partial bankruptcy, but this was excluded not only by Louis's pledge at the start of his reign but also by the wider basis of public credit which had developed in the course of it: mulcting the old-style financiers had been popular but international bankers could not be treated in so cavalier a fashion. It has been argued recently that the recall of the Parlement in 1774 had removed the accusation of royal despotism only to see it transformed in the public mind into one of ministerial despotism. This accusation the reforms of 1783 sought to allay by reasserting conciliar control over financial decisions which had tended to be decided by the finance minister alone. The agency for these reforms was the *comité des finances* and it sought to achieve 'budgetary control, reform of direct taxation and the abolition of the general farm'.[6]

However, the driving force behind these reforms was not Louis but Necker's successors, Joly de Fleury and d'Ormesson, and above all Vergennes who was given Maurepas' old post of *chef du conseil royal des finances*: 'The part that the king played in the events of 1783', a recent historian concludes, '. . . is difficult to define, since the main impression one gets from the records is one of absence' – though he adds, 'this could be deceptive' and shows how Louis moved to set limits to Vergennes's authority.[7] The reform initiatives failed through divisions within the government and a credit crisis (which the old-style financiers, threatened by the proposed end of tax-farming, may have exacerbated) and caused near panic in a king who consistently proved himself vulnerable to any threat to the supply of credit. Calonne, the spokesman of these financiers, was appointed controller-general and quickly restored confidence.

A recent historian of the Parlement, lamenting that the Parlement was kept in the dark about the critical state of the royal finances, even added that 'the king was not among the initiated'.⁸ This is not true. Joly de Fleury instigated an inquiry into the veracity of Necker's *Compte rendu* and reported its unfavourable findings to the king. His successor, d'Ormesson, in a memorandum to the king of August 1783, pointed out that key taxes would expire in 1787 and planned to make a virtue out of necessity by overhauling the entire tax system and placing it on a more equitable basis, both between regions and among social groups. This was, in its essentials, the programme Calonne was to lay before the Notables in that very year, 1787, a programme for which Louis could not have been as unprepared as is generally stated.

Whilst these subterranean currents were percolating through the geological strata of the *ancien régime*, the public's attention was captured by two events, one of happy, the other of less happy, augury: the king's visit to Cherbourg to inaugurate the enlargement of the port and the diamond necklace affair. In August 1786 Louis XVI for the only time in his life saw the sea which so exercised his mind. He travelled to Cherbourg to inaugurate the construction of a breakwater which would enable a large fleet to assemble within sight of England. It was a massive undertaking which was not completed for 60 years. The king enjoyed himself directing naval manoeuvres and socializing at all levels. For historians as widely differing in their estimation of Louis XVI as de Tocqueville and Michelet, it was the high-water mark of the reign. Louis, swapping '*vive mon peuple*' for the people's acclamations of '*vive le roi*', exclaimed, according to de Tocqueville, 'this visit was the only happy period of my life'.⁹

Michelet, the republican, anti-clerical historian, with nevertheless a soft spot for Louis, having listed the king's failings such as 'duplicity' and 'mental reservations', during the Revolution, added:

> With all that, let us not forget that he had been sincerely anti-Austrian and anti-English; that he had truly, fervently desired to improve our navy; that he had founded Cherbourg at eighteen leagues from Portsmouth.¹⁰

Michelet has Louis, in the mayor's coach, on the way back to prison after appearing at his trial in 1792, lapsing into a reverie on his favourite subject, the navy, on that glorious period of his reign, already far distant, when his ships were triumphant in every corner of the globe, when he personally gave La Pérouse his instructions, and designed the port of Cherbourg. Ah! if ever there was a contrast, it was this no doubt, the memory of that day when the king, young, powerful, in the bloom of life, wearing the dazzling costume of an admiral (red and gold), amidst the smoke from a hundred cannons, crossed the roadstead of the great port he had created, visited the famous dike by which France had conquered not only the English but the ocean![11]

Louis's visit to Cherbourg followed hard on the heels of the conclusion of the diamond necklace affair and immediately preceded the Assembly of Notables, the curtain-raiser to the Revolution. No one's reputation has emerged unscathed from the necklace affair which caused incalculable damage to the king and queen and indeed to the regime. The brief facts of the case, as they are generally understood, are that the cardinal de Rohan, the descendant of the autonomous dukes of Brittany, was duped by Mme de La Motte-Valois, a supposed descendant of Henri II, into believing that the queen wanted Rohan to act as her agent in buying a diamond necklace worth 1,600,000 livres secretly from the court jewellers. When Böhmer, the jeweller, presented Marie-Antoinette's forged promissory note for payment, Rohan, who had handed the necklace over to La Motte-Valois, was arrested in his pontificals as he was about to celebrate high mass and thrown in the Bastille. Louis allowed him the choice of venue for his trial and he elected trial by the Parlement, which acquitted him. Neverthless, Louis stripped him of his offices and exiled him to his abbey of Père-le-Chaise, high in the mountains above Puy-de-Dôme.

The standard interpretation of these facts, both at the time and later, is that Louis behaved both foolishly and unjustly. Foolishly because if he wanted to punish Rohan he could have done it by *lettre de cachet*, without the embarrassment of a trial in which, to be acquitted, Rohan had to argue that it was plausible that the queen, without the knowledge of the king, should seek to buy a costly necklace through the intermediary of a cardinal. And if the king nevertheless wanted a trial, it should have been by a special tribunal, as the foreign and naval ministers advised, rather than by the Parlement which would relish the opportunity to curry popularity at the expense of the king. Unjustly because, as the minister of justice warned Louis, he must distinguish between his role as king-judge and that of husband. As for the exile of Rohan after the verdict, de Tocqueville observed: 'when the law absolves, the sovereign should not punish; because then he is merely exercising a personal vengeance'.[12]

New evidence however has recently come to light which alters the whole complexion of the case. A letter from Louis XVI to Vergennes the day after Louis had ordered Rohan's arrest reveals that Rohan, during his initial interrogation by the king, confessed to forging the queen's signature to obtain the diamonds in order to discharge his enormous debts.[13] This new information also throws into relief the fact, which has always been known, that shortly before his incarceration in the Bastille, Rohan had time to get a message to his secretary to destroy all his papers: which suggests that the evidence for the crime he confessed to the king vanished at this time. It also highlights the point Marie-Antoinette herself made: was it likely that she would ask the cardinal, a man whom she hated, and had not spoken to for eight years, to perform so compromising a commission? Again, if Louis believed that Rohan was incontrovertibly guilty one can understand why he was prepared to risk a trial in Parlement which would carry more conviction with the public than one in a prerogative court; and why he punished despite the acquittal.

None of this cut any ice with the public. The question of civil liberty was raised in many a pamphlet. Moreover this could not even be passed off as ministerial despotism. Vergennes, who was working for Rohan's acquittal behind the king's back, supplied the *Gazette de Leyde* with copious details of his search for defence witnesses. This was naked royal despotism.

The affair marked a decisive stage in the development of Marie-Antoinette's unpopularity. The gutter press poured out a stream of political pornography against her, one *libelle*, for example, claiming that she had contracted venereal disease from Rohan and proceeded to infect half the court, and others that the duc de Normandie was illegitimate. One might have thought that such libels were too gross to be credible, but Vergennes took them seriously, writing, in 1782, 'as many letters to England about the need to suppress a smut factory run by *émigré* French *libellistes*' as about the peace negotiations. The police minister thought 'the Parisians had more of a propensity to believe the malicious rumours and *libelles* that circulated clandestinely' than official information. He added that his effort to suppress these writings 'was undercut by courtiers who had scandalous works printed and protected the printers'.[14]

|8|

Watershed

The Assembly of Notables

At this point, the autumn of 1786, after the denouement of the diamond necklace affair and the triumphant visit to Cherbourg, we approach the watershed of Louis XVI's life and reign. This concerns the comprehensive package of reforms which in February 1787, after six months' examination by the king, the controller-general Calonne presented to a specially convoked Assembly of Notables in the name of the king. Hitherto, outside the field of foreign affairs, Louis had not exhibited a distinctive personal policy, beyond seeking to establish a new moral tone in public affairs, symbolized by his rejection of bankruptcy as an instrument of government. He had taken a detached view of the operations of many of his ministers (a tendency which was to increase during the Revolution), even, Véri wrote in 1783, 'himself setting the example of showing contempt for them'.[1] Calonne's programme, however, became personal to the king, so that Louis's identification with his minister came to be as much of a constitutional embarrassment as had been his previous detachment. Moreover the defeat of the king's cherished plans wrought in him a change so profound that one can talk of two Louis's, the one before the Notables, the one after. There is a simultaneous personal and political watershed and it occurs in 1787 rather than 1789.

The programme which Calonne outlined to the king in August 1786 covered the whole spectrum of administration and had political and constitutional implications. Internal customs were abolished, the grain trade freed, the *corvée* commuted, and the phasing out of the *gabelle* (salt tax) and the *taille* announced. But the linked heart of the programme was the replacement of the *vingtièmes* by a single land tax payable by all sections of society and every region without any privileged exceptions, and its assessment by a three-tier system of assembly (parish, district and provincial), membership of which would be determined by the sole criterion of the possession of landed wealth. The traditional division of French society into orders (clergy, nobles, Third Estate) was ignored because it was felt that an assembly dominated by the privileged orders would rig the assessment of the tax.

There are several problems in explaining Louis's indentification with such a programme. Disregarding d'Ormesson's flippant and sour observation that the programme was presented by Calonne to the king with typical insouciance and accepted by the king with an insouciance which was typical of him too – Louis pondered the measures for nearly six months – why did Louis embrace such a programme from Calonne when, we are told, he had jibbed at the far more modest proposals of Turgot and Necker? Why strain at a gnat and swallow a camel? Then again the programme, especially the provincial assemblies, was closely based on Turgot's memoir on 'municipalities' – both the memoir and Calonne's legislation were drafted by Dupont de Nemours. Yet, as we have seen, Louis, in copious marginal comments, roundly rejects Turgot's assemblies and makes the cynical point that self-assessment, no matter what the composition of an assembly, will always be biased. Finally, given Calonne's reputation for fast-living and sharp practice, why did Louis stake the future of the monarchy on the plans of such a man rather than those of such undoubted men of integrity as Turgot, Necker and d'Ormesson? Or had he fallen for the contemporary jibe (directed at d'Ormesson) that brains and integrity were incompatible?

First of all, although the convocation of the Notables seemed such a bolt from the blue that people thought it betokened either a financial calamity or some imbecility in the king, we have seen that Louis was aware that a crisis had been brewing for some time, was almost, as it were, scheduled for 1787. This crisis had been prefigured by the report that Necker's *Compte rendu* was false (July 1781), the near disintegration of the war machine (1782) and a major credit crisis (1783). In 1787 the third *vingtième* was to expire but we also know from a memorandum Louis himself drew up in April 1787 that he did not intend to extend the second *vingtième* (which Necker had prorogued for 10 years in 1781) when it expired in 1791 (La Fayette, in the Notables, was to ask for a meeting of the Estates-General to coincide with this event).[2] So the most efficient taxes of the monarchy, the *vingtièmes,* were in any case in the melting pot. One of the great attractions of Calonne's proposed tax for Louis, who unlike all but a handful of *parlementaires* was aware of the ravages of inflation, was that as a fixed proportion of the annual crop, and paid in kind, it would not have to be renegotiated. This recognition he also makes clear in his April 1787 memorandum.

As we have seen, Calonne's proposed assemblies (like Turgot's) ignored the traditional division of French society into orders in favour of one based solely on landed wealth. Louis specifically criticized this feature of Turgot's proposals. 'The composition of the three orders', he writes,

> is too essentially connected with the privileges of Frenchmen, and the mission of the *intendants* is too closely concerned with royal authority, to allow of their being metamorphosed into deputies of the people . . . The administration of the *intendants* is, with the exception of certain abuses, the best administered branch of the national government.[3]

However, as we have seen, the king's marginal comments are dated 15 February 1788, that is at a time when Louis had already promised to summon the Estates-General and was conscious that the very existence of the old society was beginning to be challenged.

As regards the relative powers of the *intendant* and the provincial assemblies, on Louis's reading of Calonne's proposals, as defined in his memorandum of April 1787, the latter

> will only have the authority to order the execution of what has already been ordered [by the *conseil d'état* or the *intendant*] and will not even have the power of simulated consent enjoyed by the *pays d'états.*[4]

Calonne was, of course, himself an ex-*intendant* and his programme, though in many ways egalitarian, had little to do with liberty or liberalism. If it was revolutionary, it was the revolution of Napoleon, not of the Rights of Man.

As regards Calonne's dubious reputation, much of this depended on certain practices, which were deemed to be sharp by his opponents, at the expense of the *parlements* both as a young crown lawyer under Louis XV and more recently as controller-general. This, however, served only to endear him to the king as one of a dwindling band of loyal servitors of Bourbon absolutism. Calonne's view of the *parlements* was very similar to the one we have seen Louis XVI express in these same marginal comments on Turgot's proposals, when he said the *parlements* would yield when the 'people at large' had to do the paying but would suffer 'hardship and exile' rather than suffer in their own pockets.[5] The band of 'the king's good servants' had already been dealt a blow by the recall of the Parlement in 1774 and if Louis wanted to modernize the Bourbon state his choice of agents was strictly limited: had not Terray said that, having been pelted by stones and burnt in effigy, he was not game for another try? This, as Julian Swann observes, 'was the price paid for the abandonment of the king's party in 1774'.[6]

Calonne had reached an impasse with the Parlement by 1786. The Parlement was not prepared to register any more of the annual loans which had kept the regime afloat for the past 10 years. The head of the Parlement, as Miromesnil told the king, was 'always disposed to undermine ... [Calonne's] administration', yet, Miromesnil advised, he could not be dismissed without putting him on trial.[7] This impasse could perhaps have been solved by Calonne's resignation, but at the price of the crown's submitting to the grinding tutelage of the Parlement which had darkened Louis's adolescence. And since Calonne was embattled with the Parlement precisely because he was an exemplary servant of the crown, his fate could never be merely personal. Louis did contemplate sending a portion of the reform programme before the Parlement as insurance, but Miromesnil advised him that the attempt was not even worth making. By this advice he was admitting that the settlement with the Parlement of 1774, of which he was the architect, had failed; that the classical political system of the *ancien régime* was dead; and that something would have to be put in its place. The Assembly of Notables was the first in a long line of experiments.

The story of the Notables' rejection of Calonne's measures is well known. Cynics observe that a body, even a nominated one as this was, consisting almost entirely of members of the privileged orders, was hardly likely to approve the destruction of fiscal privilege. Others point out that the Notables were liberal aristocrats who disliked the authoritarian nature of Calonne's programme and would have been prepared to sacrifice their financial privileges in return for representative institutions, in which no doubt they hoped to play the leading role. Some, like La Fayette, had just come back from fighting in America in defence of the slogan of 'no taxation without representation'. He specifically asked for the Estates-General.

What needs to be emphasized is how hard Louis fought to defend Calonne, that he did not weakly cave in. J. Egret, in *The French Pre-Revolution* is surely wrong in saying: 'The venture on which Calonne had embarked the monarchy was beyond Louis XVI's abilities.'[8] Calonne, well aware of Louis's reputation for climbdowns (*reculades*) courageously insisted at the outset that if the king was not prepared to back him through thick and thin it would be better not to introduce the measures. Louis gave his word and kept it. Joseph Droz, whose *Histoire du règne de Louis XVI pendant les années ou l'on pouvait prévenir ou diriger la Révolution française* was published in 1839, maintained that at this point (autumn 1786) Louis should have dismissed Calonne 'who had deceived the king [over the deficit] and through him his subjects' and entrusted the implementation of his reforms to Necker, who was so popular that he would not even have needed to summon the Notables.[9] This judgement ignores two salient factors. First, that Louis believed that Necker and not Calonne had deceived the people and himself about the deficit, whose existence Necker denied. Second, that Necker's pilot provincial assemblies had exercised true delegated executive authority, something Louis was not yet ready to apply across the country. Necker was the opponent of the *intendants*, Louis their champion.

The turning point in the meeting of the Assembly of Notables was the publication of Calonne's measures preceded by an *avertissement*, which connotes both 'preface' and 'warning'. Lafayette characterized this preface, ironically praising the work of the Notables, as an 'appeal to the people which would be considered seditious even at Boston'.[10] This first of many attempts to put popular pressure on an assembly in the revolutionary period badly backfired. It made Calonne desperate with the Notables yet elicited little response from the people, despite its having been read from every pulpit in Paris on Palm Sunday 1787. Louis's personal role in this needs to be elucidated. Egret notes that hitherto Louis had supported ... [Calonne] with a constancy that was undoubtedly accompanied by some fear in the face of such a revolutionary innovation as the confusion of orders in the provincial assemblies. But this constancy ended abruptly with the scandal of the preamble ... terrifying the timid king.[11]

However, we now know from the diary of the naval minister Castries, that Louis, who read the *Avertissement* and may even, as was his wont, have corrected sections, defended the move and hoped to exploit it during the Holy Week recess. Castries indeed accused Louis to his face of egging Calonne on: 'Is it your majesty who is causing M. de Calonne to act so imprudently?'[12] Part of Calonne's difficulties stemmed from opposition from within the ministry, notably from Miromesnil, the conservative keeper of the seals, and Breteuil, the minister for the interior, divisions which flowed over into the Notables. Louis had excluded these men from the cabinet committees which discussed Calonne's projects, learning from the way Maurepas had manipulated him in committees before the recall of the Parlement, and ignoring Miromesnil's plea for a wider debate; and they were now taking their revenge.

Calonne asked the king to replace the whole ministry with his nominees with the exception of Montmorin, the foreign secretary who had been appointed on Vergennes's death in February. The king momentarily acceded to his request. For as Droz observed:

Louis XVI had come to realize that the members of a ministry should be united as to interests and policies; he found this new request [of Calonne's] conformable to the principle he was adopting.[13]

In other words, faced with a quasi-representative assembly, Calonne had to have powers analogous to those of an English prime minister, who had to deal with Parliament. The independence of the king *vis-à-vis* the ministers, best served by internal divisions, must be sacrificed to the overall independence of government. Miromesnil was replaced by Lamoignon, a long-term advocate of judicial reform who, though a president in the Parlement, promised Calonne that if necessary he would countenance strong measures against his corps. Breteuil was replaced by Lenoir but Louis told Calonne that since the queen was Breteuil's patron, she should be informed first as a matter of courtesy. At this point the king weakened and rather than dismissing Breteuil, dismissed Calonne instead, the appointment of Lamoignon remaining (8 April 1787).

'Typical Louis', is the stock reaction, 'caving into pressure from Marie-Antoinette at the first whiff of opposition'; which ignores the fact that this was the first time Louis had been deflected from his purpose by Marie-Antoinette on a matter of importance. Calonne was opposed by almost the entire political class; the people not having responded to his appeal, what was the king to do? The wonder is not that he weakly caved in but that he held out so long, until the retention or dismissal of Calonne was equally damaging to the monarchy. The king was, as Castries observed, totally isolated. Miromesnil told the king that Calonne was opposed by the whole establishment, 'bishops, nobles, ministers'.[14] Louis hoped by dismissing Calonne to save his programme and appointed a successor, Bouvard de Fourqueux, who had collaborated on Calonne's projects. This appointment served only to reveal that Calonne had failed because of his projects, not the projects because of Calonne. Bouvard was nearly 70, which caused Loménie de Brienne to remark 'that if they were choosing from among the dead, they would have done better to pick Sully or Colbert'.[15]

Calonne was the first minister Louis had been forced to dismiss; indeed the first minister any king of France had been forced to dismiss since another *révolte nobiliaire*, the Fronde, in the 1640s. Not only the monarch but the institution of monarchy suffered accordingly. The fall of Calonne was likened to the fall of Strafford at the start of the English civil war, an analogy Louis, with his obsession with English history, would have been likely to draw himself. There was also a constitutional embarrassment caused by the fact that Calonne was known to retain the king's confidence. As Mercy-Argenteau put it:

> The king's authority is all the more grievously compromised by the abandonment of . . . [Calonne] in that he had scarcely left himself any way of disowning him.[16]

To make the system work this confidence had to be turned into resentment: Louis's 'dear' controller-general had to become his 'expensive' controller. In what was still in many ways a personal monarchy, a conventional loss of confidence in Calonne was not sufficient, as it might have been in England. It had to be actual. The effects on Louis's psyche can only be imagined.

The job of converting Louis was accomplished by the man who succeeded Bouvard, Loménie de Brienne, archbishop of Toulouse, who became first *chef du conseil royal des finances* (Maurepas's and Vergennes's old appointments) and then on 1 August principal minister. Brienne set up a committee which accused Calonne of malversation, and he fled to England. Brienne was the nominee of Marie-Antoinette who had been pressing his candidacy for years but had hitherto come up against Louis's rooted objection to prelate-ministers in general (because they would have to be made cardinals and thus take precedence in council) and to Brienne in particular as an atheist: Louis's only reported witticism concerned his veto of Brienne's appointment as archbishop of Paris on the grounds that an archbishop of Paris must at least believe in God!

Droz realized the significance of Brienne's appointment: 'It was from this day that the queen played a large part in affairs of state.'[17] At this point also, Louis became uxorious, which he had never been before. He would frequently come to the queen's apartments to weep over the state of the country. His depression engendered apathy which in turn engendered dependence, largely on Marie-Antoinette. He was baffled. He believed his policies were right – and many historians would agree – yet they had been almost unanimously rejected. He wanted to alleviate the burden on the people, which had been his constant goal – 'the nobility pay nothing; the people pay everything', he complained to Miromesnil;[18] he had appealed beyond the elite to this same people but there had been no response. What more could he do?

The outward and visible signs of Louis's inner torment were clear to see and the Austrian sources revelled in describing them. Mercy-Argenteau told Joseph II:

> Against such ills the king's low morale offers few resources and his physical habits diminish these more and more; he becomes stouter and his returns from hunting are followed by such immoderate meals that there are occasional lapses of reason and a kind of brusque thoughtlessness which is very painful for those who have to endure it.[19]

Suddenly, Louis became the king who is remembered in history: dazed, dependent, tearful, vacillating; but out of this reduced material the tragic events of the Revolution would carve a third Louis: the compassionate and forgiving Christian king of his imprisonment.

Brienne and the ascendancy of Marie-Antoinette

Brienne had acted as a 'leader of the Opposition' in the Notables and Louis had hoped that they would endorse the reform package if their criticisms were incorporated. He was quickly undeceived and on 25 May the Notables were dismissed, carrying anger and despondency to the provinces. The crown had to fall back on its narrow and sterile dialogue with the *parlements* which, stung by the crown's attempt to bypass them, raised the stakes by admitting their own incapacity to consent to new taxation, for which, they argued, the Estates-General alone were competent. Since the Parlement proved as uncooperative as the Notables, the government, by the *coup d'état* of 8 May 1788, exiled the Parlement and transferred the legislative functions of the 13 *parlements* to a plenary court responsible for registering legislation for the whole country. In time, regional variations and privileges would have withered away. The measures provoked widespread discontent in the provinces, particularly those of Dauphiné and Brittany, which sent a deputation to protest to the king – they were thrown in the Bastille. The troops, or at least their noble officers, were unreliable. Brienne promised the Estates-General for 1789 but this did not prevent a run on the treasury, which led to the resignations of Brienne (August 1788) and Lamoignon (September 1788) and the triumphant return of Necker, who lost no time in recalling the Parlement. Our guide through these events will once again be Soulavie.

Soulavie's anti-Austrian thesis intensifies in this period. After the failure of the Assembly of Notables, he argues, the influence of Marie-Antoinette on her husband, which had been increasing since the almost simultaneous birth of the dauphin and the death of Maurepas, became preponderant, given the demoralized state of the king. This preponderance resulted in the appointment of two disastrous prime ministers, one in name (Brienne), the other (Necker) in fact. Brienne carried out despotic measures, culminating in the *coup d'état* of 8 May 1788 against the *parlements*. (Why Soulavie who condemned the recall of the *parlements* in 1774 laments their destruction in 1788 is a mystery.) These despotic and alien (Austrian) policies aroused a patriotic protest from every section of society from dukes to artisans. Even the clergy, the traditional opponents of the *parlements*, patriotically leapt to their defence against one of their own – Brienne was

archbishop of Toulouse. The general assembly of the clergy
piously and prophetically told the king:

> We had hoped that if such a revolution were to happen [the
> destruction of the *parlements*] it would have been the
> consequence rather than the origin of the Estates-General.[20]

This 'rainbow' coalition forced Brienne out of office. Once this
happened, the Parlement was restored and the Breton deputies
released. The country took Louis to its bosom once more:

> The sentimental cry of *vive le roi* which the French during
> two years had not pronounced, was once more reiterated
> with tenderness and joy. The queen alone was deprived of
> our esteem, and she never recovered it.[21]

Refering to Brienne's memoirs, which he publishes, Soulavie
describes the intervention not merely of the queen but of the
Austrian ambassador in the negotiations for Brienne's 'golden
handshake' and Necker's reappointment. 'This extract from . . .
[Brienne's] memoirs', Soulavie argues,

> proves, and it is a man of the queen's faction, an oracular
> witness who speaks, that Marie-Antoinette had bent Louis
> XVI to her will, and degraded the nation even to employing
> the ambassador of the house of Austria in the direction of
> the general concerns of France. It is no longer Louis who
> appoints and dismisses his ministers. The ambassador of
> Joseph II determines their fall; promises a cardinal's hat [for
> Brienne] and a return to the ministry at a future period. The
> king suspects M. Necker's fidelity; he dislikes his manners:
> the queen and M. de Mercy appoint him . . . and the king
> agrees to it. . . . Consequently the queen punctually
> followed in 1788 the instructions she had received from
> Maria Theresa in 1771.[22]

Development of a revolutionary situation

There still remain many mysteries concerning the development of
the revolutionary crisis between the recall of Necker in August
1788 and the fall of the Bastille in July 1789, and many of these
concern the king's inner thoughts. By common consent the starting point is the Parlement's declaration, on its recall by Necker in
September, that the Estates-General must be convoked 'according

to the forms of 1614', the date of their last meeting. That is usually taken to mean that the three orders or Estates should each have roughly the same number of seats, as in 1614. This pronouncement led to protests from the Third Estate which the king heeded in the ruling known as the '*résultat du conseil*' of 27 December in which, besides promising to make major constitutional concessions, he ruled that the number of deputies for the Third Estate should equal the combined total of the other two, whilst leaving open the question of whether they would be allowed fully to profit from this through counting the votes in the Estates-General by head rather than by order as they had been in 1614.

However, the froth of this debate conceals deeper waters. The deeper question was whether the deputies should have been elected by order in the first place. Brienne and Malesherbes, who was recalled to the ministry in 1787 and wrote a memorandum on the subject, considered that the division of society into orders should be ignored for electoral purposes so that 'a truly national assembly' could be formed[23]. Turgot had already advocated this arrangement as, at the provincial level, had Calonne. On this reading the very doubling of the representatives for the Third Estate implictly accepted the case of the traditionalists on the fundamental issue, which is probably what the Parlement had in mind.

Moreover, in one respect the electoral arrangements intensified the maintenance of tradition: there was regional variation, but in general there was in the electoral arrangement for the nobility a bias towards exclusivity. Many of the recently ennobled were reclassified, for electoral purposes, as Third Estate, despite having been assured in their expensively purchased patents of nobility that theirs was legally as good a nobility as a duke's. There was no question of their now having to pay the *taille* or of being excluded from jobs where nobility was a prerequisite, but there was still considerable resentment, and it is no accident that some of the radical revolutionary leaders, such as Mirabeau and Le Chapelier, fell into this category.[24] Involuntary defections from the nobility were just as important as the more celebrated secession of the 'liberal' nobility, after the Estates had met. At the same time as the nobility became more aristocratic, for electoral purposes, the clergy and the Third Estate became more democratic: the regulations for the clergy favoured the election of parish priests at the expense of the bishops, and the elections for the Third Estate, held on virtual manhood suffrage, threw up many radical lawyers as deputies. An explosive mixture.

So far we have viewed the matter in purely political terms. But the antiquarian resurrection of a political structure deriving from a social one – the society of orders, which had almost been forgotten – put the removal of its remaining traces on the agenda, as 1788 slipped into 1789. And this was a matter of some concern to Louis XVI. Provided the nobility and clergy started paying their fair share of taxes to the state – which they had refused through the Assembly of Notables and the Parlement – he thought they should retain their position in society, and maybe in politics for that matter. Indeed their new-found willingness to pay their share was linked to their successful demand for the meeting of an Estates-General so organized that they could hope to dominate it. There are parallels with the English experience.

There were two conflicting ideas struggling for dominion over Louis's mind. The first was the instinctive and traditional political alliance between the king and the commons against the magnates which had formed the stuff of politics throughout the *ancien régime*. This alliance, however, had come to grief during the *révolte nobiliaire* of 1787–88 when the commons, in so far as they had shown a preference, had sided with the rebels. Michelet, one of the few historians to treat this question, has a different slant. He notes the doubling of the representatives of the Third Estate but attributes this to a false analogy drawn by Marie-Antoinette between the contemporary clerical and aristocratic revolt in the Austrian Netherlands against her brother Joseph II and the French situation:

> M. Mercy-Argenteau, the Austrian ambassador, believed at first, and doubtless made Marie-Antoinette believe, that in France, as in Belgium, the peril was on the side of the aristocracy. Hence many false steps.[25]

For whatever danger the monarchy had faced from the nobility in 1787–88, with the *réveil du tiers* in the autumn of the latter year, the danger to the monarchy stemmed from the Third Estate. And yet the streets resounded to the cry of, *Vive le roi et le tiers-état*.

This brings us to Louis's second idea, which stemmed from his personal cogitations on political theory. I am not concerned here with his lifeless, youthful paraphrases of his tutors' *dévot* discourse. But with ideas he hammered out for himself on the anvil of crisis and dated 15 February 1788. He took as his text the memoir on 'municipalities' of the most radical and intellectually distinguished of his ministers, Turgot, which had been published in a pirated edition of 1787. This may have been Louis's first sight of the memorandum, which would explain why he made his comments at this time. But also the memorandum had suddenly become topical, as fundamental questions about the regime were now raised with a more than academic urgency following the king's promise to convoke the Estates-General. Louis sought to clarify his thoughts as the denouement approached on the questions which were being agitated in 1788, notably the link between society and politics and their impli-cations for the royal authority. As was his wont, Louis under-lined or marked with a cross the passages he found most controversial. The better to absorb them. Then he added his own reflections, mostly rebuttals of Turgot's ideas, for his private use – Turgot was dead.

The Louis of these reflections is more conservative than the young reformer at the start of his reign. He considers the current division of France into provinces which have retained an element of self-government based on the society of orders (the *pays d'états*) and those ruled directly by the king's agent, the *intendant*. If the latter were to be phased out (which Louis regretted) and if representative institutions were to be introduced at the national level, then, he considered, it was essential that the *pays d'état* model should be used. Turgot, 'the enemy of the variety of orders', had proposed 'a hierarchy based on power' – actually on landed wealth, such as the National Assembly was to introduce for parliamentary elections in 1791. This would replace a 'hierarchy of . . . assemblies which preserves in France the faculties and honours of different individuals and forms the hierarchy of my subjects without which monarchy can exist nowhere . . . [a political hierarchy] is chimerical unless it is based on a hierarchy of birth'. Louis realized that the political super-structure must be derived from the social or the latter itself is doomed, as was proved by the event.

Then Louis advances a more original idea: 'This composition [of society] into three orders appertains too essentially to the privileges of Frenchmen, and the mission of the *intendants* to the royal authority to admit of their metamorphosis into deputies of the people.' What Louis means, as he elsewhere makes explicit, is that the king has greater authority over an assembly based upon orders, such as the Estates-General traditionally organized, than over one based on 'deputies of the people' such as it became. That was why Louis rejected the proposals of Brienne and Malesherbes for 'a truly national assembly'.

He also considered the risk of counter-revolution. Turgot's proposals would lead to

> a new France very promptly regenerated and met in an assembly. But meanwhile the old France, by which I mean the *grands* of the kingdom, the *parlements*, the assemblies of the *pays d'états*, the aldermen, the mayors, the *capitouls* [their Provençal equivalents], would hold a separate counter-assembly and would perhaps revolt, wanting to know for what crimes they were being stripped of their authority.[26]

Ten months later, in December 1788, Calonne, from his London exile, would raise the dangers of a 'revolution followed by a counter-revolution'[27] and his supporter the king's brother the comte d'Artois expresses similar ideas in the *Mémoire des princes*. Calonne had tried to do something which Louis now thought impossible: to build a new politics on an old society.

Soulavie also muses on the implications for royal authority of changes in the nature of the Estates-General. He castigates Louis XVI for doubling the representation of the Third Estate. In the sense that this concession gave the Third Estate the leverage which enabled it later to impose voting by head – that is, the destruction of the division of the Estates into orders – Louis may be said to have acted contrary to his own analysis. But the double representation was a change in degree not in kind, though the one ultimately led to the other. The objections Soulavie makes are pragmatic not theoretical ones. He argued that dominance by the Third Estate was appropriate in local assemblies (he cites the estates of Languedoc) to ensure an equal distribution of taxation and other such purely administrative matters. However, in a national and legislative assembly, unless the upper orders formed a strong counterbalance – a numerical supremacy sufficient to prevent dominance by the popular element – the royal authority would be marginalized.

Soulavie drew the parallel with the English civil war, when the destruction of the House of Lords facilitated the destruction of the monarchy; with this difference, that whereas the destruction of the Lords came about as a result of war,

the doubling of the *tiers* and the destruction of the superior
chambers [26 June 1789] in opposition to the absolute will
of the people, were cool and deliberate measures, adopted
on reflection by the king himself who signed in his council
a conspiracy against the French monarchy.[28]

Soulavie is unfair on Necker. Necker made no secret that he
favoured an English-style government. Not, however, a
Cromwellian unicameral system, but two chambers, Lords and
Commons. This can be seen as a logical development of the
doubling of the Third Estate. Moreover, if the clergy and nobility
formed a separate (upper) chamber they would not need to
worry, as they did, that defections from their liberal brethren
would give the Third Estate a permanent majority if voting were
by head. Such an arrangement might have been accepted by all
parties at the end of 1788 and would have reorganized, even
rejuvenated the nobility by giving them a political function. The
stumbling block, however, was the king. In *De la Révolution
française* Necker says:

> And why again should I dissemble that both my first and
> last thoughts have leaned in favour of a system of govern-
> ment like that of England, with which neither states in three
> orders, nor any form of monarchy, can compare.
> The king, unfortunately for any views I might have
> entertained of this kind, had a prejudice against whatever
> might resemble the usages and institutions of England. His
> opinion afterwards altered, but by then it was too late.[29]

This was written in 1797, but in 1788, on Turgot's observation, 'The cause of the evil sire is that your nation has no
constitution', the king had commented: 'The lovers of innovation
require even more than an English France.'[30]
Soulavie believed that Louis XVI and Necker were responsible
for stirring up the Third Estate against the aristocracy. If, he
argues, Necker had left well alone, the national patriotic
coalition, operating through the Estates-General,

> would have united to favour the universality of imposts
> established on all lands throughout the kingdom; annulling
> the *lettres de cachet*, assigning the court a civil list, tolerat-
> ing all religious worship, and granting liberty to the press
> and to mankind.[31]

The conventional view is simply that having achieved its aims, the defeat of the king symbolized by the concession of the Estates-General, the coalition fell apart over the division of the spoils, that is over the question of who would dominate the Estates – nobles or commoners?

Soulavie, however, believed that Necker caused these dissensions by 'inventing political questions' and 'creating terms of opprobrium'. By the former Soulavie understood raising the question of whether the number of deputies for the Third Estate in the Estates-General should be doubled to equal that of the clergy and nobility together. And by the latter he meant transforming the word 'aristocrat', which in its original Greek sense meant merely 'rule of the best', into the term of abuse it became in the Revolution.

By so doing, Necker 'annihilated the patriotic activity established through every rank, to create an exclusive one in the *tiers-état*'.[32] This theme of exclusivity was developed at the time by the abbé Siéyès in his famous pamphlet, *Qu'est-ce-que le tiers-état?* and in our own times has been taken up by the 'discourse school' of historians of the Revolution. This is the process whereby those who do not belong to the Third Estate (on an increasingly narrow definition) will soon be deemed to lie outside the sovereign body and by 1794 will be called 'the enemies of the people'.

This all seemed ample confirmation of Soulavie's general thesis that the *ancien régime* fell through oppositional policies being pursued by government. Louis is castigated for walking into this with his eyes open:

> The monarch, although he was neither deficient in penetration nor sagacity, though he had but a very short time ago treated as visionary ... [Turgot's memorandum, which he characterized as 'a beautiful vision, the utopia of an individual'] ... Yet he had the inconceivable weakness to abandon his destiny to M. Necker, on the vague hope of future and uncertain happiness. He was still king of France in August 1788 and yet ... [Brienne] affirms that he dreaded M. Necker to such a degree as to fear lest that minister should have discovered the prejudice he had before entertained against him. It was in these circumstances that the king granted M. Necker's desire that the Estates-General should be convened, not to make a reform in the

administration, but for a more than Genovese revolution, which deprived the king of all legislative power, which incapacitated the privileged orders, the true supporters of the crown, which transformed into a legislative authority the popular powers, confined by their nature to a concurrence in the law, and which annihilated in France a constitution and a code of laws which till then had rendered her the most flourishing state in Europe.[33]

Lord Acton, however, in the *Lectures on the French Revolution*, which he delivered in Cambridge in the 1890s, gives this approving summary of Louis's liberal concessions in the *résultat du conseil*:

religious toleration, Habeas Corpus, equal incidence of taxes, abolition of torture, decentralization and local self-government, freedom of the press, universal suffrage, election without official candidates or influence, periodic convocation of parliament, right of voting supplies, of initiating legislation, of revising the constitution, responsibility of ministers, double representation of the commons to the Estates-General. All these were acts of the Crown, yielding to dictates of policy more than to popular demand.[34]

In one crucial respect, though, both Soulavie and Acton are mistaken about the extent of the king's concessions: Louis had no intention of surrendering the initiative in legislation and to make this clear he removed an ambiguous passage from the draft of Necker's speech to the Estates-General. He was to flee Paris in 1791 in defence of this principle.

Acton stresses that the *résultat du conseil* is a purely political text which leaves the nobility's position in society intact:

The modern absolutism of the monarch had surrendered; but the ancient owners of the soil remained with their exclusive position in the state and a complicated system of honours and exactions which humiliated the middle class and pauperized the lower.

For Michelet, too, it was natural and inevitable that the king should endorse and protect the society of orders of which he formed the apex:

It was evident that the king being besieged by them and their prisoner to a certain degree, would belong to them entirely, and show himself more and more what he was, a partisan of privilege at the head of the privileged classes. The situation of parties became clear and easily defined – privilege on one side and right on the other.[35]

PART
II

LOUIS XVI
AND THE
FRENCH REVOLUTION

Overview

Different criteria apply to a consideration of Louis XVI's reputation for the period of the Revolution than those applicable to the personal reign. Before the Revolution, Louis must take responsibility for the acts of his government. There is debate for example about his precise input to the preambles which preceded his edicts but he was responsible for them and their explanatory nature – a new feature of his reign. Until 1781 some of his ministerial appointments were suggested by Maurepas, but all the dismissals were his personal work. In the king's person resided both the executive and legislative powers, undivided as the kings always stressed, though the *parlements* had some practical if not theoretical input. The *conseil d'état* also had considerable judicial powers, especially in the realm of 'administrative law'.

From early on in the Revolution the king's power was substantially reduced. In the *résultat du conseil* of December 1788, the king had unilaterally conceded consent by the Estates-General to taxation but he planned to retain the initiative in legislation, presenting laws to be passed by the Estates-General. This he was stripped of, and he was left merely with what he termed 'an illusory' suspensive veto. Similarly with the constitution: he was merely to be presented with a *fait accompli* to accept or (which amounted to abdication) refuse. These matters were decided by the Assembly in the period 20 June to September 1789. The executive was theoretically in the king's hands, but again the Assembly diminished it by shadowing the departmental ministers with parliamentary committees. And since officials were now elected, the king lost his control over them. So obviously Louis can take neither the praise nor the blame for the legislative achievements of the Revolution.

This means that the issues by which Louis's reputation can be judged are essentially reduced to just four, which form the chaptes of the second part of this book: 1) his conduct of the Estates-General/National Assembly up to his forced removal to Paris on 6 October 1789; 2) the so-called flight to Varennes, the town where the royal family was stopped after their successful escape from Paris on the night of 20/21 June 1791; 3) Louis's responsiblity for the war with Austria and Prussia, declared by France in April 1792 and, in particular, the question of the existence and/or extent of his treasonable correspondence with these enemies of France; 4) his behaviour during his imprisonment, after dethronement on 10 August 1792, in the Temple (August 1792–January 1793), his trial by the National Convention and his execution on 21 January 1793.

Different yardsticks are also applied to this smaller area. People are less interested in Louis's skill (or lack of it), except perhaps in the first era, the summer of 1789, and more interested in a moral standpoint. This is usually considered dangerous territory for historians; in their discipline the moral high ground yields a restricted view. However, the Revolution was the founding act of modern France and, until recently, French historians have been unduly protective towards it. In England, the moral strictures of Edmund Burke have also played their part, at least with conservative historians who deplore all change that is inorganic.

So the central question, for the French at least, is: did Louis accept the Revolution and, if not, what did he propose to do about it? Most conclude that he did not accept the constitution and that he tried to suppress it himself, whilst he still had troops at his command, and later by calling in foreign troops, particularly those of Marie-Antoinette's Austrian relations. Rare indeed is the historian who argues that Louis wanted to suppress the Revolution by force, and that it was right to suppress it. Mme de Coursac, for example, argues at length that Marie-Antoinette went behind Louis's back (and forged his letters) in her attempts to enlist Austrian pressure on France.

|9|

1789

Having examined in the last chapter the evolution of Louis XVI's thinking on society and representative government, we are in a better position to understand the complexity and with it the tragedy of the king's position during the crucial months, for him and for the Revolution, between his opening of the Estates-General on 5 May and his forcible removal to the capital on 6 October. Though the king's position was complicated, the issues were relatively simple. As soon as it became clear, with Necker's reappointment in August 1788, that the Estates really would meet, there developed a power struggle between the nobility and Third Estate, or 'commons' as they were beginning to call themselves, both as a reference to their English counterparts and as an implicit rejection of the society of orders, a struggle for the ground vacated by the king.

However, it was a struggle not only for power but also for social and legal equality, parity of esteem and access to office. And in some respects these inequalities had actually increased during the reign of Louis XVI. It was harder for the bourgeoisie to obtain ministries, bishoprics and army commissions under Louis XVI than under Louis XIV. Infamously the Ségur *ordonnance* of 1781 had restricted commissioned entry into the army to those with four generations of nobility. And the *résultat du conseil*, despite promising, as one duke put it, 'all that the Estates-General on bended knees would have dared to hope for',[1] did nothing to address the social question. Moreover, as Lord Acton shrewdly observes, the king may have had an ulterior motive in making constitutional concessions. Acton quotes with approval the Prussian ambassador's analysis that Louis was 'willing to weaken the executive at home in order to strengthen it abroad'. In other words, consent to taxation would yield more taxation for the conduct of foreign policy, which after all was the *métier* of kings. If there had been consent to taxation, Louis might have avoided the humiliation of having to abandon his Dutch allies after the Prussian invasion.

Acton concludes:

> The modern absolutism of the monarch had surrendered; but the ancient owners of the soil remained with their exclusive position in the state and a complicated system of honours and exactions which humiliated the middle class and pauperized the lower.

He felt that the commons had a right to feel aggrieved. From their point of view Louis 'after skirmishing with magistrates and prelates', decided to 'call in the outer people to compel a compromise with the class which filled his court'. However, 'it was the act of a man destitute of energy and gifted with an uncertain and indistinct enlightenment ... the enterprise was far beyond the power and quality of his mind'. And the Third Estate could be forgiven for interpreting the king's position as follows:

> Let us combine to deprive the aristocracy of those privileges which are injurious to the Crown, whilst we retain those which are offensive only to the people.

Moreover the king 'was determined that the upper class should lose its fiscal privileges with as little further detriment as possible'.[2] A view borne out by Louis's marginal comments on Turgot's memorandum.

Acton is one of the few historians who capture the sense of betrayal felt by the Third Estate. Most assume, with Michelet, that as the most privileged man in France Louis was bound to support privilege. However, in 1787 Louis had fought privilege and the privileged and this was traditional royal policy. So there is a historical problem here. If Louis sided with the aristocracy in 1789 it was not inevitable. Indeed it was precisely because it was unexpected that it created a sense of betrayal, of a conspiracy, which was the major factor in the growth of a revolutionary climate. Lord Acton is the only historian seriously to address and try to explain this volte-face. He will be our guide through this early phase of the Revolution.

From Estates-General to National Assembly

When the Estates-General opened at Versailles, neither the king nor Necker gave a ruling on the burning issue, the key to all the others: whether voting should be by head or by order. A slip of the tongue in Necker's speech revealed his preference for an English-style solution of two chambers, but the king vetoed this. With no guidance coming from the government, the orders continued to wrangle for six weeks until on 17 June the Third Estate, which had already renamed itself the commons, constituted itself the National Assembly and invited the other orders to join it or be ignored. What precisely went on in the king's mind during these crucial weeks can only be guessed and Acton's guess is as good as any. As the privileged classes became aware that a political revolution implied a social one, since 'a free community making its own laws would not submit to exactions imposed of old by the governing class on a defenceless population'

> in the presence of imminent peril [they] closed ranks and pressed the king to resist changes sure to be injurious to them. They became a Conservative party. The court was on their side, with the comte d'Artois at its head and the queen and her immediate circle.
>
> The king remained firm in the belief that popularity is the best form of authority, and he relied on the wholesome dread of democracy to make the rich aristocrats yield to his wishes. As long as the commons exerted the inert pressure of delay, he watched the course of events. When at the end of five tedious and unprofitable weeks they began their attack, he was driven slowly, and without confidence or sympathy, to take his stand with the nobles, and to shrink from the indefinite change that was impending.[3]

Louis planned to impose a compromise on the Estates by means of a royal session. Necker drafted a formula which was favourable to the Third Estate but still a compromise. On 20 June, however, the National Assembly went one stage further when they swore not to separate until they unilaterally had given France a constitution (Tennis Court Oath). This Louis could not accept. He had reminded Necker just before the Estates opened that the Estates 'cannot make laws by themselves' – still less a constitution.[4] 'The surprise of the Tennis Court [oath]', in Acton's words, 'frightened him into an alliance with the nobles and he linked his caused to theirs.'[5] The 'hawks' were now able to persuade Louis to redraft Necker's programme. It was still a compromise, but this time one favourable to the privileged orders. In both versions the king promised to be a constitutional monarch. That was no longer at issue. But in the version actually delivered on 23 June, the king annulled the National Assembly's proceedings and stipulated voting by head only when neither privileges nor the constitution were involved.

The programme of the *séance royale* marked the high-water mark of the aristocratic reaction: power was taken from the king and none was yielded to the people. It is sometimes said that it was the king's last free act. Sometimes he said it himself. The confusion is epitomized by two conflicting statements concerning it in Michelet, two in as many pages. 'Here', we are told, 'is, according to every appearance, the king's manifesto, the one he fondly cherished *and wrote himself*'; and, on the next page, 'The king read, with his usual plainness of manner, the speech *composed for him* – that despotic language so strange from his lips.'[6]

The commons ignored the king's command that each order should proceed to its appointed chamber, and on the 27th Louis capitulated, to the scandal of Soulavie, by ordering the nobility and clergy to take part in the National Assembly. At the same time, however, he brought up troop reinforcements to the Paris region, thereby indelibly staining his reputation with the taint of duplicity. Not quite at the same time: Louis actually signed the first order for troop movements, that of the Swiss Reinach regiment, on 22 June, that is the day that Necker's project was jettisoned. In other words, the summoning of the troops is linked to the *séance royale* rather than to the royal capitulation of the 27th.

To understand the importance of this distinction, we must once again return to Louis's reflections on Turgot's memorandum on 'municipalities', made, in February 1788, in the light of the promise he had just given to convoke the Estates-General. Louis assumed that Turgot's proposed national municipality, elected by the provincial municipalities, would be 'the assembly of the French people' in a way that the *parlements* and the Estates-General themselves could never be. This meant that 'there would no longer be any intermediate agency between the king and the nation but that of an army'. Troops could and had been employed against, say, a refractory *parlement*, but 'it is a horrible and painful extremity to entrust to an army the defending of the

authority of the state against the assembly of the French people'.[7]
It would be legitimate to use force, if absolutely necessary,
against the traditional Estates-General, such as Louis had summoned and strove to preserve in the *séance royale*. Such a body
was a congeries of interests which could be played off against one
another, balanced, reconciled, coerced if need be. If Louis considered that Turgot's proposed national municipality, which was
based on a narrow landed franchise, was 'the assembly of the
French people', how much more so was the real National
Assembly? Louis's reflections also answer another mystery: why
Louis, who had put down the 'flour war' of 1775 with what
many regarded as brutality, was unprepared, as I shall demonstrate, to employ force against the National Assembly.

A further criticism Louis made of Turgot's assembly is relevant
to the situation in June 1789. Louis objected that the proposed
'national municipality' would become in effect 'a *perpetual* [my
italics] Estates-General' which would be 'subversive of the
monarchy which is only absolute because its authority does not
admit of a partner'.[8] In the *résultat du conseil* Louis had
promised regular but not perpetual Estates-General. They might
meet for a few months of the year as in England, leaving the king
to get on with running the country, particularly its foreign policy.
The National Assembly, however, made it quite clear, for example by pledging that it 'would not separate until it had given
France a constitution', that it would be perpetual. Indeed so
determined was the Assembly that the king should not steal a
march on it that it worked every day of the week as well as every
month of the year. This was a factor in Louis's losing the exercise
of the legislative and much of the executive power. What rights
and what power would the king have against such a Leviathan?

To what use then did Louis intend to put the troops? On 11
July the *Moniteur*, not a coarse journal like Hébert's *Père
Duchesne*, nor a sanguinary one like Marat's *L'Ami du peuple*,
but a sober if radical broadsheet like *The Times*, regaled its
readers with the following story: four items had been discussed
in the *conseil [d'état]*:

1. How to wind up the Estates-General and carry off the
   deputies at midnight . . .
2. The sale of Lorraine to the emperor, who naturally will
   pay for it with the 6 million [livres] which have been
   sent to him.

3. The holding of a *séance royale* at which the king will present four declarations.
4. A declaration which will instantly dissolve the Estates-General.[9]

This was the widely accepted view and, with the exception of the imaginative second article concerning the sale of Lorraine, this is also the consensus among French historians up to this day.

This is surprising because in 1906 the republican historian Pierre Caron published the orders of the generalissimo, the duc Broglie, to his field commander in Paris, the baron de Besenval. The orders are strictly defensive. On 5 July Besenval is told that if there are food riots he must use his 'habitual circumspection' and 'avoid getting entangled with the people except to prevent arson and pillage which threatens the safety of the citizen'. On the 11th, he advises that he has been warned of 'a violent insurrection at daybreak tomorrow': correct information which shows that the rising had been planned before the dismissal of Necker on the 12th. Besenval is told that 'if there is a general insurrection, we cannot defend the whole of Paris and you must confine yourself to the plan for the defence of the Bourse, the Royal Treasury, the Bastille and the Invalides'. If this line fails to hold, the troops must fall back on Versailles for the defence of the chateau.[10]

The military orders are the only hard evidence which we possess for the government's intentions at this time but they are surely enough to exonerate Louis from the accusation of planning a *coup d'état* against Paris. This is important because even Edmund Burke, whose praise for Louis we have already noted and who was to be the most eloquent scourge of the Revolution, conceded that

> If it could be made clear to me that the king ... of France ... had formed a deliberate scheme for massacring the National Assembly ... such a person would ill deserve even that subordinate executory trust which I understand is to be placed in him.[11]

Only one historian, Munro Price, has seriously attempted to piece together the objectives of the short-lived Breteuil ministry whose appointment, we are told, sparked off the insurrection leading to the attack on the Bastille. Price highlights the divergence of views within the royal family with only the king's youngest brother, Artois, in favour of a military solution. He shows that the new government was chiefly concerned with raising loans to cover the emergency and that they met with some success in this thanks to the support of the traditional financiers, the ones whom Soulavie had said were 'tied to the maintenance of the machine'. Apart from that, Breteuil conducted two sets of negotiations, one with the king's *frondeur* cousin, the duc d'Orléans, whom many held and hold responsible for the disturbances in Paris, the other with leading deputies in the National Assembly with a view to endorsing a modified version of the royal programme of 23 June. Breteuil had family connections both with Orléans, who wanted to make his peace with the court, and with the president of the Assembly, his cousin the duc de Clermont-Tonnerre. These negotiations reached a climax on 13 July but were overtaken by the events of the 14th.[12]

Lord Acton also mentions Breteuil's negotiations:

In one day he brought round twenty-six of the minority [liberal nobles?] to his views. A few remained, who would make a light day's work for a man of his *conviction and resource* [*sic*, my italics].

Yet on the previous page he paints a picture of an uncharacteristically belligerent king:

The king refused [the Assembly's request] to send away troops which there had been good reason to collect, but he was ready to move, with the Assembly, to some town at a distance from the turbid capital. The royal message was tipped with irony. ... After this first thrust Louis threw away the scabbard. That day he was nervous and uneasy and disguised his restlessness by feigning sleep [in the council]. At the end, taking one of the ministers aside, he gave him a letter for Necker, who was absent. The letter contained his dismissal, with an order for banishment.[13]

Three points here. The king's letter to the Assembly (personally drafted by him) was not 'tipped with irony': it represented his settled view (which was to recur for the short remainder of his reign) that if the Assembly moved to Soissons, with him nearby at Compiègne, the balance of power between him and the Assembly would be restored, by the removal of pressure from Paris on the one hand and the royal troops on the other. Second, the king did not 'throw away the scabbard' for he had no offensive plans, believing them to be inappropriate against a national assembly. Finally, Louis's letter to Necker was not a harsh order of banishment because, as Necker himself noted, the king did not think he still had the power to issue *lettres de cachet*. It was a gentle suggestion with the hope that he might soon be able to return.

Acton is full of contempt for the 'incompetent, helpless and insincere' king. He despises him for his climbdown on 27 June:

> A king who deserted his friends and reversed his accepted policy because there was no force he could depend on was a king with a short shrift before him. He became the tool of men who did not love him, and who now despised him.[14]

In any case, Louis's 'brief alliance with the aristocracy was dissolved' when on 17 July he went to Paris to give his official, superfluous endorsement of the change in power which had taken place in the capital: a bourgeois National Guard replacing royal troops, an elected municipality replacing the one he had appointed – developments which were soon replicated throughout the country. A frosty reception for him by the Parisians became no more than respectable when he agreed to place the new tricolour cockade on his hat (red and blue for Paris imprisoning Bourbon white in the centre).

The French do well to make Bastille day their national holiday. No amount of revisionism can change the fact that it was the decisive turning point in the Revolution. Robespierre, then an obscure deputy for Artois, immediately realized that this event 'as wonderful as it was unexpected', changed the whole political balance: it was no longer, he wrote home, merely a question of consent to taxation but of the Assembly's seizing the initiative in legislation.[15] For Louis XVI the fall of the Bastille was the beginning of the end; the rest of his reign consisted in a series of steps to the Temple, where he was imprisoned in August 1792 and which he left only for the days of trial and execution. It is not only with the benefit of hindsight that we can say this; Louis had little doubt that this would be his fate: this or assassination. He made his will, heard mass and took communion before setting out for Paris on 17 July.

Louis was never trusted again. People could not be expected to work out the nuances of his position, which appeared as one of vacillation and treachery. They could not work out that he signed his first orders for troop movements on 22 June rather than the 27th; and even if they had the archival evidence it would not have mattered: the main thing was that he summoned troops and that most of them were foreign, if already in royal service. When he fled Paris in the night of 20/21 June 1791 – and as Mirabeau had said, a king does not flee in the night if he wishes to remain a king – then incredible as it seems, people in the National Assembly seriously considered replacing him with his brother Artois, even though he had emigrated after the fall of the Bastille and was amassing troops for a forcible restoration of the *ancien régime*. At least, it was said, he was honest.

In July 1789 the talk was of replacing Louis with his cousin Philippe d'Orléans, a man for whom very little can be said – weak and worthless in every particular, whatever the (still debated) role his money and organization had played in the revolt of Paris. In an interval of the crisis meeting of the *conseil d'état* during the night of 15/16 July even the reactionary keeper of the seals, Barentin, said to Louis's youthful mentor, Moreau, now the royal historiographer, 'I believe we must have a recourse to a change of dynasty.' When Artois told the diehard noble deputy Cazalès that Louis's life would be endangered unless the nobility joined the National Assembly, Cazalès replied: 'Perish the monarch but not the monarchy!'[16]

It would perhaps have been better if Louis had abdicated so that the Assembly, not saddled with an incumbent king they distrusted, could have given their nominee powers sufficient to govern the country; powers, for example, such as the English parliament allowed the incoming Hanoverian dynasty. The constitution which the Assembly constructed piecemeal between 1789 and September 1791 was a monument to its distrust of Louis XVI. Moreover, that distrust also made it difficult for him to exercise those few powers which the constitution allotted him, such as his suspensive veto (for two parliaments) over legislation, ministers having neither the right to sit in parliament nor initiate legislation. Although the king remained theoretically head of the executive, in accordance with the cult theory of the separation of powers, this doctrine was honoured more in the breach than the observance. For the king could no longer appoint or dismiss his agents of execution, who were elected except in the diplomatic service, and therefore had little control over them. Moreover, parliamentary committees shadowed the work of ministers and virtually superseded them, particularly in finance, after the resignation of Necker (whose popularity scarcely survived his recall after the fall of the Bastille) in September 1790.

Yet there is reason to doubt whether even a change of king would have led to a constitution more in keeping with the needs of France, instead of 'a metaphysical and philosophical government which cannot work', as Louis was to describe it.[17] Edmund Burke quickly latched on to this 'metaphysical' quality and it is the key to his blanket condemnation of the Revolution at a time (1790) when most of his countrymen thought with Wordsworth that it 'was bliss in that dawn to be alive'. Many found Burke's stance inconsistent with his earlier defence of revolutions in America, Poland and Corsica, and with his harrying of George III. But Burke quarrelled with the inorganic nature of the changes instituted by the National Assembly; changes which ignored French history and traditions which he believed reflected the permanent character of a nation. For this reason he considered that the French Revolution at no point resembled the Glorious Revolution of 1688 in England.

Given this *tabula rasa* on which the Assembly engraved its immutable laws, an incumbent king had no automatic rights deriving from, as Louis put it, 'a long succession of centuries',[18] for, as the cant phrase went, a thousand years of injustice could not confer a single moment of legitimacy. The Assembly was inconsistent in giving Louis any role at all and, as the socialist historian Jean Jaurès argued, was dishonest in trying to have its cake and eat it. The minimal role the Assembly assigned Louis was demonstrated in a controlled experiment when he was suspended from his functions after his flight: for nearly three months the constitution worked perfectly well without him. If the Assembly gave Louis any role, it was partly out of habit, partly, as Jaurès thought, out of hypocrisy, and largely out of the realization that for all the Assembly's theories the king still retained a strong following both at home and abroad – from the émigrés and the 'trades union' of kings, and in particular Marie-Antoinette's brother, the Holy Roman Emperor. Louis had only to raise his hand to unleash civil war. Because he didn't, violence took new forms.

The October Days

Once we reach 1789 Louis's reputation is subjected to a double scrutiny, that of history and that of his judges in his trial in December 1792. There is even a third scrutiny, for as Louis's counsel reminded his judges, 'history will judge your judgement'. In recent years, this third role has been assumed by

> a Committee for the study of Louis XVI and of his Trial, founded under the presidency of the late Gabriel Marcel, the great Christian philosopher. In the works published by this committee, in its quarterly review, *Découvert*, are to be found studies on the reforms and policies of Louis XVI and on his role during the Revolution.[19]

The words are those of the leading lights of *Découvert*, Paul and Pierrette Girault de Coursac, whom we encountered when discussing Louis's education. Their work for *Découvert* is summed up by their massive *Enquête sur le procès du roi Louis XVI* (Investigation into the trial of Louis XVI) of 1982, which examines the truth of each of the charges levelled at Louis for his acts since 1789. The leaders of the French Revolution were so self-absorbed, so convinced that they had inaugurated a new era that no one, from the king down, was praised or blamed for acts committed prior to 1789, the 'year one of liberty'. (Later the declaration of the Republic on 22 September 1792 was officially designated the year one, and for 12 years replaced the Christian calendar.)

The indictment against Louis XVI took the form of a potted republican history of the Revolution, with the king intervening malevolently at the key junctures. The de Coursacs take up the gauntlet by systematically investigating the charges in chronological order. Some space is devoted to the October Days – when a Paris mob invaded the chateau of Versailles and forcibly removed the royal family to the Tuileries in Paris – because Louis is accused of 'necessitating' the mob's action by vetoing the Assembly's decrees of 4 August and the Declaration of the Rights of Man. The de Coursacs observe the *Alice in Wonderland* logic involved in blaming the king for violence done to him (the same logic was applied to the storming of the Bastille and of the Tuileries, twice, in 1792) and preface each of the chapters of the *Enquête* with a quotation from Lewis Carroll's work.

The August decrees dismantled the feudal regime, abolished privilege in taxation, tithes, sale of office and the different privileges of the towns and provinces of France. The entire 'corporate' organization of France disappeared overnight. The de Coursacs observe that so far from vetoing these decrees, Louis specifically said that 'he approved the general spirit' and approved 12 of the 15 articles. After all, the decrees were the logical extension of the programme Louis had laid before the Assembly of Notables in 1787. However, he gave only a 'conditional adhesion' to three articles which had foreign policy implications. These concerned the seigneurial rights of foreign princes with possessions in Alsace which were guaranteed by international treaty when that province was ceded to France in 1648; and the suppression of annates, that is, the Pope's right to the revenue of vacant sees which, as Louis told the Assembly, 'derived from the Concordat of France with the Holy See'. The de Coursacs observe that this flouting of international law 'was the pretext for a war which lasted for 23 years, from which France emerged vanquished, exhausted and diminished'. Louis, for whom the observance of international treaties was a sacred duty, said that he would renegotiate these treaties, but his observations were, as he put it, 'treated with contempt'. Louis also criticized article five, which suppressed tithes to the benefit of the land-owners. He thought that rather than have this random redistribution of wealth, the money should go to the fisc to tackle the deficit on account of which the Estates-General had been called.[20]

On 4 October Louis presented his observations on the first 19 of the constitutional articles and the prefatory Declaration of the Rights of Man. Despite his objection to the 'metaphysical' nature of the latter, he contented himself on this occasion with the observation that a declaration of principle should not precede its practical embodiment.

The Assembly worked once more the engine of Paris to force complete acceptance on the king. On 5 October a crowd of Paris market women, followed at a distance by a contingent from the National Guard, carrying their reluctant general Lafayette in their wake, invaded the chateau of Versailles. At 10 p.m. on the 5th, with the women milling round the chateau, Mounier, the president of the Assembly who disapproved of the articles himself, asked for Louis's sanction to the disputed decrees in writing. Louis 'went to his desk, wrote it out in full and handed it to him, weeping'.[21] During the night the mob sought out Marie-Antoinette and would have murdered her but for the rearguard action of the bodyguards who were hacked down as she sped to the king's apartments. Disappointed of their quarry, the attackers slashed the queen's bed to ribbons. The council sat intermittently, considering and rejecting flight to Rambouillet, then considering it again when it was too late, the traces of the ready-harnessed carriages having been slashed.

Such are the facts, which are more or less embellished as the
tale is retold. For Michelet, the patriotic republican, the trigger
for the October Days, which enabled Paris to break the deadlock
in the political process, was 'an act of folly' on the part of the
court; namely the imprudent behaviour of the officers of the
Flanders Regiment which had been moved to Versailles for the
personal protection of the royal family. These officers had drunk
royalist toasts and, crime of crimes, trampled the new tricolour
cockade under foot. (At his trial Louis denied being present on
this occasion.) 'An act of folly', Michelet continues, 'was
necessary.'

> That was the real remedy, the only means of getting rid of
> the intolerable position in which everyone seemed
> entangled. This folly would have been done by the queen's
> party long before, if it had not met with its chief stumbling-
> block and difficulty in Louis XVI. Nobody could be more
> averse to a change of habits. To deprive him of his hunting,
> his workshop, and his early hour of retiring to rest; to
> interrupt the regularity of his meals and his prayers; to put
> him on horseback *en campagne*, and make an active
> partisan of him, as we see Charles I in the picture by
> Vandyck, was not easy. His own good sense likewise told
> him that he ran much risk in declaring himself against the
> National Assembly.
> On the other hand, this same attachment to his habits, to
> the ideas of his education and childhood, made him against
> the Revolution even more than the diminution of the royal
> authority. He did not conceal his displeasure at the
> demolition of the Bastille. The uniform of the National
> Guards worn by his own people; his valets now become
> lieutenants – officers; more than one musician of the chapel
> chanting mass in a captain's uniform; all that annoyed his
> sight: he caused his servants to be forbidden 'to appear in
> his presence in such an unseasonable costume'.
> It was difficult to move the king, either one way or the
> other. In every deliberation he was fluctuating, but in his
> old habits, and in his rooted ideas, insuperably obstinate.
> Even the queen, whom he deeply loved, would have gained
> nothing by persuasion. Fear had still less influence on him;
> he knew that he was the anointed of the Lord, inviolable
> and sacred; what could he fear? [22]

Lord Acton takes up the narrative at the point between the invasion of the chateau by the Parisian crowd and the arrival of Lafayette and the National Guard. Relying on the memoirs of Saint-Priest, the minister for the interior, he draws a dispiriting picture of Louis's weakness:

> The command at Versailles was in the hands of d'Estaing ... who at this critical moment showed no capacity. He refused to let his men defend themselves and ordered them to withdraw. Saint-Priest grew impatient. Much depended on their having repressed the riot without waiting to be rescued by the army of Paris. He summoned ... [d'Estaing] to repel force by force. D'Estaing replied that he waited the king's orders. The king gave none. The minister then said: 'When the king gives no orders, a general must judge and act for himself'. Again the king was silent. Later, the same day, he adopted the words of Saint-Priest and made them his own. He said that the comte d'Estaing ought to have acted on his own responsibility. No orders are needed by a man of spirit who understands his duty. It was the constant wish of Louis XVI to be in the hands of stronger men, who would know how to save him in despite of himself.
>
> Mounier had obtained his unqualified assent to the Rights of Man, and urged him to seize the moment to seek refuge in some faithful province. It was the dangerous, but the honourable course, and there was hope that the Assembly, standing by him, would prevent an outbreak of war.

Acton follows this last, pious hope with a scathing comment on Louis's reaction to the arrival of La Fayette:

> Louis received him with a sensation of relief, for he felt that he was safe. At that moment indeed the sovereign had perished, but the man was safe.[23]

Acton considered that the October Days marked the decline also of the Assembly, which followed the king to Paris:

> The power was passing from them to the disciplined people of Paris [the National Guard] and beyond them and their commander [La Fayette] to the men who managed the masses [foremost of whom he counted Danton].[24]

|10|

Varennes

I propose to move straight from Louis's forcible installation in the Tuileries on 6 October 1789 to his escape from Paris on the night of 20/21 June 1791 and his recapture at Varennes, in the Argonne, the next day. My reason for omitting this period of nearly two years (a long time in a revolution) is that, as Louis said in the declaration he left behind in the Tuileries, he regarded his actions during this period as provisional because 'his palace was a prison' and promises made under duress were not binding.[1] Moreover, since he was allowed no say in the framing of the constitution – the main occupation of the National Assembly during this period – he could hold no more than a watching brief. The deputy Alexandre de Lameth quipped that the executive was playing dead but it remained the fact, as Louis observed in his declaration, that the Assembly's committees shadowed the ministries to such an extent that the Assembly virtually engrossed the executive as well as the legislative power. Louis played no part in the construction of the new France: the replacement of the historic provinces with 83 departments with geographic rather than historical names, the confiscation of the churchlands, which became the collateral for a paper currency, the *assignats*, the Civil Constitution of the Clergy or the abolition of nobility and armorial bearings. So there was not much for Louis to do and that little he regarded as provisional.

I concentrate on the so-called 'flight to Varennes' because all sides regard it as the fulcrum of the Revolution and the test of Louis's character. It is also a great escape story and provides a classic forum for counterfactual speculation: what would have happened if the position of the change of relay horses in the little town had not been altered without Louis being informed, which would have enabled him to reach his destination? 'Varennes' also provides comfort to those who believe in the primacy of accident in history (especially of the French Revolution, as is currently fashionable). But it also provides material for a refutation of such a view, since the little town – village really – became, on 21–22 June, a microcosm of France: if Louis couldn't pass Varennes there was no point in passing it. The fact that Louis was stopped at Varennes suggests that his whole enterprise might have failed.

There is, and there was, enormous disagreement over the nature of that enterprise; even over Louis's destination, though that much is clear: he was heading for Montmédy, a small fortress on a hill, some 40 miles from Varennes, where General Bouillé had assembled troops. It is difficult to deny this, there is abundant evidence, and as Louis said after he and his family had been ignominiously returned to Paris, anyone who didn't believe him could always check on the arrangements which had been made at Montmédy for housing the royal family. However, without denying this point blank, many have insinuated that Louis planned to flee the country. So Jules Flammermont, writing in 1885 an article designed to show that Louis XVI was a traitor, says in his mealy-mouthed way that Louis was travelling 'towards the border with Luxembourg'. He later says that in 1792 'there was a new attempt to escape to foreign soil'.[2] This can be disproved just as easily as it can be proved that he was heading for Montmédy. For the route Paris–Clermont–Varennes–? was a very inefficient and dangerous way of leaving France. Better to go to Brussels, as the king's brother, Provence, did.

Provence was then to have gone to the rendezvous at Montmédy, but Louis chose the inferior route to avoid leaving the country even momentarily. His reason: that James II of England had lost his crown by emigrating. These factual questions about destination have become controversial because there is a rider to the accusation of the king's wanting to leave the country. Louis wanted to emigrate *in order to* put himself at the head of foreign and French *émigré* troops and bring about the restoration of the *ancien régime*. This is an extreme position, but also the one most commonly held.

Girault de Coursac

The most extreme opposite position is held by P. and P. Girault de Coursac. Their starting point is that there were two escape plans, one masterminded by Marie-Antoinette and the other by Louis, and until the last minute neither spouse knew of the intentions of the other. Louis, according to the de Coursacs, had no plans to escape from Paris until 18 April 1791. On that date the royal family, sitting in their carriages in the courtyard of the Tuileries, had been forcibly prevented by a mob from spending Easter at Saint-Cloud, a smaller palace at the gates of Paris, where they had been allowed to spend a few months the previous summer. Louis now believed that the fiction that he was free in Paris had finally been exploded. 'It was thenceforth impossible', the de Coursacs argue,

> for [Louis] to prove he was free. On 19 April he went down to the Assembly to convey to the deputies that by their refusal [to guarantee safe conduct to Saint-Cloud] they themselves had tainted with nullity all the sanctions ... he had given to their decrees since 6 October 1789.[3]

The king therefore was 'left with no alternative but to make himself free by leaving Paris'. At Montmédy he hoped that public pressure, through petitions, would demand that 'the Constitution be modified and above all submitted article by article for the free acceptance of the king'. Having come to this decision, Louis applied to General Bouillé who had showed character in putting down a serious mutiny in his command at Nancy the previous year. On that occasion, Louis had written to Bouillé: 'nurse your popularity, it may be useful to me and to the kingdom'.[4]

The king's letter, according to the de Coursacs, put Bouillé in a quandary. For six months he had been working on the details of the queen's escape plan in the mistaken belief that the king was privy to it. Now he had to put the original plan to the king as something newly devised but, in order to prevent the king from finding out what he had put his pen to (reader, prepare to take a sharp intake of breath), Bouillé caused the escape to miscarry by making sure Louis ended up in a cul-de-sac at Varennes.

The queen had originally planned to leave Louis behind in Paris as an encumbrance. She would escape with the dauphin, who would be proclaimed king as Louis XVII with herself as regent. A woman on a horse with a child, like her mother Maria Theresa in 1740, she would rally her troops. Both these accusations, against Bouillé and Marie-Antoinette, are so far-fetched that it is tempting to dismiss all the de Coursacs' evidence, except to note, in a book on Louis XVI's reputation,

that the de Coursacs have a wide following in France and a
journal, *Découvert*, devoted to their findings: on the delayed
publication of one of their works a red band was placed round
the cover with the word *enfin* emblazoned in white. Moreover,
that following is not only or even principally composed of right-
wing *Action française* readers: the de Coursacs present Louis as
loyal not only to France, but to the Revolution.

Such a blanket rejection of the de Coursacs' work, however,
would involve that of some excellent archival work and textual
exegesis, albeit placed at the disposal of a false premise. For
example, the de Coursacs demonstrate from several *lapsus* – such
as 'I' crossed out and replaced with 'the king' – that in speaking
for the king, Marie-Antoinette is really putting forward her own
ideas. The de Coursacs also observe that there are only two
extant letters of the king's with a bearing on the escape: a letter
to Breteuil giving him plenipotential powers and a letter to the
Emperor Leopold II dated 20 June 1791. However, their claim
that the former is a forgery and that the latter has been tampered
with is highly controversial.

Where they are undoubtedly right is in saying that the king's
actual declaration of 20 June has nothing in common with the
one Marie-Antoinette says (in February) he is working on. In
particular, Louis makes no mention, as Marie-Antoinette does, of
punishing rebels, still less of recalling the *parlements* and exploiting the religious schism. Such measures would have been
anathema to him, as would her claim, just before the departure,
that 'he' was going to declare a bankruptcy, which would have
overturned the most distinctive feature of his reign, the principle
which caused him to summon the Estates. But to say that Marie-
Antoinette was putting words into Louis's mouth is not to say
that she planned to abandon him to his fate in Paris.

The de Coursacs' interpretation of the queen's role in the flight
to Varennes is only a part, though perhaps the culmination, of
their general thesis that even before she set foot in France, Marie-
Antoinette was designated by her mother to be a tool of Austrian
foreign policy. Once there, she set about, with the help of the duc
de Choiseul, a native of Lorraine like her father the Emperor
Francis, to denigrate her husband, often deny him conjugal
rights, and rule over him, finally planning to dump him in Paris
and rule through her son. Similar views (except for the
proclamation of Louis XVII) were expressed by Soulavie and, of
course, were prevalent throughout France, which had never

taken the Austrian alliance to its collective bosom and where even before the Revolution the queen, *L'Autrichienne*, was dangerously unpopular. The process was to culminate in the declaration of war on Austria in 1792 as a means of embarrassing the king by making his wife an 'enemy alien' in order to make him choose between his wife and his country.

It can be seen then, that the debate about Marie-Antoinette's input into the escape plans is a lively one less because of the de Coursacs' obsession with her treachery towards the king, than because of its bearing on the king's putative treachery towards France. After all, the accusation that he was plotting to restore the *ancien régime* by means of foreign, that is Austrian, troops is not just a matter of historical debate but formed one of the actual charges which he had to answer at his trial. So apart from devoting a book to the Varennes question, *Sur la route de Varennes* (1984), the de Coursacs also devote a chapter to it in their massive *Enquête sur le procès du roi Louis XVI* (1982). And, apart from the question of force, some of the proposals for the cession of French territory revealed in the correspondence between the queen and her mentor the former Austrian ambassador to France, Mercy-Argenteau, are not only treasonable but fanciful in the extreme.

So fanciful are they that one is tempted to think that perhaps Marie-Antoinette really did plan to make the dauphin king! More to the point, they are so fanciful that they amount to proof that the king, with his excellent grasp and long experience of diplomacy, could have had no knowledge of them. Their premise is that the post-1787 alliance of England, Prussia and Holland would not allow Austria to restore the power of the French monarchy. England, therefore, must be bought off by territorial concessions – the West Indian sugar islands or all the French possessions in India, leaving only trading counters, are suggested. Alternatively, an alliance of Spain, Sardinia and Denmark(!) must be formed, by means of smaller concessions, to contain the triple alliance. The king is said, in this correspondence, to be unhappy about these concessions. It is more likely he had never heard of them.[5]

Acton and Sorel

Two late-nineteenth-century historians, Lord Acton and Albert Sorel, give a specific reason for the royal flight. One of Marie-

Antoinette's secret agents had been sent to see Leopold II at Mantua to discover what aid the emperor would afford his sister. The agent, however, was suborned by Calonne and Artois, also at Mantua, and returned with a false document which precipitated the flight. The 'Mantua forgery' stated that Leopold was about to invade France with 150,000 men on 15 July and that the royal couple should sit tight in the Tuileries. This, however, apart from the obvious personal danger of remaining (the same faced in August 1792), did not suit the queen. 'She', in Acton's words, 'was for a counter-constitution, they [the *émigrés*] for a counter-revolution.'[6] In Sorel's words, 'the king, reduced to the neutral and passive role of a hostage, would lose the character of arbitrator and and pacifier that he wanted to assume'.[7]

Timing: the completion of the constitution

My own view is that Louis's flight was governed by his reading of domestic politics. Two things in particular, apart from his enforced residence in Paris, distressed the king. The first was the Civil Constitution of the Clergy which provided for the election of priests and the redrawing of dioceses to coincide with the new division of France into 83 departments. According to canon law, the latter required papal institution which was refused by Pius VI who condemned the Civil Constitution (tardily) in bulls of March and April 1791. This established a national schism, with half the *curés* and all but seven of the bishops refusing to take an oath accepting the Civil Constitution which the Assembly required. Apart from his distress at schism and coercion, Louis, on off days, regarded himself as standing in mortal sin for having given his sanction to the Civil Constitution (July 1790) and to the oath (December 1790). When he asked the bishop of Clermont whether he could still make his Easter communion in 1791 because he had acted under duress, he received the uncompromising anwer that the king's sanction 'has had the most disastrous consequences for religion' and that, as 'Your Majesty knows, it was only resistance to force which produced the martyrs'. In view of this, the bishop said, the king had better not communicate.[8]

The question of Louis's Easter communion is a vexed one. The most commonly accepted line is that Louis wanted to go to Saint-Cloud for Easter so that he could take communion, in private, at the hands of a non-juring priest. If he remained in Paris, he would have to take it at Saint-Germain l'Auxerrois, the parish church of the Tuileries, where the priest had taken the oath – which he did, together with Marie-Antoinette, after the aborted departure for Saint-Cloud. Louis returned in a profound state of depression. Lord Acton, however, argued that the point of going to Saint-Cloud was precisely *not* to communicate. 'At Easter the king of France used to receive communion in public.' However, if he did take communion (Acton does not specify whether from a juring or non-juring priest) that would show that neither he nor the priest who administered the sacrament felt any guilt which would in turn seem to sanction the schism.[9]

In fact it is likely that Louis did take communion from a non-juring priest, despite the direction of the bishop. At any rate he hired people to deny, in the Cordelier Club, the rumour that he had communicated in the private chapel of the Tuileries.[10] To complete the complications, Acton suspected and Michelet was convinced that Louis had hired the crowd which prevented his departure so that he could argue that he was unfree and thus gain additional freedom of movement. At all events, Clermont's letter, the Pope's bulls and the aborted departure for Saint-Cloud, all occurring in April, are often seen as the linked catalysts for Louis's decision to escape. The de Coursacs, as we have seen, argue that the decision was taken then.

The second of Louis's complaints – and the one which I think has most bearing on his flight – was his exclusion from the legislative process. From the autumn of 1790 there had been a new disposition in the Assembly's constitutional committee to strengthen the executive in the final revisions to the constitution. Some of the radicals of 1789, notably Barnave, Duport and Alexandre de Lameth, the 'triumvirate', now wanted, as Barnave said, to 'stop the Revolution' before it degenerated into a general attack on property. They saw a strong constitutional monarch as the best way of preventing this. Louis watched these developments with interest. In his declaration he states that 'he placed his confidence in the wise men of the Assembly' who 'when speaking about the revision of the [constitutional] decrees' showed a disposition to strengthen the executive and guarantee property and security so that the *émigrés* could return.

However, in the spring, the constitutional committee began to lose ground to the radicals: it was decreed that the king could never place himself more than 20 leagues from the Assembly, that members of the Assembly were ineligible for future ones and that the king should lose the prerogative of mercy (which he cherished). As Louis put it:

> the nearer the Assembly approached the end of its labours, the more the wise men were seen to lose their influence, together with a daily increase of clauses which could only make government difficult . . . the mentality of the [Jacobin] clubs dominated and pervaded everything.

The development of the network of Jacobin clubs to which Louis refers was arguably the biggest political development of 1790–91, restoring the dynamic to the Revolution at a time when former radicals, such as Barnave, thought they could stop it like a bus. In his declaration, Louis, who recognized the enemy, compared the network, with its 'mother society' in Paris corresponding with affiliates throughout the country, to the *parlementaire théorie des classes* whereby the concerns of one are the concerns of all. The Jacobin network, Robespierre's most original creation, transforming this obscure provincial deputy into a household name and a force throughout the land, pressurized the Assembly by collective petitions and posted 'slates' of candidates for the elections which were held for most offices. It was the unexpected rise of the clubs which was responsible for the rapid deterioration of royal authority in the months preceding the king's flight.

The Assembly was expected to finalize the constitution in July, so Louis had to get out of Paris before that date or be forced to accept it as it stood. As the individual constitutional articles had been drafted they had been presented to the king for his 'sanction'. But the process was a solemn farce. As Adrien Duport told the Assembly after the king's flight, had the king refused his sanction to any of the decrees, 'you would have declared what you declare now that you had no need for any sanction on the king's part to establish your constitution'. But, he added, it was fortunate that the king had not forced them to try conclusions too furiously because his sanction had smoothed the passage of legislation which the country would otherwise have regarded as too radical 'until it was ready to trust its destinies to your zeal'. By the same token, Duport added, the king was not bound by his sanction of individual articles when it came to giving his sanction to the constitution as a whole. He was free to take it or leave it, though the latter implied abdication.[11]

Apart from the constitutional question, there was also that of the elections to the successor assembly to the Constituent, the Legislative. The primary assemblies for these elections had already begun and the final round was due to start on 5 July. These, Louis gloomily noted, under the influence of the Jacobin clubs – putting up 'slates' of candidates and applying pressure – were likely to produce radical candidates. Louis's flight had the effect of suspending the meetings of the primary elections and they were held, in conditions more favourable to him, at the end of the summer. Louis, as we know, was an eternal procrastinator: with the constitution almost completed and the primary elections begun, 20 June was the last possible moment to go.

Louis's flight had negative and positive features. It was designed to paralyse the system – his ministers were left instructions to sign nothing. It had the effect of paralysing constitutional and electoral matters but government continued without him, the Assembly ordering that ministerial signatures were not necessary, which proved Louis's point that the country was effectively being run as a republic – an opinion endorsed by Sorel:

The monarchy ... was now only a fiction. ... This conclusion in a manner can be derived from the constitution itself. It would not have been otherwise conceived if the aim had been to demonstrate that a constitutional monarchy was infeasible.

Sorel thought that the option of dissolving parliament was a necessary prerogative of a constitutional monarch:

Recourse to the nation, which is the necessary resource and the legitimate solution to all the crises in constitutional regimes, was forbidden in France.[12]

Louis explained the more constructive reasons for his flight to the duc de Choiseul (nephew of Louis XV's minister) who was responsible for providing troop detachments to escort the king's carriage between Châlons and Montmédy. From Montmédy, Louis told Choiseul, he would have 'accepted reasonable proposals from Paris [for a revision of the constitution] and he would have imposed obedience on Coblenz', where the *émigrés* were concentrated. For Choiseul, the escape was the difficult part, the rest would have followed – had started to follow:

As soon as his departure was known, all the wise men of
the Assembly, ignoring the speeches from the popular
orators . . . and even a momentary outburst of anger from
the people, took immediate steps to profit from the event to
give a better turn to affairs.[13]

The Assembly was preparing to send a deputation to the king
at Montmédy to renegotiate the constitution when news of his
recapture at Varennes caused them to cancel their plans.
Alexandre de Lameth lamented: 'What a disaster! . . . I hoped
that a negotiation with the king from a position of demonstrable
and complete independence could, through reciprocal concessions, give France peace.'[14] Once a constitution had been agreed,
Choiseul informs us, Louis planned to install himself at
Compiègne, 'for a long time' and summon the Assembly to him,
only returning to Paris once the constitution was bedded in. A
receipt exists for furniture for Compiègne 'for the estates' dated
December 1790.[15]

The sort of modifications to the constitution Louis would have
insisted on can be gleaned from his declaration. First and fore-
most the king would be given full partnership in the legislative
process, which the Assembly 'in contempt of the *cahiers*', the
electoral mandates for the Estates-General, had denied him. In
practice this would have meant the initiative in legislation and an
absolute veto, as in England, rather than the suspensive one
which he dubbed as 'purely illusory'. This was the verdict on the
suspensive veto of the radical deputy Pétion in a private letter to
the deputy Brissot. 'The people', he said,

> would complain if the king were stripped of all his pre-
> rogatives. There aren't twenty *cahiers* which don't instruct
> the deputies to make laws in conjunction with the king. The
> suspensive veto only leaves him with the appearance of
> power which I think it is impossible that he can abuse given
> permanent assemblies.[16]

Louis would have had a bodyguard under his own control and
the prerogative of mercy. The Civil Constitution of the Clergy
would be modified in discussion with the Pope. Whether
ministers would have seats in the Assembly is not discussed in the
declaration, but it would seem to follow from the revised legislative framework and also from what may be said to have been
the unstated premise of Louis's proposals: the inauguration of an

English-style form of government. Necker had said that in 1789 Louis rejected his proposals for such a system but that he 'afterwards adopted it when it was too late'. I would suggest that this was the moment of adoption; a point reinforced by the comte de La Marck's observation that Bouillé's

> opinions tended towards a form of constitution similar to England's. The king was not unaware of this viewpoint and this did not stop him from designating the officer most worthy of his confidence, which proves once again that Louis XVI had sincerely opted for a constitutional system of government.[17]

My analysis of Louis's plans is shared only by Robespierre and the Robespierrist historian Georges Michon, whose *Adrien Duport et le parti feuillant* was published in 1924. (We agree on the facts, disagree on the moral value to be placed on them.) Robespierre did not think that the king's flight was meant to bring about the restoration of the *ancien régime*. Nor, Robespierre adds, 'could it have been upon Leopold and the King of Sweden and on the army [of *émigrés*] beyond the Rhine, that he placed his hopes'.[18] No, Robespierre argued, something more dangerous because more insidious was afoot: the king intended to do a deal with the National Assembly which would enable the *émigrés* to return voluntarily to France. (Louis mentions this objective in his manifesto.) The triumvirs, according to Robespierre, would 'at first ask for very small sacrifices to bring about a general reconciliation'; and they would have little 'trouble in inducing a weary people to accept a deal, a half-way compromise'. 'You will have observed', he added 'how [the king] distinguishes between those things in the constitution which he finds offensive and those he deigns to find acceptable.'

Robespierre also appreciated the timing of the king's flight: four times he employs the rhetorical refrain 'why did he choose this precise moment' to go? And answers: 'he chose the moment' when the primary assemblies were in progress and with the prospect of a Legislative Assembly more radical than its predecessor and prepared to 'revoke a portion of its measures'. (This lends me to doubt the de Coursacs' supposition that Louis planned to order elections for a new assembly rather than gather elements from the existing one round him.)

Robespierre states and Michon implies that the 'triumvirs' and even La Fayette colluded or connived in Louis's escape. 'The king', Robespierre proclaimed, 'fled with the consent of La Fayette.' He had seen how the 'triumvirs' had striven to revise the constitution in order to strengthen the executive and had witnessed the measures they had taken to attack the Jacobins. At the beginning of March 1791 the king was given the right, in certain circumstances, to replace local officials – to the chagrin of the local Jacobins who had often been instrumental in their election. On 11 May Le Chapelier introduced a law banning wall-posters and collective petitions, which as Robespierre's unsuccessful intervention made clear was aimed at the Jacobin Clubs. No evidence for such collusion over the flight has survived but in a sense the question is irrelevant: everyone knew, particularly after the Saint-Cloud departure, that Louis was bound to try to escape; it was only human nature.

Choiseul's assumption that once Louis had got to Montmédy the rest would be plain sailing – 'apart from the danger of the actual journey, there was scarcely any doubt that such a wise plan ... would have been successful'[19] – may have been optimistic. Whatever the support for the king's plans from among the political leaders, the history of the Revolution shows that once they tried to 'stop the Revolution' they lost their popular authority. As Louis's declaration said, the Assembly was under increasing pressure from the clubs. What the dispersal by suspicious crowds of the troop detachments placed along the king's route and the final arrest at Varennes shows is that civilian militants were able either to prevent the military from taking any action or to seduce them from their allegiance through the by now familiar process of fraternization – getting them drunk. Bouillé himself was increasingly doubtful about the loyalty of his own troops, even though the majority were Germans in French service.

This posed the problem that, whatever Louis's good intentions, if things turned nasty he would be forced to rely on Austrian troops. This is the sense of Michelet's dictum that the escape plan started as a French one but finished 'entirely foreign'.

Michelet[20]

Though ultimately Jules Michelet condemns Louis XVI, he also presents him as a tragic figure, whose instinctive honesty is finally overruled by his royal and sacerdotal education. Unlike many historians, he does not present Louis as inanimate, unfeeling and unthinking, and so can restore to the Revolution, through its central figure, a sense of drama, even of tragedy.

Although Louis, according to Michelet, was formed by the Jesuits, there were other more salutary infuences which weighed in the balance in the months preceding the flight to Varennes. First was Louis's reading of English history from which

> he had retained this much: that Charles I had been put to death for having made war on his people, and that James II had been declared to have abdicated for having forsaken his people. If there was one fixed idea in his mind it was not to expose himself to the fate of either: never to draw the sword, and never to quit the soil of France. ... This resolution of not acting in order not to compromise himself was moreover perfectly consonant to his natural indolence.

Second, Louis did not want to be dependent on foreign assistance, regarding Prussia as ambitious and Austria as treacherous. His distrust of Austria derived from both his parents: from his father the dauphin who detested the Austrian alliance and Choiseul its architect, and from his mother, Marie-Josèphe of Saxony.

This meant that Marie-Antoinette, who was intent on flight, had an uphill struggle in bringing her husband round. To convince him

> it was ... necessary that Louis XVI, cleverly tutored by the clergy, should ... allow his kingly scruples to give way to his scruples as a Christian and as a *dévot*; for the idea of a superior duty could alone make him fail in what he believed to be a duty.

The clerics' task was facilitated by the Civil Constitution of the Clergy and the subsequent persecution of non-juring priests. The abortive Saint-Cloud departure allowed Louis to ask rhetorically, 'how was it that he, who had granted toleration to the Protestants, could not enjoy it in the midst of his own palace? He considered himself freed from every oath and absolved from every duty; and he believed he saw both God and reason arrayed against the Revolution.'

Initially (October 1790) Marie-Antoinette and those who planned the escape – Breteuil, Fersen, Mercy – 'in order not to alarm the king, merely spoke to ... [him] in terms of taking refuge' among Bouillé's faithful troops. Nothing was said of the Austrian stipulation that it would not intervene until there was '*civil war begun*'. By December the chance of the purely French solution's succeeding was evaporating 'when Bouillé confessed that he needed German troops to retain the few French that remained with him. He *requested* . . . assistance from foreigners'. Earlier it had been hoped, after Bouillé's crushing of the Nancy mutiny,

> that a great party both in the army and the National Guard, would pronounce for the king and that France would be divided . . . meanwhile a fact became manifest which changed the face of things – the unanimity of France.
> The affair then became entirely foreign.

After the abortive Saint-Cloud departure Louis sent a circular to all the French diplomatic agents stating that he was free, that he was no more than the 'first functionary' of the people and that he rejoiced in the constitution and the Revolution. This invites Michelet's contempt:

> This entirely novel language, wherein everybody perceived the stamp of falsehood, and this false jarring voice, did the king incredible harm; and whatever attachment was still felt for him could not withstand the contempt inspired by his duplicity. . . .
> The king had received a royal education from M. de la Vauguyon, the leader of the Jesuit party; his natural honesty had gained the upper hand in ordinary circumstances; but, in this crisis, where religion and royalty were at stake, the Jesuit reappeared. Too devout to have the least scruple of chivalrous honour, and believing that he who deceives for a good purpose cannot use too much deception, he outstepped all bounds, and did not deceive at all.
> Austria does not seem to have believed, any more than France, in the honesty of Louis XVI; and perhaps, in reality, he still remained patriotic enough to wish to deceive Austria in availing himself of her assistance.

A distressing feature of the flight for Michelet was that the king fled at night disguised as a servant, the factotum to the governess of the royal children who was posing as a Russian baroness. Michelet has Louis directing:

'you will put in the carriage box . . . the red coat with gold lace that I wore at Cherbourg'. . . . What he thus hides in the box would have been his defence. The dress the King of France wore when he appeared against England, amidst his fleet, was better calculated to consecrate him than the holy ampulla of Rheims. Who would have dared to arrest him if, throwing open his dress, he had shown that coat? He ought to have kept it, or rather kept his French heart, as he then possessed it.

Louis's disguise as a servant enables Michelet to make a brilliant point:

This disguise, which appeared so unseemly, placed Louis XVI in the private condition for which he was formed. Judging from his natural abilities he was calculated to become, doubtless not a valet – for he was educated and accomplished – but the servant of some great family, a tutor or a steward, dispensed – as a servant – from every kind of initiative; he would have been a punctual and upright clerk, or a well-informed, strictly moral and conscientious tutor, as far, however, as bigotry admits. A servant's costume was his most appropriate dress; he had till then been disguised in the inappropriate insignia of royalty.

As the king's *berline* rattled along the fine roads his grandfather had constructed, Louis applying himself to his map as the towns and villages flashed by – La Ferté-sous-Jouarre, Montmirail, Vauchamps, Etoges, Châlons – Michelet observes, 'All goes well – but for France or Austria? For whither is the king going?' He has Louis telling one of the bodyguards who accompanied the carriage, 'tonight I shall sleep at the Abbaye d'Orval', out of France, *on Austrian territory!*

M. de Bouillé [in his memoirs] says the contrary; but even he shows, and states clearly, that the king having no longer any safety to expect in the kingdom, must have changed his mind, and have at length fallen, in spite of his former resolution, into the Austrian net.

The arrest

There is much truth in this observation of Michelet's and in a sense the arrest at Varennes can be seen less as an accident than as the substance of the enterprise. Louis was stopped whilst searching for fresh relay horses placed in the other half of the town, across the river Aire (which, worryingly, David Jordan, *The King's Trial*, has marking the border with Luxembourg; the border is instead some miles away). But even when he revealed his indentity and asked for an escort from the local National Guard to take him to Montmédy, he was not obeyed. At Varennes he was no more obeyed than in the Tuileries when he tried to depart for Saint-Cloud. Although the troop detachments along the route had dispersed, some 150 ended up, by a rare favourable chance, at Varennes and in time to rescue the royal family before the numbers summoned by tocsin from the surrounding villages had become too great. But there would have been some risk: the bridge was barricaded with furniture and the royal family would have had to ford the river, on horseback, surrounded by cavalry. Louis hesitated: 'Can you guarantee', he asked Choiseul, 'that in this unequal struggle a bullet will not hit the queen, or my sister or my children?'[21]

This hesitation was not just typical of Louis; it also typified the situation. Wouldn't Louis have hesitated all the more before giving orders to storm or starve Paris? If he had given them, would he have been obeyed? And isn't this the point of his hesitation, that he had already witnessed so much disaffection along the route that he doubted of the success of the enterprise, had come to share Michelet's analysis. The 150 dragoons were themselves becoming more disaffected with every passing minute. The exquisite moment of hesitation is marvellously captured by John Wilson Croker, an arch-Tory minister in Wellington's cabinet but also, arguably, the first 'scientific' historian of the Revolution:

> No one present except Louis had any right to command; and the only orders that Louis could be induced to give were to do nothing. The boldest thing he said was to M. Deslons, who had come into town to receive his orders – '*I am a prisoner and have no orders to give*'! If Deslons had been in command he might have taken this hint and acted without those orders which a *prisoner* could not give; but he was only a captain and his own colonel and two other superior officers were present. They happened, unluckily for this purpose, to be too intimate with, too much personally devoted to their amiable and kind-hearted

master to venture to do him the salutary violence which his complaint, more than once made, of being a *prisoner*, was perhaps meant to suggest. Everyone was intimidated. Even the high spirit of the queen herself seems on this occasion to have failed before the *strenua inertia* of the king.[22]

The state of being a prisoner, then, constituted for Louis the excuse for constructive inaction he had always sought, an inaction which implies action by others on his behalf. It was a dramatic variant of a stock situation in his reign, similar to the one we saw Saint-Priest describe during the October Days. 'Passing the buck' would be too coarse a way of defining a necessary prerogative of kings. As Shakespeare's Pompey says to a servitor:

> Ah! this thou should'st have done,
> and not have spoken on't.[23]

Louis also saw his prevarication as a safety play, giving Bouillé, who had been informed, time to reach him. Bouillé's failure to reach the town before 8 a.m., when the commissioners from the National Assembly ordered the return of the royal family to Paris, needs explaining. The de Coursacs suggest treachery on Bouillé's part but Michelet is nearer the mark:

> The few troops which Bouillé still possessed were so little under his control that, after having gone forward a few leagues to meet the king, he was obliged to return to be among his soldiers, to watch over them and keep them in order.[24]

In other words we come back to the same problem of disaffection which would probably have doomed the exercise. As Croker puts it, Bouillé's

> strong distrust of the general spirit of his troops . . . leads us to doubt whether, even if he had gotten the king to Montmédy, he would have eventually been better obeyed by his army than Lafayette [in 1792] and Dumouriez [in 1793] subsequently were, when they appealed to their troops against the violence of the National Assembly.[25]

Louis, I believe, hoped that force would not be necessary and that he could have negotiated with the Assembly without it. But if the Assembly was preparing, at news of Louis's escape, to send a deputation to treat with him at Montmédy, why, when news arrived of his recapture at Varennes, didn't they equally send a deputation thither, instead of La Fayette's aide-de-camp, and the three deputies who joined the carriage between Epernay and Dormans, to bring him back to Paris? True, the situation was different, notably that the king instead of being free at Montmédy was just as much (though no more) a prisoner at Varennes as he had been at Paris. As Michelet put it:

> The *monarchien* Malouet would have been the natural intermediary, the negotiator with a free king; to guard a prisoner-king, the Left had sent three men who expressed its three complexions, Barnave, Latour-Maubourg and Pétion.[26]

The aftermath

'The journey back to Paris was', in Croker's words, 'a lingering agony of insult and danger' for the royal family.[27] Several occupants of the coach, that moving prison, including the king's daughter and the deputy Pétion, have left a record of the journey. Here is Pétion's description of the king:

> The king tried to strike up a conversation. . . . He asked me if I was married; I said I was; he asked me if I had any children. I told him I had one who was just older than his son. I said to him from time to time, 'look at the country-side, is it not fine? . . . What a fine country France is! There is no kingdom in the world that can compare with it.' I let out these ideas deliberately; I examined the impression they made on the royal physiognomy, but his expression is always cold, unanimated to a devastating degree, and, truth to tell, this mass of flesh is insensible.
>
> He wished to speak to me of the English, of their industry, of the commercial genius of that nation. He formulated one or two phrases, then became embarrassed, noticed it and blushed. This difficulty in expressing himself gives him a timidity I noticed several times. Those who do not know him would be inclined to take this timidity for stupidity; but they would be wrong: very rarely did he let out anything misplaced and I did not hear him utter any-thing stupid.

He applied himself greatly to following his maps and he would say: 'We are in such and such a *département*, or district or spot.'[28]

Pétion then describes Louis's return to Paris, a calculated insult, a coronation in reverse, vast silent crowds, hats on, National Guard with reversed arms. The king was taken back to the Tuileries, where he was placed under the strictest house arrest, guards standing at open doors. A few minutes later, Pétion went into the king's bedroom:

> Already all the valets had preceded there in their usual costume. It seemed as if the king were returning from a hunting party; they did his toilet. Seeing the king, contemplating him, you never could have guessed all that had happened: he was just as phlegmatic, just as tranquil as if nothing had happened. He immediately put himself on show.

Opinion is sharply but unequally divided on the effects of the king's flight. The Girault de Coursacs take the view that the flight actually strengthened the king's position. I consider that the flight polarized opinion concerning the monarchy. It gave rise to the first serious expression of republicanism but also to a rallying of social conservatives, including former political radicals, around the monarchy as the only means of 'stopping the Revolution'. The most commonly held view is that the flight fatally compromised the king and made his fall inevitable.

The de Coursacs make the valid point that after the king's return, even whilst he was put under strict house arrest in the Tuileries and suspended from his royal functions, the constitution was revised to take account of some of the objections he had raised in his declaration. Thus he became the 'hereditary representative' rather than merely the 'first functionary' of the nation; he was given a bodyguard of 1800 men paid and appointed by himself; and the Civil Constitution was reclassified as ordinary unentrenched legislation subject to repeal. So Louis could take an oath to observe the constitution without including the Civil Constitution, which everyone knew he detested. The de Coursacs do not give any credit for these changes to the 'triumvirs' and their party who seceded from the Jacobins, formed the rival Feuillant club, and dispersed a crowd which had assembled to present a republican petition (massacre of the Champ de Mars). Any arrangements the Feuillants had were with the queen not the king, they were 'Feuillants but still Jacobins' and their aim was to 'eliminate Louis XVI and proclaim the republic'.[29]

That may at one stage have been the aim of La Fayette – Lord Acton suggests that he may have deliberately allowed Louis to escape, knowing that the proclamation of the republic would be a likely consequence; but it was not the aim of the 'triumvirs' who planned to give Louis XVI all the powers of a king of England, initiative in legislation, veto, right of dissolution, but were thwarted in this objective by the 300 deputies of the extreme Right pursuing a *politique du pire*, who cared nothing for the personal position of the king and feared that an improvement in the constitution would lessen the chances of a return to the *ancien régime*.

The de Coursacs also correctly note that the elections to the Legislative Assembly in August returned only 206 deputies who joined the Jacobin Club, whereas a majority in the Constituent Assembly had been members. They cite the department of Pas de Calais where the electoral assembly proclaimed that 'it would not nominate any member of the clubs'.[30] One of Louis's explicit objectives in flight had been to diminish the influence of the clubs on the elections and in this he can be said to have succeeded.

However, Barnave's proclaimed intention of 'stopping the Revolution' could not be predicated on Louis's flight, which restarted it. This point is made by Croker with reference to Robespierre's career. Believing the Revolution to be indeed finished, Robespierre had in the spring induced the Assembly to pass its famous 'self-denying ordinance' whereby members were ineligible for seats in the next two legislatures. He was about to be elected to a lucrative judicial post and retire from politics which could now be left to second-rate men. The king's flight upset his plans. For, he now realized with bitterness, he had miscalculated: an even more divisive phase of the Revolution had been inaugurated. Sorel offers a brilliant analysis of the still mysterious 'self-denying ordinance'. The Constituent Assembly was as discredited in 1791 as the monarchy had been in 1788. Both were exhausted, both had lost the will to govern. The Constituent had been worn out by its legislative activity, just as Louis XVI's government had been exhausted by constant innovaion, from Turgot's reforms at the beginning of the reign to Calonne's 'expedients' in 1787.

Lord Acton's analysis is typical of the many hostile commentaries on the consequences of the king's flight, which,

> while it broke up the conservative party, called the republican party into existence. For Louis had left behind him a manifesto, meditated during many months, urging the defects of the constitution, and denouncing all that had been effected since he had suffered violence at Versailles. Many others besides Louis were aware of the defects, and desired their amendment. But the renunciation of so much that he had sanctioned, so much that he had so solemnly and repeatedly approved, exposed him to the reproach of duplicity and falsehood. He not only underwent the ignominy of capture and exposure; he was regarded henceforth as a detected perjurer. If the king could never be trusted again, the prospects of the monarchy were hopeless.[31]

Jaurès believed that, knowing these to be the king's sentiments, the Assembly was just as dishonest in reinstating him as he had been in sanctioning decrees since October 1789.

Michelet believed, in company with the deputy the marquis de Condorcet, that the republic should have been proclaimed on 21 June. He quotes Condorcet's prophetic words:

> The king at the moment no longer has a following; let us not wait until he has acquired so much power that it will require an effort to overthrow him; this effort will be terrible if the Republic is made by a revolution, by a popular uprising.

Instead of seizing this moment:

> The politicians waited, hesitated and the moment was missed. A sentiment no less natural gained ground on the king's return – pity for his misfortune. He could not be put together again as a king, so he was restored as a man ... by bringing him back a captive, humiliated, unfortunate, generous and tender-hearted folk were so carried away that through their tears they no longer saw the false and double-dealing king. Instead they saw a man full of resignation and they made a saint of him.

This will henceforth be the great theme of Michelet and one can see across his contempt for royalty and especially priest-ridden royalty he too is affected by Louis's misfortunes. That, however, does not prevent him from indulging in a bout of popular mysticism:

> The impression made by the king's flight, his desertion to the enemy, this major, this capital fact, with its decisive significance, might be obscured to the gaze of the idle, chattering classes which feed on daily gossip. But for the bulk of France, hard-working and silent, the same fact retained its freshness as an ever-present threat. This France, gathering in the harvest of its toil, could think of nothing else, and if the ploughshare struck a stone, and perchance stopped the plough, it was always this same stone, positioned in every furrow.[32]

|11|

The fall of the monarchy

The constitutional monarchy lasted less than a year. Accepted by the king on 13 September 1791, it was brought down by the *journée* of 10 August 1792, when the Tuileries was stormed and the king took refuge in the Legislative Assembly before being imprisoned in the Temple. The cause of the fall of the monarchy was the war which France declared on Austria on 20 April, Prussia entering in alliance with Austria on 3 July. It was the war which, in Marcel Reinhard's words, revolutionized the Revolution. National crisis intensified the Revolution and left no space for waverers. It would be a further year before Saint-Just was to ostracize the 'lukewarm' as well as the 'enemies of the people'; but the idea was already there.

Most prominent among the lukewarm stood the king, as can be seen from the words he addressed to Bertrand de Molleville on appointing him minister for the marine:

> My opinion is that the literal execution of the constitution is the best way of making the nation see the alterations to which it is susceptible.[1]

At a time of national crisis such an attitude (Louis carried a pocket edition of the constitution around with him to quote chapter and verse) was clearly unacceptable. As Vergniaud, the best orator on the Left Wing of the new assembly, the Legislative, privately reminded the king, 'he had been sadly deceived if he had been led to believe that not to depart from the letter of the constitution was to do all that he should'.[2]

This, to my mind, is the most serious accusation that can unequivocally be made against Louis XVI. True, pursuing a *politique du pire* – that is, deliberately making a situation worse in the hope that good will come of it – is a particularly French vice, for which there is no phrase in English. And many politicians followed such a chimera during the Revolution, starting with a spectrum from the Right to Mirabeau in the Constituent. The policy was perfected, in the Legislative, by the Left grouping to which Vergniaud himself belonged, known to history as the Girondins from the department (capital, Bordeaux) which many represented. But it was no less dangerous a strategy for being so prevalent. One ministerial candidate was dissuaded because, as Marie-Antoinette put it, 'he is a man to put by for better times', and the king and queen were said to 'have regretted appointing M. Bertrand because they are satisfied with him'.[3] By such actions they ensured that the 'better times' would never come.

Nevertheless it was not because of his negativity that Louis was dethroned – that could even be an advantage in a *roi fainéant* – but because he was suspected of conspiring with the 'foreign powers' to bring about the forcible restoration of the *ancien régime*. That was the major accusation at his trial before the National Convention and before history. The logically possible defence of Louis that he did ask for foreign intervention but that this was necessary to end bloody anarchy in France is rarely made. It is mainly confined to the two periods of royalism following national defeat in 1815 and 1870 which ended the two Bonapartist adventures. From the latter period, Jules Flammermont, professor at Poitiers, cites a candidate for the *baccalauréat*:

> 'It was the crimes of France', he told me, 'which forced the Prussians and Austrians to enter France in the month of August 1792 to restore order.' One can see here that the spirit of Father Loriquet still hovers over the teaching of history in certain secondary schools.

Flammermont wrote this in 1883 in his seminal article, *Négociations secrètes de Louis XVI et du baron de Breteuil avec la cour de Berlin (décembre 1791–juillet 1792).*[4] Flammermont chooses to write about Prussia because the case against Louis XVI depends on just one letter, purportedly written to Frederick William II on 3 December 1791. The rest of the voluminous correspondence seeking foreign intervention is conducted by Marie-Antoinette, through Fersen – her alleged lover who organized the escape from Paris in June 1791 – Breteuil and Mercy-Argenteau, the former Austrian ambassador, since 1790 resident in the Austrian Netherlands. Marie-Antoinette believed that nothing could be expected from the internal resources of the monarchy; the flight to Varennes had convinced her that 'there was not a single town, not a regiment on which they could rely'. She favoured an 'armed congress' of the Powers. That is, diplomacy backed up by an international force or, as she put it, 'not war but the threat of war'. Louis would then be asked to mediate with the European Powers who would disarm once he was restored to his former prerogatives.[5]

The letter to the king of Prussia specifically asks for 'a congress of the principal Powers of Europe, supported by an armed force, as the best means of ... restoring a more desirable order of things'. It also mentions that the king has written to the rulers of Russia, Spain and Sweden as well as to the emperor and asks for secrecy. Flammermont notes that until recently (he is writing in 1883) the letter was only known in printed form and only in collections which contained many forgeries.[6] And 'the defenders of Louis XVI and Marie-Antoinette had profited from this fact to challenge the authenticity of this appeal to the foreigner'. This argument, he adds, had been used in a 'political debate' on the continuing utility of the *chapelle expiatoire* which Louis XVIII had erected on the site of his brother's burial as a place where the French nation could 'expiate' their sin of guillotining their king.

This 'political debate', Flammermont notes, had ignored the recent archival discoveries of the German historians Leopold von Ranke and Heinrich von Sybel who, whilst acknowledging the authenticity of the letter in question, played down its significance since it showed Prussia to have been an aggressor in the war. In writing his article, Flammermont strayed from his main field of *ancien régime* politics in order to score a point not just against Louis XVI but against the Prussia which had recently defeated France. Prussia, he implied, was the aggressor in both 1792 and 1870.

Flammermont's conclusions have passed into the mainstream of Revolutionary historiography, confirming as they seem to do what had always been suspected, namely that the king was conspiring, if not with the *émigrés*, then certainly with the 'foreign powers' to influence the internal arrangements of France. Thus Sorel: 'royalty appealed to force from abroad; the Revolution appealed to popular force', on 20 June and 10 August 1792.[7] T. C. W. Blanning also in *The Origins of the French Revolutionary Wars* (1986), the best of the modern treatments of this subject, argues that the 'paranoid' fear of betrayal was justified because 'The court *was* conspiring against the Revolution and *was* seeking the armed intervention of the European powers.'[8] Both these writers sometimes accuse Louis in person of treason, but usually they employ the more mealy-mouthed term of 'the court' or 'the royal family'.

Sorel also is sometimes inconsistent, or rather he prints conflicting evidence, often on the same page, without comment. He cites a letter from the king to his *émigré* brothers of December 1791:

> I am aware that you are thinking more of yourselves than of me. . . . I see that you are asking for the restoration of the former regime, which cannot be effected without shedding torrents of blood. You make me shudder with horror! I would rather the monarchy fell than ever subscribe to such a project!

Then, on the same page, Sorel cites another letter of Louis's, to Breteuil, written a fortnight later:

> It is clear to anyone who walks on two legs that, privately, I cannot approve the Revolution and the absurd and detestable constitution which places me below the former state of the king of Poland.

Louis goes on to welcome foreign intervention, since 'instead of a civil war it will be a foreign war [*une guerre politique*] and things will be all the better for that'.[9] Can these two letters – neither of them for public consumption – have been written by the same pen within a fortnight of each other? Were they?

These are the sort of questions addressed, as one would expect, by the Girault de Coursacs, who offer the major modern challenge to the conventional view. These revisionist historians do not permit themselves the defence offered by Flammermont's Poitevin schoolboy (quoted above) but needs must argue that Louis was a patriot who simply did not seek foreign intervention. They demonstrate, to my mind convincingly, using the same arguments deployed in discussing the flight to Varennes, that the letters written in the king's name but in the hand of Marie-Antoinette were composed by the queen. But when they come to the letter to the king of Prussia they have a harder task since it is in the king's hand. They have to argue that it is a forgery.

In seeking to prove this the de Coursacs rely on a curious feature of the correspondence. On 25 December 1791 Fersen tells Gustavus III of Sweden about the letters being sent to the various rulers to promote the congress. 'The letter to the king of Prussia', he adds, 'is in the *queen's* hand, as is that to the empress', Catherine II of Russia. The letter to the king of Prussia, he adds, will be delivered by the chevalier de Bressac. On 1 January, however, Fersen writes that since Bressac

> has not yet arrived, the baron de Breteuil has decided to send the letter to the king of Prussia by a courier. *It is in the king's hand.*[10]

The reason the de Coursacs give for the perpetration of the forgery is that with all the conflicting signals coming out of Paris about whether the king accepted the constitution or not, the king of Prussia had insisted on having something which demonstrated Louis's personal dispositions 'in an authentic manner', a matter on which the other rulers had been less exigent. Finally, the de Coursacs argue, the forgery was perpetrated by a German-speaking engraver who in the key phrase *'une ordre de choses plus desirable'* made *'ordre'* feminine (which is the German equivalent) – an error of gender which no francophone could commit.[11]

This is all very speculative: it is to be hoped that Munro Price's forthcoming book on Louis XVI and Breteuil during the Revolution will shed some light on these long-standing questions. But, even supposing that the entire correspondence relating to foreign intervention was conducted by Marie-Antoinette, can one assume that her husband was ignorant of even its general drift? May he not have found it convenient to let others act in his name, as Croker observed when he told Choiseul at Varennes that he was a 'prisoner'. Added to Croker's idea of a calculating inertness, there is also the consideration that the symptoms of depression, and notably dependence, which Louis first exhibited after the failure of his reform programme in 1787, intensified as the political situation deteriorated further.

Sorel captures this well:

> Louis XVI left Paris as a prisoner and returned as a hostage. Captive in the Tuileries, the royal family had only one thought, that of all captives, to be free. Its history, during this period, can be summed up by a perpetual plot to be

delivered. Louis XVI appeared more insignificant and crushed than ever; his heavy spirit resolved itself, as it were, into a sort of gentle haze. The moment for great sacrifices, which would be the moment for his ennoblement, had not yet come. Meek in spirit and resigned, he expected the queen to think for him, and his servitors to act in his cause, and God at last to have pity on the House of France.[12]

But Sorel also concludes: 'Louis XVI had no secrets from [Marie-Antoinette]; and she had none from their [foreign] allies.[13]

The best evidence for Louis's patriotic and pacific intentions adduced by the de Coursacs – and arguably the finest thing he ever wrote – is the secret letter he sent to his brothers explaining why he had accepted the constitution. Here he explains, prophetically, that a foreign invasion would lead to a 'massacre of the so-called aristocrats' in France. Even if the invasion were successful against badly armed national guards and regular soldiers left (by emigration) with few officers, were the allies prepared for a permanent occupation? For 'one can never govern a country against its inclinations'. And those inclinations were overwhelmingly in favour of the Revolution because

> the lower portion of the people see only that they are reckoned with; the bourgeoisie sees nothing above them. Vanity is satisfied. This new possession makes them forget everything else.

Only by 'executing the principles' of the constitution 'in good faith will the people come to know the cause of their misfortunes; public opinon will change' etc. Sorel characterizes this letter as 'wise and moving'.[14]

In a postscript Louis bitterly blames his brothers Provence and Artois for inducing the emperor and king of Prussia to issue the Declaration of Pillnitz of August 1791 pledging intervention to restore order in France, with the important proviso that the other sovereigns joined in the venture – a condition which was not likely to be met but which was ignored by the firebrands in France. Aware that his brothers constantly spoke in his name without consulting him, Louis sent a copy of his secret letter to the emperor, who used it to catch out the brothers in a lie.

The question therefore is whether Louis's attitude towards the Revolution had hardened between the sending of this letter in

August and the time of the letter to the king of Prussia in
December 1791. There is a passage in the letter to Frederick
William which seems to be at once characteristic of Louis's
attitude and of the development of the situation. It runs:

> despite my acceptance of the new constitution, the men of
> faction openly display their project of entirely destroying
> the remains of the monarchy.[15]

Louis is referring to the moves by the Girondins – a republican
minority in the Legislative Assembly but one which could often
carry the constitutional monarchists with them – to depopularize
the king by introducing measures he was bound to veto. The
measures were against the *émigrés* and the non-juring clergy. The
former were required to return to France on penalty of death and
confiscation of their lands. The latter unless they took an oath to
the constitution were to lose their pensions and be held responsible for religious disturbances in their vicinity.

Blanning, harsh on Louis, considers that the objective of the
Girondins was 'the subversion of the constitution which had just
been introduced'.[16] Michelet, kinder to the king, nevertheless
thinks that if the measures against the priests offended his
conscience, he should have abdicated. For Michelet, the fervent
anti-clerical, believed that the measures against the priests were
necessary for national salvation, since they were at the heart of
resistance to the Revolution.[17] Sorel, on the other hand,
perceptively observed that the measures actually harmed the
Revolution by uniting two causes which were naturally
disparate, that of the nobility and that of the Church. The decrees
made possible the rising in the Vendée, the most serious one the
Revolution encountered, in March 1793. My own view is that
the decrees were, in Blanning's phrase, cynically designed to
'subvert the constitution' and in support of this I adduce the fact
that a week before introducing the law against non-juring priests,
the Girondins had proposed the abolition of the Civil
Constitution itself!

In view of this my instinct is to suggest that Louis's attitude to
the Revolution had hardened as support for the constitutional
monarchy crumbled. (Why did the Feuillant majority in the
Assembly not have the courage to throw out these bills – against
the spirit of the constitution not to mention the rule of law –
rather than leave it to the king to court the unpopularity of
vetoing them?) And that accordingly he did indeed write the

famous letter to the king of Prussia. I say this fully aware of the implications for Louis's reputation, for as the de Coursacs say:

> One cannot insist too much on the incalculable consequences of this false [*sic*] letter which dissipated the King of Prussia's doubts. Without it he would never have taken part in the coalition of the Powers. . . . And without it the school textbooks could not say that Louis XVI's treason is proved by a letter in his own handwriting.[18]

Flammermont adds for good measure:

> Louis XVI and Breteuil were clearly the first to recognize how criminal were their approaches to Prussia. To require secrecy so insistently is to admit that one is guilty.

And he concludes:

> Having surveyed the documents, whose authenticity is incontestable, and which can be added to those published by MM. d'Arneth, Klinckwostrum and Feuillet de Conches, it is, I believe, impossible for any man of good faith to deny that Louis XVI and Marie-Antoinette provoked the invasion of France by the foreigner.

He also quotes from a letter of Breteuil's to the Prussian minister to show that the purpose of that invasion was to restore Louis XVI to his '*antique autorité*', to the '*plénitude de cette autorité*' and, lest there be any mistake, there must not be '*la moindre altération*' to that authority. And, Breteuil adds, the king wants the invaders to press on to Paris without being restrained by considerations of the personal safety of himself or the royal family.[19]

Between his consideration of the letter to the king of Prussia and this conclusion, Flammermont enters into a long discussion of Marie-Antoinette's secret diplomacy in which the king only figures as presented by the queen. This is unfair, since even accepting the genuineness of the former letter, there is a big difference between an armed congress to introduce a 'better order of things' and an implacable march on Paris to restore the absolute monarchy *tout court*. One has to assume a total repudiation of the sentiments he expressed in his letter to his brothers on accepting the constitution and also, once again, to assume an identity of views between the king and queen.

Peace and war

The letter to the king of Prussia had asked for an armed congress, not war. Historical opinion is divided on the question of whether Louis wanted war. Most of those (the vast majority) who think that Louis was in league with the foreign powers conclude that he sought war, whereas those few – including the Girault de Coursacs and Louis's last foreign secretary, Bigot de Sainte-Croix – who believe that he was not in collusion with the foreign powers, conclude logically that he did not seek war with them. Two exceptions are Jaurès and Michelet. Jules Michelet proclaims at the start of his sixth book:

> the main theme of this book is the gradual discovery of this certain truth: *that the king is the enemy*, the epicentre (voluntarily or involuntarily) of all the enemies, whether internal or external.

Nevertheless he states:

> The king, whom the Jacobins accused of wanting war, had done everything to prevent it. The best outcomes which it presented were very bad.

If the war went badly, an angry populace would storm the Tuileries. Even if the allies had time to rescue the king, the *émigrés* would hold him in tutelage and put Marie-Antoinette on trial. In doing this, Provence, the regent of the kingdom, 'would satisfy his personal hatred and that of the nation'.[20]

Michelet, however, is wrong in his belief that 'the queen in particular had everything to fear' from war. We know from her secret correspondence that her only fear was that Leopold or the Feuillant ministry would back away from it. At the end of March 1792 she sent an envoy to her brother saying that she was going to be put on trial by the revolutionaries. Leopold, according to Sorel and Blanning, was undecided right up to the moment of his sudden death on 1 March 1792. Bigot argues that Leopold and de Lessart, the foreign secretary, acting in accord with Louis' wishes, both strove to preserve the peace. De Lessart was a constitutional monarchist, the protégé of Barnave, who believed, correctly, that the constitutional monarchy could not survive a war with Austria.

Bigot himself, whose *Histoire de la conspiration du 10 août 1792*, was published days after Louis's execution, was at this stage de Lessart's envoy to the electorate of Trier, the epicentre of the conflict between France and the empire, because the small army of French *émigrés* had taken refuge in the elector's dominions. The Girondins had been stridently demanding their dispersal but, in Blanning's words, 'the war-party were wrong-footed by Louis XVI's response' when on 14 December he announced to the Legislative that he had already given the elector an ultimatum.[21] He also reminded the Assembly that it was trenching on his constitutional territory. Bigot supervised the evacuation of the electorate by the *émigrés*. His mission accomplished, he wanted to return, but de Lessart told him to stay put to give the lie to any Girondin claims that the *émigrés* had returned.

Whatever his ulterior motives, it suited Louis's book to clamp down on the *émigrés* since they compromised him with the Jacobins and ignored his own wishes. When the Varennes débâcle prompted a further wave of emigration, Bigot heard Louis instructing a confidant, 'dissuade them; tell them from me that they do damage and that they will do much more'.[22] Moving the *émigrés* on from Trier was a rare issue on which the king's action could be effective.

Given his own role in the dispersal of the *émigrés*, Bigot asked rhetorically:

> To whom should it fall to testify to the constant care and effort of the king for the maintenance of peace if not to myself, the one who devotedly sacrificed himself in its cause? No, the king did not have the *émigrés* in his pay, he did not promote their arming nor the coalition of the Powers; and it is those alone who accuse him of these things who by design provoked both the emigration and the war.

Bigot's thesis is that from 1789 there was a faction aiming for a republic. In order to further their designs, the assemblies 'invented a raft of new oaths in order to supply the legislators with acts of resistance to punish or perjuries to presume' – and royal vetoes to apply. And, as Bigot elegantly put it, 'The first Assembly had deprived the king of the power to resist the incursions of the second.'[23]

The emigration achieved the dual purpose of creating 'an imaginary connivance with those who aspired to save the king' and 'the external threat which was necessary in order to propagate terror at home'. War achieved this on a much bigger scale. To make his point, Bigot cites a pamphlet published in September 1792, after the declaration of the republic: 'without the war France would not be a republic'. This was virtually admitted by the deputy Brissot as early as December 1792 when he proclaimed:

> I have only one fear; it is that we won't be betrayed. We need great treasons, our salvation lies there, because there are still strong doses of poison in France and strong emetics are needed to expel them.

The war, he hoped, would reveal the king to be a traitor, in league with those 'who aspired to save him'.[24] Lord Acton, who also gratifies Louis with the epithet traitor, realized at least this:

> The calculations of the Girondins were justified by the event. Four months after the declaration of war the throne had fallen and the king was in prison.[25]

When it appeared that Leopold and de Lessart together might succeed in preserving peace, the Girondins had the latter impeached and sent for trial at Orléans for the new crime of *lèse-nation*. Vergniaud set a precedent which would soon be visited upon himself when he proclaimed that suspicion was sufficient for such a charge.

De Lessart's impeachment is a curious as well as an ugly incident. Basically he was accused of seeking to preserve peace, whilst at his own trial Louis was accused of seeking war before France was ready for it. This inconsistency perhaps explains why de Lessart was never brought to trial – he was massacred together with the others accused of *lèse-nation* in September. The Legislative's diplomatic committee seized de Lessart's papers, though in terms of the constitution they belonged to the king, and refused to forward them to the High Court at Orléans, despite repeated demands from that court. The de Coursacs see this as suspicious and perhaps it is. Certainly it makes it more difficult for us to get to the bottom of the question of war and peace.

De Lessart himself prepared a defence document in which he claimed:

> The harassment of M. de Lessart can have had no other aim but that of isolating the king by substituting a ministry friendly to the republican faction for one which supported

the constitutional party; to destroy the king's influence and prestige by stripping him of the secret conduct of foreign relations and thus of progressively despoiling the executive power of its most precious attributes to give them to the legislative body.[26]

Alarmed by de Lessart's impeachment, all the ministers but one resigned and Louis appointed a basically Girondin ministry committed to war with Austria. Acting on their advice, on 20 April Louis again went down to the Legislative to propose the declaration of war against Austria, which was voted by acclamation, with only seven dissentient voices. Louis, as he made his proposal, was white in the face and stammered. He took what he thought was the precaution of getting all the ministers to sign their opinions and *published* them, together with his own précis of the opinion of Dumouriez, the new foreign secretary.

Marcel Reinhard, in *10 août 1792: la chute de la royauté*, attributes conduct to Louis which would have put Machiavelli to school. Louis, according to Reinhard, was desperate for war so he appointed a ministry which could carry this in the Assembly. This achieved, he planned to dismiss the Jacobin ministry before the foreign invasion reached Paris.[27]

20 June

Louis gambled that the appointment of Girondin ministers would make them responsible, following Mirabeau's dictum that a Jacobin minister was not the same as a Jacobin in the ministry. He was disappointed in this hope because the new ministers fitted instead into another pattern, noted by Soulavie for the whole reign, that of ministers acting as an opposition in government. So the new ministers sponsored further measures to embarrass the king: decrees to disband his constitutional guard, to form an armed camp of 20,000 provincial national guards (*fédérés*) at Paris to intimidate him thus defenceless, and to deport the non-juring priests.

This was foolish (to say no more) of the Girondins: since the king needed a ministerial counter-signature to exercise his veto, if he wanted to exercise it, he would have to dismiss them. Louis sanctioned the decree dissolving his guard, but, exploiting a split between Dumouriez and his colleagues, dismissed the three most radical of these, including Roland, the henpecked and naively portentous minister of the interior. When Dumouriez left shortly afterwards to take up a command at the front, Louis formed another Feuillant ministry. As Soulavie puts it, 'in this forsaken state he with difficulty found a few men sufficiently attached to him to fill the places of administration; but he could meet with none capable of repressing the wild and revolutionary spirit of the times'.[28] Barnave thought that the dismissal of the Jacobin ministry was a mistake because they would have supported the unpopularity of the military defeats which punctuated the summer.[29]

I have said that Louis's biggest failing (apart from his disputable treason) was his attempt to discredit the constitution by his literal observance of it. Nevertheless, his conduct after the acceptance of the constitution was different from that before. In the earlier period, after his criticisms in August and September 1789 had been greeted first with derision and then with violence, Louis had sanctioned everything, allowing the Revolution to caricature itself. After his acceptance, however, Louis attempted to stick up for his rights, for example in the conduct of foreign policy as we have seen. The best example of this new policy can be seen in his determination to defend what he regarded as the true Catholic clergy of France (in 1792 Pius VI excommunicated the constitutional priests). He reproached himself for the rest of his life for sanctioning the Civil Constitution and the earlier oaths but was now finished with such expediency.

This is the background to the *journée* of 20 June when a mob occupied the Tuileries and demanded the withdrawal of the veto and the reappointment of the 'patriot' ministers. For four hours, Louis was squeezed into a window embrasure, protected by just four national guards, with the Assembly and the mayor doing nothing to invervene. The king was prevailed upon to don the *bonnet rouge* and to drink the health of the nation, but he would not give way and at 8 p.m. the mob retired defeated. This episode briefly rallied support for the monarchy and Louis has elicited praise even from hostile historians such as Michelet, Sorel and Acton, whose colourful accounts will be given now.

Sorel writes that, the mob having come to dominate the Assembly,

> it was a small thing, it seemed, to force the king to cry mercy. The organizers of the *journée* did not know their Louis XVI. Because they had always seen him timid and

reluctant to employ force, they imagined that he was
personally pusillanimous – in which they were deceived.
Louis considered that he had sinned, through feebleness
and political calculation, in having formerly sanctioned
impious laws. He reproached himself with it bitterly. He
was determined to suffer everything rather than to cede
again on a matter of conscience and his resignation, on
other occasions bordering on nonchalance, was here
transformed into virtue. To this he added a dignified bearing: modest in the exercise of power, indolent as regards the
affairs of state, he only felt himself to be truly a king in the
presence of danger, and his easy-going nature gave an
indefinably touching quality to his courage.

The Christian in him supported the prince. He had no
fear of death. He was ready for it. The day before he had
written to his confessor: 'I have finished with men. Time to
turn towards God!' . . .

Louis remained impassive whilst nearby Marie-
Antoinette made of the council table a sort of rampart for
her terrified children. The queen was unshaken and the king
would not give way. He stood his ground with these furies,
at once horrible and grotesque in their brute impotence
against the abnegation of a disarmed and defeated king.[30]

On the cowardly behaviour of the Assembly and the municipal
authorities in leaving to the king the defence of the constitution,
Sorel quotes 'a republican', Edgar Quinet, with approval: 'The
journée was more fatal to the republic than to the monarchy. The
republic was strangled at birth and the revolution miscarried.'

Another republican account, that of Jules Michelet, is more
ambivalent:

An officer said to him, 'Sire, have no fear'; the king grabbed
his hand and put it on his heart and said what the early
martyrs would have said: 'I have no fear; I have received the
sacraments; they can do what they please with me.'

This moment of heroic faith lifts Louis XVI's historical
reputation infinitely. What injures it a little is that at this
very moment (singular effect both of nurture and nature)
the royal habits of duplicity resurfaced. . . . To those who
apostrophized him, he replied: 'that he had never strayed
from the constitution', hiding in a pharisaic literalness
whilst betraying its spirit.

Michelet also recounts that when the crowd departed Louis forgot that the *bonnet rouge* was still on his head. When it was pointed out to him

> he threw it down violently, indignant to find, on this day when he was moreover heroic, this badge of his duplicity on his person.

Michelet eloquently evaluates the consequences of this *journée*:

> Many, in France and in Europe, were moved by the tragic image of the royal *Ecce homo*, under his *bonnet rouge*, but firm in the face of outrage, saying, 'I am your king'. So much for sentiment. But nothing had changed. The struggle between two ideologies had only sharpened. The revolutionary masses, hurling themselves at the Tuileries, had counted on finding merely the idol of despotism. Instead, they found themselves in the presence of the old faith of the middle ages, intact and still living and, even with the prosaic face of Louis XVI, beautified by the poetry of the martyrs.[31]

Lord Acton, who believed that the plan was to kill the king if he did not give way, also thought that this was Louis's finest hour:

> Louis XVI had not the ability to devise a policy or vigorously pursue it, but he had the power of grasping a principle. He felt at last that the ground beneath his feet was firm. He would drift no longer, sought no counsel, and admitted no disturbing enquiries. If he fell, he would fall in the cause of religion and for the rights of conscience. The proper name for the rights of conscience is liberty, and therefore he was true to himself, and was about to end as he had begun, in the character of a liberal and reforming king. . . .
> That trying humiliation marks the loftiest period in the reign of Louis XVI. He had stood there with the red cap of liberty on his powdered head, not only fearless, but cheerful and serene. He had been in the power of his enemies and had patiently defied them. He made no surrender and no concessions whilst his life was threatened. The Girondins were not recalled and the movement failed.[32]

10 Août

Most of Louis XVI's historians and contemporaries have seen the period between the declaration of war and the storming of the Tuileries on 10 August, as a race against time for the 'royal couple'. They were banking on deliverance by the allied armies, particularly by the Prussians. Prussia shocked the Girondins by declaring war on France on 3 July in accordance with the defensive treaty concluded with Austria in February. The Girondins had fondly imagined that they would have to contend with Austria alone, though even this proved too much for the French troops who fled at the first sight of the enemy. The Austrians, however, had not followed up their victories in Belgium, whereas the Prussians invaded France in August, with the intention of marching on the capital. The invasion was prefaced by a manifesto, in the name of the Prussian commander the duke of Brunswick, threatening Paris with destruction if the *journée* of 20 June were repeated.

In this highly charged situation, the status of the king changed from that of *de facto* prisoner to that of *de facto* hostage. There was also a fear that the Prussian march on Paris would be synchronized with a royal breakout from the Tuileries and the taking over of the capital by royalists. In these circumstances the dismissal of the Girondin ministry on 12 June evoked similar fears and a similar reaction to the dismissal of Necker on 11 July 1789. With this difference: that in 1792 the fears had some foundation. For La Fayette, now a general at the front, had written to the Assembly to condemn the *journée* of 20 June and then had come to Paris with the intention of using the National Guard to close down the Jacobins. This had failed through lack of royal support. Nothing deterred, La Fayette devised another scheme.

In this, La Fayette's army of the Rhine and Luckner's army of Flanders would exchange positions. This meant that at one point, at Compiègne, La Fayette's army would pass within 20 leagues of Paris. In terms of the constitution, the king could not step outside this limit and this strategem would satisfy his conscience. The plan was for La Fayette to come to Paris (again) and escort the king to Compiègne under the protection of the Swiss guards and loyal units of the National Guard. Though La Fayette's first two actions were open and the third suspected, the Legislative, which Louis's courage on the 20th had removed from Girondin dominance, refused to censure him. No wonder the Girault de Coursacs are able to entitle chapter 22 of their *Enquête*, 'Victoire en Juillet'.

La Fayette's plan, however, would not have favoured the counter-revolution. For he intended that the king should issue a proclamation from Compiègne forbidding his brothers or the foreign troops to advance any further. So it is crucial for Louis's reputation to know where he stood on this question. What we get is a repeat performance of the debates at Marly in 1789, when the queen's influence distorted Necker's planned intervention in the Estates-General. Louis at first adopted La Fayette's proposal on the recommendation of his council but then, we must presume, the queen, who by this stage relied solely on outside help, prevailed on him to stay put. The difference betwen Louis and Marie-Antoinette is preserved in a letter of hers to Fersen:

> The Const.[itutionalists] in conjucntion with La Fayette and Luckner want to conduct the king to Compiègne on the day of the Federation [15 July]. For this purpose the two generals are going to arrive there. The king is disposed to lend himself to this project; the queen is against it. The outcome of this venture which I am far from approving is still in doubt.[33]

This brief, coded note reveals a clash, *in extremis*, between the royal couple which is not just a tactical one of whether to leave Paris or stay put but a symbolic one over whether to rely on the Prussians or the internal forces of the constitutional monarchy.

Marie-Antoinette's position is absolutely clear. She refused to contemplate La Fayette's first plan, to use the National Guards to close down the Jacobin Club, and, it is said, she even tipped off the mayor, Pétion – Pétion who had stood idly by whilst the terrified royal children crouched under the council table on 20 June! Through Fersen, she had an input into the Brunswick manifesto. As soon as she got an inkling of the French military strategy, she betrayed it. Sorel most eloquently develops this unanswerable accusation:

> Marie-Antoinette did not scruple to spy on her opponents and to reveal their plans to the enemies of France: France, for her, was the king, was her children. It was a question of saving and rehabilitating them. Louis had no secrets from her; she had none from their allies. Everything that she

could glean of the war plans – the attack on the Low
Countries – she communicated to Montmorin, to Fersen, to
Mercy.[34]

Sorel has a marvellous description of the delusion of the royal
couple in mistaking the rock of disaster (the allied invasion) for
the rock of salvation:

> Each day's delay [in the allied march] carried off a portion
> of their hopes and placed them further from the chimerical
> port in which Marie-Antoinette and Louis XVI thought
> they would find refuge. As the crisis intensified, the rock to
> which they were being dragged by the current, by the
> tempest and by their own faulty navigation, emerged little
> by little from the fog, and revealed itself to them, nearer
> and more formidable. Yet they imagined that they could
> squeeze round it and that at the moment of ship-wreck
> some providential miracle would suddenly see them safely
> to port.[35]

However, in the light of Marie-Antoinette's note to Fersen,
Sorel's assumption of identity between Louis and his spouse is
mistaken. This insight comes more easily to those who have
learned from Louis's correspondence before the Revolution how
much he concealed from his wife, how much he resisted her,
particularly when Austria was involved. The only people who
have read this correspondence are very recent historians and
Soulavie. Soulavie does not say much about the outbreak of war,
except to say that the German powers were planning on intervention and that 'Louis XVI had given the Legislature direct
intelligence of it'. After war had been declared:

> Louis gave the Legislative Assembly intelligence of the
> march of the foreign troops; and the revolutionists accused
> him to the Jacobins of having called them in to punish his
> enemies and destroy the Revolution.

Soulavie concludes that 'Louis was still a Frenchman, if he was
not a constitutional Frenchman'.[36]

In late July and early August an attack on the palace was
expected hourly. On 27 July Louis notes in his diary 'alert all
day'. In these circumstances he went down to the Assembly on
3 August to protest his patriotic adherence to the constitution.
Sorel believes that the form of words he used was perfectly

consistent with his intention to 'negotiate at a conference of the powers' and enabled his 'royal conscience' to square his promises to France with what he was asking from abroad. Sorel here joins Michelet in depicting Louis as Jesuitical. Louis's short speech is as follows:

> I will never be seen to compromise the *gloire* or the interests of the nation; nor to be dictated to by foreigners or by a faction. I owe myself to the nation, I am one with it . . . I will maintain national independence to my dying day.

Sorel believed that 'his speech passed for the public confession of the treason of which he was accused'.[37]

Bigot de Sainte-Croix, who had just been sworn in as foreign secretary, believed that the speech held no ambiguity. He records Louis's words when he kissed hands as minister:

> Whatever the outcome of this war, which I did everything in my power to prevent, I will set my face against any foreign power interfering to impose any form of government on France. My intention is to uphold the constitution unless the nation itself release me from the oath which binds me to it. . . . No one wanted the destruction of abuses more than I and I have wished to ground this on a free constitution whose principles have always been in my heart. Everyone knows what efforts I have made; anyone who is unbiased will do me this justice, I have no doubt. However I am fully aware of the dangers which surround me and I submit my fate to the sovereign master of the universe.[38]

On 10 August the attack on the Tuileries finally came to pass. Marcel Reinhard suggests that the outcome was in more doubt than appears in hindsight. He describes a civil war within the Parisian National Guard. What tipped the balance was the arrival of radical National Guards from Marseille, and, on the night of 9/10 August, the assassination of the royalist commander of the Paris guards and the creation of an 'insurrectionary' commune. The rest of the story is well known: how Louis wearing a violet, funereal costume, with the curls in his wig flattened on one side by the brief sleep which Michelet begrudges him, lifelessly tried to rally the National Guards who shared the defence of the chateau with the Swiss. How various dignitaries persuaded him to take refuge in the National Assembly which reluctantly and under popular pressure suspended him from his functions and, on the 13th, allowed him to be imprisoned in the Temple, under guard by the Commune.

Less familiar details are supplied by Bigot, who reported to the king every half-hour through the night of the 9th/10th. At 5 p.m. on the 9th, Bigot was given details of the planned attack with the names and addresses of the principal organizers and plans to place Marie-Antoinette in an iron cage! Two ministers asked the Legislative to send a deputation to the Tuileries but the Assembly replied that there was not a quorum for so important a decision and continued to debate the abolition of the slave trade. Bigot refutes Danton's claim that Louis slipped out of the palace by a back door by saying that there were 2000 witnesses to his departure. As Louis, placed in the reporters' box, listened to the various accusations levelled against him, he protested to Bigot, 'there is not a word of truth in any of this'.[39]

However, the most vexed issue and the charge which Louis most vehemently denied was that he caused the shedding of blood on the 10th. We are not concerned here with the curious Jacobin logic which equated defence with attack but more specifically with the orders which Louis gave to the Swiss guards. As is well known, after the king abandoned the chateau, the Swiss guards continued to defend it until about 10 a.m. when Louis, from the Assembly, gave the order to stop firing and return to their barracks. The Swiss were then butchered. The most general interpretation is that Louis, in the haste of his departure, simply forgot to countermand his orders to resist force with force. Michelet, however, believes that 'only when' the king realized that the fight was lost, with cannon firing on the Swiss from the Pont de la Concorde, did he order a cease-fire.[40] Bigot, on the other hand, believed that Louis's words on leaving the chateau 'evidently' implied an order not to use force. Louis's words, as recorded by Bigot, were: 'Let us go. Since we are going to the Assembly there is no more to be done here.'[41]

|12|

Trial and death

For the last phase of his life, Louis was an actual and not just a virtual prisoner. His new situation came home to him on 11 August when his attendants were ordered to leave him: 'I am in prison, then, and less fortunate than Charles I who was allowed to keep his friends with him to the scaffold.'[1] This impression was confirmed on the 13th, when the insurrectionary Commune forced the Legislative Assembly to yield up the royal family to its care and installed them in the tower of the Temple, the grim medieval habitation of the Templars, its thick walls and slitted windows yielding nothing in louring menace to the now demolished Bastille. The Temple was to be Louis's habitation for the rest of his life: he left it on three occasions only, twice in December to participate in his trial by the new Assembly, the National Convention, and on 21 January 1793 to make the journey to the scaffold.

This short phase of less than five months, when Louis had nothing to do but improvise a defence, prepare to die and educate his son in case, as he put it in his will, 'he should have the misfortune to reign',[2] was in some respects the most decisive of all in establishing his historical reputation. Though sequestered from the general public, in prison he led a life on display similar but with even less privacy than the one he had lived at Versailles. In his palace he was dressed in public, but he had already dressed in private, he processed through halls of mirrors and gilded salons, but also through a warren of secret passages and staircases. In the Temple the municipal jailers observed his every waking and even sleeping act, and reported his actions to a press avid for news. In this respect the *Moniteur* picked up where the *Gazette de France* had left off.

Louis's officious jailers submitted him to a series of petty indignities, blowing smoke in his face, because he hated tobacco, devising opportunites to call him 'Monsieur' instead of 'Sire', stopping his son's mathematics lessons or his wife's embroidery, in case their work contained codes, not allowing him to shave in case he committed suicide – an insult to a devout Christian. But gradually his gentle submissiveness won them over, despite themselves, as David Jordan recounts in *The King's Trial*.[3]

Louis's conduct in his last phase can be considered under two heads, the political and the personal, the latter now achieving an equal status in establishing his reputation. His political reputation is based on his conduct during his trial. His personal reputation depends on his family life, his relations with his captors, and above all his comportment on the scaffold. At his trial, the same historical debates we have witnessed in relation to his reign from 1789 to 1792 are continued and concluded. For the accusation against him was cast in the form of a republican history of the Revolution. His personal life culminated in a fine death no one has sought to deny him – though the socialist historian Jean Jaurès insisted that even that was conferred upon him by his enemies. Some historians, notably the Girault de Coursacs, have argued that Louis was a Christian martyr; others, like Michelet, that his identification with Christ was a piece of hubristic blasphemy.

It was not at first certain that Louis would be brought to trial. Two events facilitated it. The first was the tactically inconclusive but strategically decisive battle of Valmy on 22 September, after which General Dumouriez negotiated the unmolested Prussian evacuation of France. This meant that Louis lost his status of hostage and could be prosecuted with impunity. The previous day the new parliament, the National Convention, had formally proclaimed the republic. The second event was the announcement on 20 November by Roland, restored to the ministry of the interior on 10 August, that a safe had been discovered in the panelling of the Tuileries, full of incriminating documents, the famous *armoire de fer*. Susan Dunn, in *The Deaths of Louis XVI*, and David Jordan, in *The King's Trial*, are quite wrong in stating respectively that the safe 'contained his secret correspondence with Austria' and the letter to Breteuil I have discussed on p. 140.[4] Even hostile historians in the French republican tradition do not claim as much but rather that though his accusers rightly suspected Louis of conspiring with foreign rulers to intervene in the internal affairs of France, they did not actually produce evidence at his trial to substantiate the charge. Such, for example, is the view of the Marxist/neo-Jacobin historian Albert Soboul, who adds, 'in this respect light was not shed until after the king's death'.[5]

What the documents in the iron safe – and those captured in the sack of the Tuileries – do demonstrate is Louis's relations with Mirabeau, La Fayette, Dumouriez and what Soboul terms 'other lesser personages, all engaged in the counter-revolution';[6] also his spending of considerable sums of money to win over public support at the level of popular politics and through subsidizing the royalist press. Jaurès, however, rightly observes that one cannot accuse men such as Mirabeau and La Fayette, the heroes of 1789, or Dumouriez, the saviour of France at Valmy, of counter-revolution without condemning the Revolution itself – an observation, as we shall see, that he considers Louis should have made himself. The captured documents show that Louis and his agents, notably La Porte the *Intendant* of the civil list, were engaged in political management typical of the eighteenth century: La Porte was playing Robinson to Louis's George III – though with conspicuously less success. But what should have been taken as evidence of Louis's sincerity in trying to rule as a contemporary constitutional monarch, was, in the puritanical climate of the Revolution, considered instead as conclusive proof of his duplicity and secretiveness. For in this climate, secrecy was equated with conspiracy.

The discovery of the iron safe meant that the Girondins could no longer prevaricate about bringing Louis to judgement – the very minimum that their opponents to the Left, the Montagnards, would accept. (The Montagnards' preferred line, as outlined by Robespierre and Saint-Just, was that Louis had already been 'judged' by the *journée* of 10 August and should be put to death without more ado.) This makes even more extraordinary the accusation of the Girault de Coursacs that Roland had the iron safe constructed himself and crammed it full of incriminating evidence! They point out, correctly, that the Girondin leaders, who had served in government under Louis, had a personal dislike of the king, which was not shared by their Montagnard opponents. Michelet also makes the point that the Girondins' dislike of the king was personal whereas that of the Montagnards was abstract, as instanced in Saint-Just's famous apothegm, 'kings cannot reign innocently'.[7]

The Girault de Coursacs are also right in saying that most of the documents in the iron safe did not justify the space they took

up and that the only documents that pointed though not
conclusively towards treason were housed in ordinary desks and
cupboards; that Gamain, the locksmith who constructed the safe,
had been dismissed from Louis's service in 1790, and that
whereas Roland claimed that the safe had a special key, in fact it
was the same one which fitted three other cupboards. We must be
content, however, to leave these loose ends untied.

The trial

The trial of the king – or Louis Capet as he was now called – and
the form it took was a compromise between the warring factions
of Gironde and Mountain. The Montagnards, as we have seen,
did not want a trial at all. Those who attacked the Tuileries on
10 August had, in Robespierre's words, 'stood proxy for the
whole people'.[8] Moreover, if there were a trial, there was the
possibility of an acquittal and in that case, the Revolution would
be condemned. Indeed, Robespierre continued, if there were a
trial in terms of the Constitution of 1791 (which had not been
repealed) it was the Convention not the king which would be in
the dock. Most Girondins, however, though they were more
divided than their opponents, would have liked to keep Louis as
a hostage for the duration of the war and then banish him.
Brissot stressed foreign policy considerations, others were
actuated by compassion or by a chivalrous scruple about killing
a personal enemey – Pétion, the former mayor, considered
himself to fall into this category. Above all they feared to set a
precedent in deviating too far from the rule of law: David Jordan
observes that Louis's trial, apart from its being held in public,
flouted most of the provisions of the criminal code of 1791, in
that Louis was denied advance sight of the evidence, witnessess
and, initially, a lawyer. A debate continues to this day as to
whether the trial of the king led directly to the Reign of Terror.[9]

Louis's trial can best be described as a unicameral impeachment. In an English or American impeachment the defendant is
accused by the lower house in the upper house – Lords or
Senate. In the National Convention the same people acted as
jury of indictment and 'judges, jurors (and many of them,
prosecuting attorneys as well)' – an obvious violation of the rule
of law.[10] An impeachment is a political trial, and a fair political
trial may seem a contradiction in terms. However, there had

been examples during the earlier period of the Revolution of just that: in 1789–90 Besenval and Barentin, respectively field commander in Paris and keeper of the seals at the time of the fall of the Bastille, were tried for *lèse-nation*, the latter *in absentia*. Barentin, in particular, objected that many of the charges against him concerned motives and were not susceptible either to proof or disproof. Both men were acquitted. The fact that Louis asked to have de Sèze, the man who had defended Besenval, as his counsel suggests that he may have had these cases in mind.[11]

Louis's trial was not as fair as Besenval's but it was fairer than the subsequent show trials (beginning with those of Marie-Antoinette and the Girondins in autumn 1793) in that 'specific charges were brought against the king and evidence was collected to substantiate them'.[12] Nevertheless the general charge of 'conspiring against liberty and an attempt against the safety of the state' scarcely admitted of proof or disproof. Moroever, as the de Coursacs rightly observe, the specific charges, in the final version of the indictment drawn up by Lindet, are far vaguer than the original ones drafted by the Girondin 'committee of 21' under Valazé. In the former, there were 'questions, very brief and very clear'.

For example, in the original indictment, Louis was to be asked:

Did you pay members of your bodyguard at Coblenz in 1791 and 1792?
When you declared war, were you not sure that your preparations for it were inadequate?
Did you not negotiate with foreign powers to bring their troops to France?
Were you aware of a projected attack on Paris and did you take part in it?
Did you not give your approval to the sedition of your brothers?
Did you not raise troops without the authorization of the legislative body?

In the final version, when Louis appeared before the Convention on 11 December, he was read the indictment as a whole, a republican history of the Revolution, and then the whole thing again 'arbitrarily chopped into 32' chunks. The clear, brief questions were replaced by 'peremptory affirmations on the actions, plans and intentions of the king'. At the end of

each lengthy paragraph, Louis was asked, 'What is your answer?'
The de Coursacs give this example:

> *President*: After your arrest at Varennes, your exercise of
> the executive power was temporarily suspended, yet you
> continued to conspire. On 17 July the blood of citizens was
> shed on the Champ de Mars. A letter in your hand, written
> in 1790 to La Fayette, proves that there was a criminal
> coalition between you and La Fayette, to which Mirabeau
> acceded. The revision [of the constitution] began under
> these cruel auspices; every kind of corruption was
> employed. You payed for satire, pamphlets, journals
> designed to corrupt public opinion, to discredit the
> *assignats* and support the cause of the *émigrés*. The
> accounts . . . show what enormous sums were spent in these
> manoeuvres to destroy liberty. You seemed to accept the
> constitution on 14 September; your speeches announced
> the intention to uphold it, and you worked to overthrow it
> even before it was finished. What have you to reply?
> *Louis*: What happened on 17 July cannot conceivably have
> had anything to do with me. For the rest, I have no
> knowledge of it.[13]

Louis's plan of defence

Jordan outlines the choices which were open to Louis on his
appearance before the Convention. He could, like his direct
ancestor Charles I of England, whose life by David Hume he was
rereading at the time, deny the competence of the court and
refuse to plead; or, he could throw himself on the mercy of the
court; but these two courses 'led directly to the guillotine', so he
chose a third, to 'take seriously the offer of a trial and defend
himself, thus recognizing the right of his subjects to try him'. He
would 'force his accusers to prove him guilty, which he believed
they could not do without violating the legal procedures and
guarantees created by the Revolution itself'. 'Let them give me a
fair trial, he thought, and he would be exonerated. Unlike Mary,
queen of Scots, unlike Charles I, Louis thought the moral victory
worth fighting for, and he certainly had no interest in the glories
of martyrdom.'[14] There was actually a fourth line of defence open
to Louis: simply to say that the Constitution of 1791, still in
force, envisaged only three acts for which the king was

responsible: retracting his oath to uphold the constitution, leading an army against the forces of the nation and leaving the kingdom; that he had done none of these things and had, in any case, already incurred the only penalty provided, dethronement.

Many historians and contemporaries, of various political complexions, from the constitutional monarchist Théodore de Lameth, to Jaurès and Walzer, believed that Louis's adoption of Charles I's line would have been the only way to salvage the prestige and mystique of monarchy and the best way to secure its speedy restoration. If, they argued, the king descended to bandying words with the Convention in answer to the individual accusations, he would be legitimating the process. For, as one of Brissot's collaborators on the *Patriote française* put it, 'be it weakness, be it reason, be it the hope of making his cause better', Louis had rendered homage 'to the national sovereignty'.[15] But nearer the mark than these armchair *émigrés* and historians was Montmorin, Louis's foreign secretary, who turned up to fight on 10 August and perished in the September massacres. Shortly before his death he predicted, 'If the king is tried and formally condemned, you will not see a monarchy for a long time.'[16] By this he meant that the whole people would, by proxy, be involved in a culpable act they would find it difficult to disown. The manner of Louis's defence was irrelevant. For this reason, Louis himself would have preferred, as he expected, to be assassinated.

Louis, without a lawyer, and held incommunicado for over three months, had to improvise a defence. This was a novel situation for him because the Bourbon kings had always acted on formally delivered advice; as Louis had written when dauphin, 'counsel is of the essence of monarchy'. This conditioning made spontaneous action difficult for him in the new situations where it was required. That, apart from the fact that he was entitled to one by law, was why Louis repeatedly asked for a lawyer. He finally shamed the Convention into granting him one, though only after he had answered the charges and been taken back to prison.

Louis offered a defence based on the laws in force at the various times he was supposed to have committed the crimes.[17] Thus to the charge, 'You caused an army to march against the citizens of Paris' (in June–July 1789), he replied: 'At that time I could order troops to march where I pleased.' For the period between the fall of the Bastille and his acceptance of the constitution, he relied on the amnesty for political offences issued at the time. For the period when the Constitution of 1791 was in force, he invoked ministerial responsibility where appropriate.

Jordan considered this a clever defence, 'noble even cunning'.[18] I think myself that it brought out the worst in the king, that technical rectitude which had caused Vergniaud to despair in the dying days of the monarchy. Louis's stance seemed almost to justify Robespierre's strictures against 'legal niceties', though, as his subsequent career was to illustrate, legal forms are necessary for the protection of innocence. After making some general comments about the legal/constitutional position, Louis should have gone further into his motives. When asked about the troop movements in 1789, for example, could he not at least have given the explanation he gave the National Assembly at the time – that they were needed to preserve order and that if the Assembly felt threatened he would translate it to Soissons? Louis only really comes alive when accused of shedding blood at the Champ de Mars and notably on 10 August. At the latter charge, tears sprang to his eyes.

At the end of the interrogation, Louis asked to see the evidence upon which it was based. As each piece of evidence was presented to him, the president, honey-tongued Barère, asked Louis if he recognized it. Louis infuriated his judges by denying all knowledge of the majority of them. When he came to Louis's letter to the bishop of Clermont about his Easter communion in 1791, even the impassive Barère had to ask: 'Don't you recognize your signature?' 'No.' 'The seal bears the arms of France.' 'Lots of people had it.' Jordan defends Louis's approach on the grounds that 'his papers had been illegally seized and it was up to his accusers to prove that they were the king's papers, written in the king's hand'.[19]

After his appearance, as Louis was waiting in the conference room of the Convention for the mayor's coach to take him back to prison, there occurred a charming little scene, an emblematic anecdote, typical of many which were recorded by his captors and helped to spread a legend. Chaumette, the *procureur* of the Commune, took a piece of bread and some brandy from a guard and started to eat. Louis, who had eaten nothing since breakfast, said: 'My dear Chaumette, I have had no more to eat than you. Do let me have a bit of bread, please.' Chaumette obliged and Louis was munching his bread as he got in the coach. Another official took the bread from the king's hand and threw it out of the window. 'Ah!', Louis sighed, 'it is not good to throw bread away, especially when it is so scarce.'[20]

During his reign Louis had been tongue-tied, morbidly shy; he could not find the right words when they might have saved his throne, as at Varennes or on 10 August. Now it was too late, the spell was broken. The silent king became almost garrulous. The first evidence of it occurred as he was being transferred to the Temple on 13 August. A communard drew his attention to the overturned equestrian statue of Louis XV and observed, 'that, sire, is how the people treats its kings'. 'It is fortunate', quipped the king, 'that it confines its attention to inanimate objects.'[21] Walzer comments on the 'extraordinary grace' which Louis displayed after 10 August, though he puts it down to court manners.[22] Jordan considers that 'all Louis's public utterances after his fall from power … have a note of pathos that springs from his inability to accept that the people he sincerely loved would deliberately take his life'. And he adds that 'for the first time in his reign he was interesting not only because he was king'.[23] In stripping the king of his dignities, the Convention and the Commune had unexpectedly revealed his dignity.

The day after Louis's appearance, the Convention granted him a choice of lawyers. In fact he had three, Tronchet and Malesherbes to supervise the case and de Sèze to present it. De Sèze's speech adhered to the guidelines Louis had laid down at his first appearance. It offered a royalist history of the Revolution, but also touched on the early reforms. After his two-hour performance Louis made a short speech stating that his counsel had spoken nothing but the truth and once again protesting his innocence of the blood shed on 10 August. He had always 'exposed himself to spare the people's blood'.

Jaurès considered that both Louis's and de Sèze's defence were lamentable. For him, all spontaneity was crushed by the habit of mendacity Louis had acquired, causing him to 'reduce the flank exposed to the enemy'. According to Jaurès, Louis

> had contracted over three years a sort of duplicity. He gave the impression of accepting the constitution whilst continually betraying it. But there was always a muted quality to this lie. Louis XVI believed that by never pursuing any of his contradictory policies to its logical conclusion, he would absolve himself from the reproach of perfidy. He had lived in a sort of flickering ambiguity, on a

strange, phantasmagorical horizon where the monarchy, setting in the west, and popular sovereignty rising in the east, had mingled their rays and their shadows. And this . . . vacillating half-light remained in his mind. So, even when his life was at stake, even before his former subjects, now his judges, he was no longer capable of a simple and violent access of sincerity. Mendacity, that anticipation of death, had already virtually turned him into a shadow.

Louis 'should have spoken as a statesman rather than a lawyer'. His 'greatest crime' was in not having understood Mirabeau, which meant that he did not comprehend the Revolution or how the monarchy could have profited by its destruction of the corporate organization of the *ancien régime*. He thought that 'all the drama of his life' was 'an accident' which did not 'affect the basic rights of royalty and which did not bind history forever'.[24] Not content merely with criticizing Louis's defence, Jaurès also provides 'the one which Louis should have given', the one which Mirabeau would have advised had he lived. It is worth quoting at some length.

Jaurès's proposed defence

You want to judge me and no doubt you will condemn me tomorrow. I do not fear death and I have not come here to wrangle with you over my life. History has taught me that the death of kings belongs to peoples as a solution to terrible crises. . . .

But I tell you that by concentrating on the head of a single man the responsibility for so vast a crisis, so deep a conflict, you are making an unnecessary tribute to the perennial prestige of monarchy. . . .

The transition from absolute monarchy, which I repre-sented, to the extreme democracy which you want to found, cannot be made without difficulty and peril. It is hardly my fault if for centuries France has lacked free institutions and if all power was concentrated in the hands of the kings. It is not even the fault of my ancestors. Do you seriously think that it is solely the volition of the kings which has created dissimilar institutions in England and in France? Perhaps, in France, that centralization of royal power was necessary to bring low the great feudal princes, those feudal despots who bound the people and atomized the nation. You think that it is you who have brought feudalism low; but only its shadow remained; it was the kings who first removed its force and substance. ... Perhaps the popular movement which threatens me and is going to carry me off, could have been postponed for fifty years if I had not given it the signal by convoking the Estates-General and by doubling the Third Estate. ...

I did not do it out of some easy-going generosity: there are scarcely any examples in the already long life of human societies of power spontaneously surrendering a portion of its prerogatives. I needed the nation to restore the finances, to force the privileged orders to make the financial contribution which the state needed and which their blind egoism denied me. Such is the mysterious causal chain that it is perhaps in indebting the monarchy by supporting American independence that in France I was obliged to appeal to the Estates-General and start the Revolution. But I was entitled to think that some precautions were necessary, given that France was not used to self-government. Too abrupt a transition risked losing everything. That is why I watched over the incipient Revolution, to control it, and what you saw fit to regard as intrigue and conspiracy, was simply the fulfilment of my duty as king towards the monarchy and indeed towards the Revolution.

Despite their faults, the nobility and clergy were the secular supports of the monarchy. I attempted to save them from total destruction as orders, whilst at the same time limiting their privileges. Have you the right to make a crime of it? And, if it be a crime to have wanted to stop the Revolution at such and such a point, why did the revolutionaries not demand the wholesale abolition of monarchy? Why did they try to reconcile the royal tradition with popular sovereignty? It was the Constituent Assembly which wrote monarchy into the constitution.

Today you all say or you all think you are republicans, and to hear you talk, one would think that the monarchy is a sort of antique monster, long buried ...

And yet two years ago there was not a republican to be found amongst you. Even when I left Paris to find a point in the east of France where I could make a stand against the men of faction, no one in the Assembly dared ask unequivocally for the end of the monarchy. Even those who proposed to suspend my inviolability and bring me to trial seemed to be thinking of another king; and the petitioners on the Champ de Mars were disowned by all the parties in the Revolution.

Nevertheless, in the letter which was read to the Assembly, I left an unequivocal testimony to my real thinking. And to those who accuse me of deceiving them, I reply that they let themselves be deceived. They were frightened of the Republic and, whilst denouncing my perfidy, they affected to believe that I was more revolutionary than I possibly could have been, to escape from the terrible dilemma of either stopping the Revolution or abolishing the monarchy. If there is a lie, it is there. It was to deceive yourselves and to deceive the nation to imagine that you could push democracy to its extremes without abolishing the monarchy, and to strip a tree of all its leaves without killing it. I am the one who should be complaining at being exploited by the deception of the Revolution to ease the transition of monarchy to republic. . . .

And if this was not a cynical calculation, if France sincerely believed that a monarchy was necessary in the new order, how can you blame a king who thought so too and wanted to maintain all the props without which, in my judgement, it could not survive. I groaned at the struggle in which you engaged against the clergy and it is true that I applied the veto which the constitution gave me to lessen the blows you rained upon it. For religion is not only my personal consolation and requirement, it is, in my judgement, necessary to regulate morality and liberty. I considered that the too vehement, too violent attacks on the clergy would lead to the overthrow of religion itself. And was I wrong? . . . It was the struggle for Christianity which had begun and if I wanted to protect the clergy against the passions which were insensibly being extended to religion itself, I was prophetic and I was serving the Revolution, which will perish the day it becomes plain to all that it is incompatible with Christianity.

To accuse me of treason, you are obliged to accuse also the majority of the illustrious men who have served the Revolution. Because all of them, La Fayette, Mirabeau, Barnave, others too, thought that the Revolution must be stopped and consolidated, that it would destroy itself if it passed the line which they themselves had prescribed. You can stigmatize and strike them. But at the same time you would be stigmatizing and striking the Revolution itself . . . Do you, in all good faith, believe that these men yielded to base passions, that they were at the mercy of a bit of gold? Surely not: they thought to serve the Revolution and liberty in opposing the excesses which could compromise it, in seeking to give the organization of the executive power the necessary strength. And if men born of the Revolution, who had neither strength, credit or hope outside of it, felt it had to be controlled and restricted, who can make it a crime for the king to have thought the same, the descendant of kings and the guardian of monarchy by virtue of the constitution and of tradition?

Take care lest in condemning the king on the pretext of betraying the Revolution, you threaten each other with death. Because henceforth you will be condemned to denounce and strike down as traitors all those who do not share your understanding of the interests of the Revolution and who do not want to bring its limits to the arbitrary and shifting point indicated by the passions of the day. . . .

It is really very strange that I should be criminalized for having thought of the possible consequences of an un-limited war and of wanting to prevent them! You who accuse me of not having hastened the rupture with Austria and of not having gone to war at the slightest offence from foreign courts, are you so sure that the Revolution can take on the whole world without risk? Are you sure that the new France will not leave behind her finances and her liberty in this colossal enterprise? Can you be sure that the un-certainties of the struggle will not exacerbate the rivalry between factions to the point where they exhaust the Revolution and tear it apart? And if I was preoccupied with the likely repercussions of the war on public opinion and on the destiny of the monarchy, who set the example? You did! Those who in the spring of this year dragged you into war loudly proclaimed that it was necessary to put the monarchy to the test and to change the constitution. . . . By what right can you reproach me with having spun out the chances of peace to the end, when you openly gave the war a partisan complexion? But beware! You have provoked war to fell the monarchy. In ceasing to accommodate the monarchy you have ceased to accommodate the world. I hold you responsible before posterity for the disasters which may follow.

If I tell you these things, it is not to save my head. You are too divided among yourselves to be just. ... After destroying me, you will destroy yourselves on my account. So far the only blood that has been shed has been shed by the impulsiveness of the people. Soon death will be institutionalized.

I have read a lot and meditated on the history of Charles I. For a long time I have had a presentiment, because of the general unrest, that I too was reserved for the supreme test. I am ready for it. But don't flatter yourselves that events in France will work out like those in England. England is an island; its disturbances are containable and Cromwell was able to contain them. You are exposed to all the pressures of the universe and this deadly struggle will raise passions and tragic happenings here. You cannot be sure that one day an exhausted France will not seek refuge in monarchy. I would have wished, if this return to the former state took place, that monarchy was not restored through pity. Pity is blind and violent: and kings brought back through it will never take the measure of a new era. In causing my head to fall, you will unleash a dangerous current of pity: it would be better to reserve the future for experience and reason.

'This', Jaurès concludes in a celebrated passage,

is what Louis XVI could have confronted the Convention with; and what condemns him the most, is that he made no effort to rise to this order of thought; that he did not for a moment enter into a dialogue with the Revolution. The persistence of royal prejudice prevented him and above all the secret weight of his treasons. Because he had not only tried to moderate the Revolution, he had also summoned the foreigner to destroy it. And he was reduced to the low cunning of an ingenious barrister. French monarchy was decidedly dead in the water. It would briefly return, but as a phantom.[25]

There is a major inconsistency in Jaurès's analyis. He expatiates on Louis's unwillingness to go to war, yet accuses him of 'summoning the foreigner'. The general line of those who accuse Louis of treason, as we have seen, is that he wanted war because, to paraphrase Marie-Antoinette, 'the fools don't know what they are letting themselves in for'. If Louis had managed to avert the war, how could he expect 'the foreigner to destroy the Revolution'?

I lament with Jaurès that Louis did not accept Mirabeau's analysis of a revolution which, by destroying the 'intermediary powers' of the *ancien régime*, created 'a surface equality favourable to the exercise of power'.[26] However, this was not because 'ideas above a certain level exceeded his mental capacity', as Véri said, nor even because he could not separate Mirabeau's ideas from his character, but rather because, as we have seen, he had reflected on this matter just before the start of the Revolution in marginal comments on Turgot's memo-randum, and come to a different conclusion. Turgot hoped that his arrangements would facilitate general legislation, as the Revolution did, by removing the need to argue the toss with a congeries of *parlements* and local estates. But Louis concluded that

> if the organization of my provinces were everywhere similar ... it would be more difficult to move at the same moment a complicated mass than to move it through the medium of the *intendants* and the *pays d'état*, as my ancestors did.[27]

Given Louis's attitude, one can seen why he was not receptive to Mirabeau's argument that the Revolution by destroying regional variations had created a medium in which the royal authority would, as Turgot put it, be 10 times more efficient. One may consider that Louis's analysis is defective – Napoleon proved it to have been – or eccentric, but he clearly comprehended the issue and did not dismiss it out of hand.

Jaurès thought that because Louis could not relate to the Revolution, he could not come up with an imaginative defence and it is certainly true that he didn't. But in fact much of what Jaurès puts into Louis's mouth can be found in his utterances on other occasions, so that Jaurès's defence is magnificent precisely because it does enter into the king's mind. The references to Charles I spring to mind. But also Jaurès's concluding section warning against pity. For Louis struck out the original emotional peroration to de Sèze's defence with the words, 'we must delete it;

I don't want to soften them'![28] Jaurès's idealized Louis is endowed with prophetic fire, which can only come from an understanding of the mainsprings of the Revolution, something denied to Jaurès's actual king. However, other writings of Louis, and in particular his letter to his brothers in September 1791, show prophetic insight. Not for nothing did Soulavie call Louis 'the Cassandra of his nation'. So whilst I share Jaurès's view of the inadequacy of Louis' legalistic defence, I would place another speech in his mouth, based on the analysis made by that letter:

'During this trial you have made repeated use of documents seized illegally from the Tuileries, quoting those which appear to paint me in an unfavourable light in an attempt to establish my duplicity and treason. You spend a lot of time dealing with the summer of 1791, since the heart of your accusation is that I perjured myself when I swore to uphold the constitution in September of that year. You also refer to the Declaration of Pillnitz which you accuse me of procuring from the emperor and the king of Prussia. Consequently I have felt that I could not better answer those charges than by reading to you a letter of mine which was not available to you, a secret letter to my *émigré* brothers dating from that time. I explain to my brothers my attitude to the constitution and to war. Some of the things I predicted then have come to pass and others may. Judge from this letter also whether I have failed to understand the Revolution.'

Louis's letter

You have doubtless been informed that I have accepted the constitution and you will know the reasons which I gave to the Assembly; but they will not suffice for you. I want, therefore, to let you know all my reasons. The condition of France is such that she is perhaps approaching a total disintegration which will only be accelerated if violent remedies are applied to all the ills which overwhelm her. The solution is to end partisan divisions and to restore the authority of the government. But for this there are only two means: force or reconciliation.

Force can only be employed by foreign armies and this means recourse to war. Can a king allow himself to call it upon his land, and would not the remedy be worse than the ill? I know that you think that you can assemble such immense forces that war will be prevented by the impossibility of resistance. But have you well considered the state of the kingdom and the interests of those who now exercise authority? All the leaders, that is those who are able to rouse the people, will believe that they have too much to fear to surrender .... . The offer of an amnesty will not reassure them. They would rather rate their chances in a fight than surrender without one. They would make use of the National Guards and other armed citizens .... . They will even begin the war by massacring the aristocrats to envenom the conflict. This example first given by Paris and the Assembly will surely be followed throughout the kingdom. ... So there we have France in arms and the people roused to every possible violence against those who are called aristocrats. ....

War will therefore be inevitable because it is in the interests of all those in authority to fight; it will be terrible because it will be motivated by violence and despair. Can a king contemplate all these misfortunes with equanimity and call them down on his people?

I know that kings have always prided themselves on regaining by force that which people have sought to snatch from them, that to fear in such circumstances the horrors of war is called weakness. But I confess that such reproaches affect me less than the sufferings of my people and my heart rebels at the thought of the horrors which I should have caused. I know how much the nobility and clergy have suffered from the Revolution – all the sacrifices which they have so generously made have been rewarded with the destruction of their fortune and their standing. ... I too have suffered; but I feel myself equal to suffering still more rather than making my people share my misfortunes.

So many injustices are beyond repair. You place much reliance on a successful war. Doubtless National Guards and regiments without officers will not be able to resist well disciplined troops and the elite of the nobility. But these foreign troops could not settle in the kingdom and, when they were no longer there, how would one govern if insubordination began anew? I know that my *émigré* subjects flatter themselves that there has been a great change in people's attitudes. I thought myself for a long time that this was happening but now I am undeceived. The nation likes the constitution because the word recalls to the lower portion of the people only the independence in which it has lived for the last two years and to the class above equality. The lower portion of the people see only that they are reckoned with; the bourgeoisie see nothing above them. Vanity is satisfied. This new possession has made them forget everything else. The losses they experience seem to them to be coming to an end. The completion of the constitution was all that stood between them and perfect happiness; to delay it was in their eyes the greatest crime because all good things were to come with it: time will teach them how mistaken they were. But their error is nonetheless profound. . . . One can never govern a people against its inclinations. This maxim is as true at Constantinople as in a republic; the present inclinations of this nation are for the Rights of Man, however senseless they are.

You say the aristocracy would be the support and refuge of the monarchy, but is it even united amongst itself? Does it not have its parties and differences of opinion? Would those who are called aristocrats in Paris be so called elsewhere? I am reliably informed that there are as many ideological differences on this side as on the other. One wants the old order; another the Estates-General and yet another an English-style government. What real strength could the government derive from these different parties, which would be even more divided amongst themselves if they came to win and several of which would rather treat with the Jacobins than with another faction of the aristocracy?

I have carefully weighed the matter and concluded that war presents no advantages just horrors and a continuance of discord. I have therefore thought that this idea should be set aside and that I should try once more the sole means remaining to me, namely the junction of my will to the principles of the constitution. I realize all the difficulties of governing a large nation in this way – indeed I will say that I realize it is impossible. But the obstacles that I should have put in the way [by refusing to accept the constitution] would have brought about the war I sought to avoid and would have prevented the people from properly assessing the constitution because it would only have seen my constant opposition. By my adopting its principles and executing them in good faith, they will come to know the cause of their misfortunes; public opinion will change; and since, without this change, I could only expect new convulsions I ... [considered] that I would be proceeding towards a better order by my acceptance than by my refusal.

I have therefore preferred peace to war, because it seemed to me at once more virtuous and more expedient. I have bound myself to my people because it was the only way of rallying them and I have preferred a course of action which can be reproached neither by my people nor my conscience. ... Let the princes so conduct themselves that I will be spared the decrees against them which the Assembly may present to me for my sanction. ... Let the nobility so conduct itself that the multitude, at present intoxicated with novelty, may cease to believe that the aristocrats are its enemies. ... The true nobility will then stand a good chance of being restored to all its consideration and to a portion of its rights. What I say of the nobility can in the same way be applied to the monarchy.

Postscript, 15 September:

... I was deeply pained to learn that the comte d'Artois had been to that conference at Pillnitz without my consent. ... People will never believe that my brothers are not carrying out my orders. So you are going to portray me to the nation accepting the constitution with one hand and applying to the foreign powers with the other. What virtuous man could esteem such behaviour? And you think you are serving me by depriving me of the esteem of decent folk?

I hope you will come to your senses. Know that victory is meaningless unless it facilitates government and that you cannot govern a great kingdom against the dominant ideology.[29]

The verdict

The Convention did not proceed immediately to a vote. For a fortnight the parties manoeuvred. Many of the Girondins, obscurely aware that the king's death would enlarge the conflict, at home and abroad, devised ways of saving his life – an appeal to the people organized in primary assemblies; a diversionary attack on the duc d'Orléans, sitting in the Convention as Philippe-Egalité. Dumouriez came to Paris to put his laurels discreetly at the king's service, but his intervention was counter-productive. Danton is said to have guaranteed to save the king's life if Pitt would give him 2 million francs, and Pitt is said to have refused. Louis himself believed that 'the majority of deputies could easily have been bought'. He had been lent money for the purpose but was scrupulous about using it for corruption. The civil list, he told Malesherbes, had been a different matter, 'being only the just equivalent of the money from my domains'.[30]

Finally, between 14 and 20 January, the Convention voted on four motions. The first was phrased:

> Is Louis Capet, former king of the French, guilty of conspiring against liberty and an attempt against the safety of the state? Yes or no.

There were 691 who voted 'yes', with 27 abstentions. No one voted against the motion. The second motion, proposed on 15 January, concerned the appeal to the people. The voting was 287 for, 424 against, with 12 abstentions. The third motion was on Louis's punishment – death, banishment, imprisonment, or whatever. The voting lasted 36 hours and could not have been closer: out of 721 votes only 361 voted unconditionally for death – a majority of just one. Given the closeness of this vote, a fourth motion was put, whether there should be a reprieve, but this was rejected by a majority of 70. The Convention decreed that Louis should be notified 'within the day' and executed 24 hours after this notification. The Convention rose at three o'clock on the morning of 20 January 1793.

At two in the afternoon Garat, the minister of justice, informed Louis that he would be executed within 24 hours. Listening to the Convention's decree, Louis displayed no emotion except at the words 'conspiring against liberty' when a 'smile of contempt' played on his lips. Garat was astounded at the king's 'super-human courage'. After Garat had read out the decree, Louis produced a document from his portfolio. In it he requested 'a three-day stay of execution to prepare myself to appear before the presence of God'; the right to see a priest of his choice and to see his family 'without witnesses'.[31]

The Convention rejected the first but granted the other two requests. Garat then returned to the Temple at 6 o'clock bringing with him the abbé Edgeworth de Firmont, Mme Elisabeth's former confessor, who had been advised by Malesherbes of the king's choice of a man 'whose obscurity may save him from persecution'.[32] The king conferred with his confessor until half-past eight when the abbé withdrew to one of the side-turrets so as not to alarm Louis's family, who were now admitted for the first time in six weeks. After the tearful reunion, Louis turned to his confessor and said, 'Let us forget everything else in order to concentrate on the one matter, it alone must occupy all my love and thought.'[33] Much to Louis's surprise and delight, the Commune not only allowed Edgeworth to celebrate mass at six next morning, but scoured the neighbouring churches for the necessary accoutrements. Thus fortified, at 9 o'clock he set off once more in the mayor's carriage, this time to the former Place Louis XV where he was guillotined within sight of the Tuileries.

No one contests the king's courage on that raw January day. There had been a heavy fall of snow in the night and the carriage crept to its destination along the troop-lined streets, Edgeworth and the king reciting alternate verses from the psalms for the dying. Louis looked 'pensive but not downcast'.

When Louis descended from the carriage, three executioners rushed forward and tried to take his coat off. He pushed them aside, removed it himself and unfastened the collar of his shirt. He was further outraged when they sought to tie his hands behind his back. He looked to Edgeworth for guidance:

'Sire, in this further outrage I see only a final resemblance between Your Majesty and the God who will be his recompense.' – 'Assuredly ... nothing less than His example would make me submit to such an affront.' Then, turning to the executioners, 'Do as you please, I will drain the chalice to the dregs.'[34]

As Louis mounted the steps of the scaffold, Edgeworth said either: '*Fils de Saint-Louis, ascendez au ciel*' or '*Allez, fils de Saint-Louis, le ciel vous attend.*' Inspired, Louis rushed forward to the front of the platform and tried to address the crowd. Santerre had ordered a drum roll; Louis commanded silence. How many drums stopped beating we do not know; nor how many people heard Louis's words; nor indeed what exactly those words were. The most characteristic version, that of the *Semaines parisiennes*, runs:

I die perfectly innocent of the so-called crimes with which I
was accused. I pardon those who are the cause of my
misfortunes. Indeed, I hope that the shedding of my blood
will contribute to the happiness of France and you,
unfortunate people——

These words may have been broken off by Santerre, by the
drum roll or by the descent of the axe.[35]

There is widespread disagreement among historians about the
long-term effects on the French monarchy of the execution of
Louis XVI. Walzer follows Jaurès in considering that 'the
principal of monarchy or monarchy itself was done to death with
the king'.[36] Louis's brother Provence came back in 1814 as Louis
XVIII (the dauphin had died in prison of studied neglect in 1795)
but the monarchy was hollowed out. Edgar Quinet, on the other
hand, held it as axiomatic that regicide is followed by
restoration.[37] Michelet, too, considered that the king's death gave
the monarchy, expiring since the reign of Louis XV, the kiss of life
– in modern academic parlance, resacralized it: 'This tired
institution was revived by two legends, the sanctity of Louis XVI
and the glory of Napoleon.'[38]

Michelet calls Louis's sanctity a legend, a fable. Was it? Many
of Louis's and Edgeworth's words were charged with religious
symbolism. That was to be expected: Edgeworth was a priest and
Louis a devout Catholic. Louis reread Thomas à Kempis's
Imitation of Christ in prison. But many read more into it than
that, and see Louis XVI as a Christian martyr, a saint. The
Girault de Coursacs' *Louis XVI, roi martyr?*, is, as they themselves explain, only the most recent in a line of such books. The
first man, they explain, to have had the idea of a 'systematic
parallel between the martyrdom of Louis XVI and the passion of
Jesus', with the title, *Louis XVI, royauté douloureuse, royauté
glorieuse*, was Armand Granel, a barrister from Toulouse.
Unfortunately, they continue, that work relied on 'historians'
rather than contemporary sources. The de Coursacs also had
'sinned' in that direction in their first treatment of the subject, *Le
Roi stigmatisé* (1950). Their 'entirely new, rigorously scientific
methodology', they explain, is that used by *Découvert*, as we
have seen. The works published under its banner

> reveal the truly satanic nature of this Revolution, the work of
> those privileged in rank and fortune who beguiled the people
> with false promises and killed the king with their calumnies.[39]

The 'parallels' the de Coursacs draw in *Louis XVI, roi martyr?*, include the famous ones on the scaffold, the man-handling of Louis resembling the scourging of Christ, and the draining of the chalice consciously quoting his words in Gethsemane. So we have: 'He was reckoned among the trans-gressors'; Louis was the 'son of Saint-Louis', Jesus the 'son of David'. But there are many others. Just as Jesus weeps over Jerusalem, so Louis, in his 'Declaration on leaving Paris' weeps over the French capital and longs to return, 'once he has freely accepted a constitution which respects our holy religion'.[40] Caiaphas' 'it is expedient for us that one man should die for the people and that the whole nation perish not' (John 11:50) sits in uncomfortable proximity with the words of a lapsed and, confessedly, 'bad' Catholic, Robespierre: 'Louis must die that the nation may live.'[41] Louis's *'marchons'*, when he left the Tuileries on 10 August and the Temple on 21 January are linked to the same words uttered by Jesus after the Last Supper and in Gethsemane.[42] One could multiply examples; these are the ones in which the parallels seem least strained. One can also ridicule this approach but a Christian interpretation of history is no less valid than a Marxist, or any other universalist theory. So, enter-ing into the debate on its own terms, was Louis XVI a saint?

The key text is Louis's correspondence with the bishop of Clermont concerning his Easter communion in 1791 (see above, pp. 120–1), which was used in evidence against him at his trial. The deputy Dubois-Crancé had insisted that Louis's letter to the bishop should be placed in the indictment because of Louis's promise 'that when he recovered his authority he would restore the Catholic cult'. Valazé read the text of the letter aloud, upon which another deputy said: 'I demand that there be no mention of religion unless you want to have him canonized one day.'[43] However, the correspondence with the bishop in fact contained, I would have thought, an insuperable barrier to canonization. Louis, it will be remembered, had asked whether his sanction of the decrees concerning the Civil Constitution of the Clergy disqualified him from making his communion. He hoped not, since 'I have always regarded my acceptance of them as acting under duress'. The bishop, however, would have none of this comfortable doctrine. The king's sanction had had 'the most disastrous consequences for religion' and he concluded that 'it was only resistance to force which produced the martyrs'. So not only could Louis not communicate but he was ruled out as a martyr. Clermont's argument is all the more damaging since the excuse of duress was the same as Louis gave in his June 1791 'declaration' for regarding as 'null and void' all the decrees to which he had consented since his 'imprisonment' in Paris in October 1789. Would Clermont have regarded this argument as invalid too? Wasn't this the reproach that the *émigrés* made against the king?

The abbé Proyart, however, excuses the king on the grounds that the Pope's missives condemning the Civil Constitution were intercepted and the two archbishops in his cabinet advised sanctioning the decree. He quotes Pius VI as accepting that Louis's signature under duress was excusable and in any case redeemed by 'his incontestable and solemn retraction', made in his will. The main thing for Pius, as he declared in full consistory on 17 June 1793, was that

> this prince was put to death particularly out of hatred for the faith and for his attachment to Catholic dogmas.

His conclusion: 'it seems to us impossible to deny him the glory of martyrdom'.[44]

Another argument against Louis's sanctity would be what Michelet called his 'strange deification of himself'.[45] This is a hard charge to refute. A Christian must seek to imitate Christ – that is the whole point; the imitation can also be self-conscious; yet to be truly holy, he must feel that he has failed in the attempt. Would a future saint have said that he would 'drain the chalice to the dregs' when the early martyrs, for example, insisted on being crucified in a posture different to their Lord's? Walzer, on the other hand, argues that in using these words, 'he knew he was acting the way kings were supposed to act. It was a triumph of ideology over mere personality.'[46] Michelet believed that Louis's jailers encouraged him in his saintly pretensions by asking for relics, his gloves, a cravat, as did his confessor on the scaffold in noting 'a final resemblance' with his Saviour. There is also the suspicion that in his last months Louis deliberately supplied the market for pithy, homely sayings, much as Christ may be said to have done and that like him, perhaps, he was consumed by an *amor fati*.

Michelet's politics moved progressively to the left as he grew older. The works he published in the 1830s were sympathetic to royalism. And he saw in Louis XVI the type of the French saint-king, epitomized by his ancestor Saint-Louis (Louis IX) and more distant kings of previous dynasties such as Louis the Debonair. Such kings were frail and gentle, meek and mild and the people saw in them at once the image of Christ and 'the image of their own servitude'.[47] According to this view, Louis would neither be an example of 'dynastic epigonism', as Trotsky argued,[48] nor, as the later Michelet argued, was the best saved for the last in order to demonstrate that the institution of monarchy itself was defective, but rather Louis was a reversion to type.

|13|

Three general perspectives and a conclusion

De Tocqueville

The great nineteenth-century aristocratic-liberal historian Alexis de Tocqueville offers a sympathetic portrait of Louis XVI in his masterpiece, *L'Ancien Régime et la Révolution française* of 1856.[1] This favourable view was partly a matter of family tradition: his great-grandfather, Malesherbes, had been guillotined for his defence of Louis XVI and most of his family with him – Alexis's parents, imprisoned with the rest in the Conciergerie prison, the antechamber to the guillotine, were only saved by the fall of Robespierre on 27 July 1794. Such a view of Louis was also partly an integral part of the linked paradoxes of de Tocqueville's main thesis: that an oppressive regime is most at peril when it lightens its touch; that 'the social order overthrown by a revolution is almost always better than the one immediately preceding it'; and that the very prosperity of France under Louis XVI hastened the Revolution.

De Tocqueville quotes with approval the preamble of an early edict of Louis's, 'we glory in the fact that the nation we govern is high-spirited and free'. And he stresses that the obedience of French people was instinctive and affectionate rather than the servile and degrading obedience many nineteenth-century monarchs obtained through their capacity to 'help or harm'. The government of the last two Bourbon kings

> so authoritative and self-assured (provided no one questioned its authority) suddenly took fright at the least hint of resistance. ... On such occasions it drew back, negotiated, tried to read public opinion – and often stopped short of its legitimate powers. The easy-going egotism of

Louis XV and the natural kindliness of his successor lent themselves to such procedures. It never entered their heads that anyone would dream of dethroning them. They had none of the anxieties and none of the cruelty inspired by fear that we find in so many rulers of a later day, and the only people they trod underfoot were those they did not see.[2]

Therefore, though Louis XVI

still used the language of a master, in actual fact he always deferred to public opinion and was guided by it in his handling of day-to-day affairs. Indeed he made a point of consulting it, feared it, and bowed to it invariably.[3]

De Tocqueville quotes an 'official pronouncement' of Necker's to the effect that opinion was 'the invisible power behind the throne'.

Louis consulted opinion in an informal way. He rejected, as we have seen, Turgot's proposal for a hierarchy of purely consultative but official bodies, the municipalities. De Tocqueville thinks that, 'great administrator though he was', Turgot was politically naive in believing that these bodies would have been content to remain purely consultative:

Often towards the close of revolutions it has been possible ... to give the people the shadows of liberty without its substance ... [as Napoleon did] but at the early stage ... such methods always fail.[4]

De Tocqueville also criticizes the widespread introduction of provincial assemblies in 1787 for introducing an element of uncertainty at a critical juncture: hitherto the kings had remained administratively absolute, however much the *parlements* had weakened their political power.

One of de Tocqueville's many fruitful paradoxes concerns the relations between classes. On the one hand, the bourgeoisie and the nobility, if not the peasantry, were coming to resemble each other in dress, education and manners. On the other, the legal barriers between the two were watertight, in the way they were taxed or the careers they could pursue. Unlike England, there was in France no all-embracing category of 'gentleman' which could span a divide which, de Tocqueville rightly argues, played a major part in the outbreak of the Revolution. The kings, pursuing a policy of divide and rule deepened this chasm:

Though in the long history of the French kingdom so many admirable monarchs occupied the throne at various periods, many of them remarkable for their practical shrewdness, some for their high intelligence, and almost all for their courage, not one of them ever made an attempt to unite classes and obliterate their distinctions otherwise than by reducing them all to a common state of dependence on the Crown. No, I am making a mistake; one of our monarchs made it his aim and, indeed, put all his heart into it, and – how inscrutable are the ways of Divine Providence! – that was the ill-starred Louis XVI.[5]

Turgot worried about these divisions in memoranda for the king:

The nation is an aggregate of different and incompatible social groups . . . no trace of any feelings for the the public is anywhere to be found.

But when Louis brought 'these isolated social units once again in touch', in the Estates-General in 1789, 'it was on their sore spots that they made contact and their first gesture was to fly at each other's throats'. The harm had already been done.[6]

Similarly with Louis XVI's recall of the Parlement in 1774. That could not undo the impression created by the destruction of 'an institution almost co-eval with the monarchy'; an impression that nothing was sacred and 'scarcely any novelty, however startling, would not seem worth trying out'. 'I am convinced', de Tocqueville added,

that from this moment the far-reaching political upheaval which was to sweep away without distinction both what was worst and what was best of the old system became inevitable.[7]

De Tocqueville criticizes Louis most severely for his '*reculades*' – that is, withdrawing measures shortly after they had been introduced with due solemnity. What aggravated the fault was Louis's otherwise exemplary habit of explaining his measures to his people in the preambles to his edicts, in his determination to create enlightened citizens out of ignorant subjects. For example the preamble to Turgot's edict abolishing the Parisian craft guilds declared that 'the existing craft corporations are unnatural and oppressive organizations stemming from self-regarding motives, greed and a desire to domineer'. De Tocqueville comments, 'It was indiscreet enough to utter such words, but positively dangerous to utter them in vain' – since on Turgot's fall the guilds were reinstated.[8]

De Tocqueville's critique of Louis's reforming impulses is worth quoting *in extenso*:

> During his entire reign Louis XVI was always talking about reform, and there were few institutions whose destruction he did not contemplate before the Revolution broke out and made an end of them. But after eliminating from the constitution some of its worst features he made haste to reinstate them; in fact he gave the impression of merely wanting to loosen its foundations and leaving to others the task of laying it low.
>
> Some of the reforms he personally put through made over-hasty, ill-considered changes in ancient and respected usages, changes which in certain cases violated vested rights. They prepared the ground for the Revolution not so much because they removed obstacles in its way but more because they taught the nation how to set about it.[9]

What de Tocqueville has in mind is Louis' search for uniformity throughout his kingdom. This was epitomized by the abortive edicts of 8 May 1788, which could be presented as illegal, a violation of the charters granted to the various provinces when they were incorporated into France, some fairly recently. De Tocqueville favoured abolishing the fiscal privileges of the various geographical and social groups but not their independent standing. He believed that an aristocracy was the best guarantee against despotism and that the Revolution, which was the *reductio ad absurdum* of Louis's policies, since all distinctions were obliterated, demonstrated his point.

The abbé Proyart

Liévain-Bonaventure Proyart, teacher and early biographer of Robespierre (under a pseudonym), author of the official life of Louis XVI's father, offers an essay in religious determinism. He devotes two books to Louis XVI, whose titles announce their thesis: *Louis XVI détrôné avant d'être roi* (Louis XVI dethroned before he even became king) and *Louis XVI et ses vertus aux prises avec la perversité de son siècle* (Louis XVI and his virtues at odds with the wickedness of his times). Proyart also believed

> that there still [in 1808] exists a tacit but real agreement to undermine the reputation of this prince. It consists of everyone in every party who needs to find justification outside themselves for what they were or what they did.

Therefore he feels it necessary to adduce extra evidence 'when it should be sufficient to relate the facts' in order to

> show Louis XVI embellished with a variety of knowledge and precious qualities which together, but for the obstacle of his century, could not have failed but to form a great king as well as a virtuous man.[10]

The 'obstacle of his century', of course, was freethinking philosophy and Proyart marshals a large and, it has to be said, well-selected number of quotations from the leading *philosophes* tending to prove how they undermined respect both for religion and for monarchy. This approach is fairly conventional, though Proyart's decision to publish his *Louis XVI et ses vertus* in 1808 in Napoleonic France was risky – he was immediately thrown in prison, leaving it only to die. Slightly more unusual is his identification not just of atheism but of Calvinism as a direct cause of the French Revolution: 'that Louis XVI went to the scaffold was uniquely because the spirit of Protestantism managed during his reign to pervert his Catholic subjects'.[11] Calvinism became a dynamic in the French polity through its Catholic variant Jansenism, which was strongly entrenched in the Parlement. In *Louis XVI détrôné* Proyart talks of 'the spirit of independence and democracy introduced into the Parlement of Paris as a result of Calvinism'. He even argues that this spirit goes back beyond the seventeenth-century heresy of Jansenism to the religious wars under Henri III the previous century. Fanciful as such theories are, they have been embraced by a modern scholar, whose work received at least a *succès d'estime*.[12]

Proyart also adopts a more conventional religious explanation of the Revolution: that Louis was the innocent agent of divine displeasure against a godless generation. Everything worked together towards this consummation so that 'the king under whom this catastrophe was set to happen, having no vice with which he could be reproached, his very virtues will often operate against him'.[13] Even if Louis's fate had not been decided before he ascended the throne, the appointment of Maurepas sealed it: 'it was all up with a sick France treated by Maurepas'. Yet none of the other candidates would have been any better, 'such was the general depravity in the educated class'.[14] Proyart dwells particularly on the appointment of Brienne during the crisis of the Assembly of Notables in 1787 when Louis 'could not find a single man endowed with sufficient talent and probity to aid him in his paternal care to relieve his people' and had to appoint a man whom he had not considered fit to be archbishop of Paris on the grounds of his atheism.[15] Brienne's crowning folly was to introduce (limited) toleration of Protestants.

It followed from the depravity of his subjects, that Louis could not be a great king:

> We will not therefore make the contradictory claim of discovering the great king in Louis XVI, *dethroned before he became king*. The dissolution of a people excludes the quality of greatness in its leader *qua* leader.

Even Peter the Great could not have forged an entity out of 'a people decomposed by philosophy'. Only when the people had been chastised in the Revolution to the extent that they 'virtually ceased to be a people' was it possible for Napoleon to create France anew.[16]

However, if Louis could not be great as a leader, he was great as a man. Like the Evangelists, Proyart collects dozens of more or less apocryphal didactic sayings of Louis, to show the king's goodness and homely wisdom. So, when a minister tells him he is authorized to foment trouble in England's American colonies because the English have behaved similarly, Louis asks him how he would qualify England's action. 'Execrable', replied the minister. 'I think the same,' said the king, 'please God we never imitate what we find so odious in others.' During the terrible winter of 1784 Louis had the inhabitants of the town of Versailles clearing snow. Encountering a group so engaged he addressed them:

> I know what you're thinking: 'we're being put to a pleasant and useless task'. And there you're wrong; it's bitterly cold and this work will warm you up and save you firewood; you were bored and this work will take your minds off things and then at the end you get a wage.

The workers were so impressed that they made a snowman-statue of the king, to which a passing poet attached some lines to the effect that Louis would rather have a statue of snow than one of 'marble paid for with the bread of the indigent'.[17]

Some of the stories about good king Louis seem modelled on the parables in the New Testament. The parable of the labourers in the vineyard seems the model for the story of Louis's sorting out the wages of women and children employed to weed the gardens of the chateau of La Muette, involving the sacking of the head gardener who claimed that the children should have more because they were nimbler and his wages going to the women. The parable of the debtors suggests another story in which Louis in his council directs that a merchant should pay his debts only to be told that the merchant in turn was owed money by Louis XV. Louis replied:

> Very well, I must set an example and I order that the king will pay immediately in order that the merchant can pay.

Proyart also puts into Louis' mouth some words reminiscent of Christ's about cutting off offending limbs. On being informed that the abbé L'Epée, the pioneer teacher of sign language to the deaf, was tainted with Jansenism, Louis proclaimed:

> He is performing a great service for his pupils; but it would be better for them to remain deaf than to open their ears to Jansenism.[18]

Leon Trotsky

The Russian Revolution was carried out in the shadow of the French. In his history of the later revolution, Trotsky draws interesting parallels between Nicholas II, Louis XVI and Charles I:

> Louis and Nicholas were the last-born of a dynasty which had lived tumultuously. The well-known equability of them both, their tranquillity and 'gaiety' in difficult moments, were the well-bred expressions of a meagreness of inner powers, a weakness of the nervous discharge, poverty of spiritual resources. Moral castrates, they were absolutely deprived of imagination and creative force. They had just enough brains to feel their own triviality and they cherished an envious hostility toward anything gifted and significant. It fell to both to rule a country in conditions of deep inner crisis and popular revolutionary awakening. Both of them

fought off the intrusion of new ideas, and the tide of hostile forces. Indecisiveness, hypocrisy and lying were in both cases the expression, not so much of personal weakness, as of the complete impossibility of holding fast to their hereditary positions. . . .

The ill luck of Nicholas, as of Louis, had its roots not in his personal horoscope, but in the historical horoscope of the bureaucratic-caste monarchy. They were both chiefly and, above all, the last-born offspring of absolutism. Their moral insignificance, deriving from their dynastic epigonism, gave the latter an especially malignant character. . . .

The historic-psychological contrast mentioned above between the Romanovs and the Capets can, by the way, be aptly extended to the British royal pair of the epoch of the first Revolution. Charles I revealed fundamentally the same combination of traits with which memoirists and historians have endowed Louis XVI and Nicholas II. 'Charles, therefore remained passive', writes Montague, 'yielded where he could not resist, betrayed how unwillingly he did so, and reaped no popularity, no confidence'. 'He was not a stupid man', says another historian of Charles Stuart, 'but he lacked firmness of character. . . . His evil fate was his wife, Henrietta, a Frenchwoman, sister of Louis XIII, saturated even more than Charles with the idea of absolutism.' . . .

If Nicholas had gone to meet liberalism and replaced Stürmer with Miliukov, the development of events would have differed a little in form but not in substance. Indeed it was just in this way that Louis behaved in the second stage of the Revolution, summoning the Gironde to power: this did not save Louis himself from the guillotine nor after him the Gironde.[19]

The comparison Trotsky made between Louis XVI and Charles I is at once apt and ironic. Apt, because everyone, especially Louis, made the comparison. Ironic because, with this knowledge, Louis strenuously tried to avoid the mistakes made by his ancestor. When people wanted to stiffen Louis's resolve, they tried to scare him with the fate of Charles. So in 1776 Turgot, in conflict with the Parlement and his colleagues over his six edicts, wrote to the king reminding him that 'it was weakness which put Charles I's head on a block'.[20] Similarly, the day before the *résultat du conseil* was announced on 27 December 1788, the conservative party substituted a portrait of Charles I for that of Louis XV in the king's cabinet to warn him against yielding to pressure from the Third Estate. But of course it was not weakness which was Charles's undoing but stubbornness.

In the autumn of 1788, at the beginning of the revolutionary crisis, Malesherbes and Louis discussed the parallels with Charles I. Despite the obvious similarities in the predicament of the two kings, Malesherbes was able to point to a consoling difference and conclude that Louis would not share the fate of the English king because in France, 'the political quarrel is luckily not aggravated by a religious one'. 'Very luckily,' the king said, squeezing Malesherbes's arm, 'so the atrocity will not be the same.'[21] When the schism over the Civil Constitution emerged, it must for Louis have been as if Birnam woods had come to Dunsinane. Nor did other talismanic safety plays – such as not levying war on his subjects as Charles had done, or emigrating as James II, or departing from the letter of the constitution – serve him any better. Nor, one feels, did he ever really think they would. For he was trapped in a formal maze of his own devising.

Conclusion: a sketch of Louis XVI's mind

Why have there been such diverse views of Louis XVI and why have the unfavourable ones predominated? The answers to the two questions are linked. Louis is hard to fathom: Mercy said of him as dauphin that he was 'impenetrable'. This characteristic trait was reinforced by his Jesuit tutor, Soldini, who advised: 'never let people read your mind'. But not only was Louis 'impenetrable', there were two men living within the same body and the same mind. And the two never fused, except perhaps in the period between his imprisonment and his death – the period of his life which has left the strongest impression.

Soulavie was on the right track when he said there were two Louis's, the man who 'knows' and the man who 'wills'. But even within Louis's intellect there is a division. The first Louis is most perfectly represented by his desolating diary, kept from the age of 11 until his dethronement. (Why did he discontinue it then, just when he had time on his hands?) Trotsky rightly comments on its 'depressing spiritual emptiness'.[22] The famous entry of *'rien'* on 14 July 1789 can be partially explained by the fact that Louis's was an engagement/hunting diary and the storming of the Bastille was not an official engagement. But it was not exclusively an engagement diary – Louis crams in details of his wife's confinements, and his own taking of medicine or a bath. Historians have been able to leap to the wrong conclusion about the significance of 'nothing' precisely because the entry seems so consonant with the 'spriritual emptiness' of the other entries. Particularly numbing – perhaps he wanted to numb himself – are the references to the move from Versailles to Paris and the flight to Varennes. Both are treated as 'trips', such as the regular autumnal removal to Fontainebleau. In his recapitulation for the year 1789, Louis writes:

> Excursions in 1789
> Marly 14–21 June (7)
> Paris 6 October–31 December (86)
> Nights that I slept away from Versailles, 93.

When he comes to the flight to Varennes, he meticulously notes that at Dormans, on the return trip, there was no '*coucher*'. He doesn't give us the reason: that there was no '*coucher*' because there was no bed – he slept in an armchair! Written across his diary for the whole month of July 1791 are the words: 'nothing all month; mass in the gallery'; and for August: 'the whole month has been the same as July'. He doesn't explain that he had been suspended from his functions and had to hear mass in the gallery because he was kept in such close surveillance that he was not allowed to go to the chapel.

But compare the diary entries with the letters the 20-year-old king wrote to Vergennes at the start of his reign. As he outlines the contours for an ethical foreign policy, gives detailed instructions for the handling of 'the Eastern Question' and the implications of English politics for its foreign policy, especially in relation to the American war, you could be excused for thinking you were dealing with a different man. Or, from the end of the reign, the letter to his brothers I quoted in the last chapter reveals anything but 'spiritual emptiness'. It alone should serve to dispel the notion that Louis never understood the Revolution. It is perfectly possible to understand something and yet be defeated by it.

Most of the time, these two men remain separate, but they fuse in Louis's declaration on leaving Paris on 20/21 June 1791. Here a brilliant early analysis of the structure of the Jacobin network and a triumphant exposition of the shortcomings of the constitution are coupled with petty complaints about the state of the Tuileries when he was forced to take up residence there and with carping about the size of the civil list in relation to the domains he had been forced to surrender. No wonder this document has been read in so many different ways.

However, it is hardly satisfactory baldly to state that there were two Louis's; one must try to explain how this came about. The key is Louis's conditioning at Versailles, and this explains not just the mechanical aspect of his thought but his inability to respond imaginatively to rapidly moving situations. Take his diary: this was an expansion, but not a deepening, of the hunting diaries traditionally kept by the kings. Louis XV had kept one. Or his famous indecision: this was reinforced by the tradition that kings should abide by majority decisions in council. In Louis's reign, where controversy was rarely absent, the council was often split down the middle. Albert Sorel said the issues were more tractable in foreign policy and the whole nation united and perhaps they were – yet it took Louis two years to decide to enter the American conflict.

Louis sometimes did break out of the straightjacket of his conditioning, to reveal another side to him. *Pace* Girault de Coursac, Louis's education in the humanities was stultifying and repressive and he did not do more than parrot and paraphrase his tutors' antiquated ideas going back to Fénelon and the duc de Bourgogne at the beginning of the century. François Furet is right here. His teaching in the natural sciences, by distinguished tutors provided by Maurepas, was a different matter, and here he showed real distinction, for example in geography.

However, what really marked Louis out was that he became a strenuous autodidact, to become, as David Jordan observes, possibly the most widely read of all the French kings. Early evidence of this came when he disobeyed his mother and taught himself English. His method was translation without bothering at first with the grammar. This method was advocated by his Latin tutor, Radonvilliers. But Louis also believed throughout his life that the act of copying (or translating) was the best way of absorbing the meaning of the text. We know this because Vergennes annotated one of Louis's many copies of letters from Charles III of Spain to this effect.

Autodidacts often have unconventional and pig-headed views. And since much of the old schooling stuck, the disparities between the two Louis's were intensified. So, side by side with the

Louis of the diary, we have the lost personal record to which Proyart alludes. And above all we have the marginal comments on his ministers' proposals to which I have made much reference. Yet these themselves contain the two Louis's. We have the highly conventional Louis arguing that the old social hierarchy must be maintained intact because the king stands at its apex, the Louis which Jules Michelet depicts so brilliantly. But beside this Louis is another with unusual even eccentric views. The man who argues, against the whole tradition of royal administrative reform, that a governmental machine with no regional variations is actually harder to set in motion than the complex one in existence. The man who argues that a perfectly representative national assembly is undesirable because the king could not morally use troops against it. These are the product of a mind unregulated by correction.

Notes

Introduction: the many faces of Louis XVI

1. J.-L. Soulavie, *Historical and Political Memoirs of the Reign of Lewis XVI from his Marriage to his Death*, London, 1802, 6 vols, II, xiv–xv.
2. J. Hardman, *Louis XVI*, New Haven and London, 1993, 226.
3. J. Hardman and M. Price (eds), *Louis XVI and the comte de Vergennes: Correspondence, 1774–1787*, Oxford, 1998.
4. A. d'Arneth and J. Flammermont (eds), *Correspondance secrète du comte de Mercy-Argenteau avec l'Empereur Joseph II et le prince de Kaunitz*, Paris, 1891, 2 vols, II, 94.
5. M. A. de Bacourt (ed.), *Le comte de Mirabeau et le comte de La Marck, correspondance, 1789, 1790 et 1791*, Paris, 1851, 3 vols, II, 211.
6. Hardman, *Louis XVI*, 126.

Chapter 1   Inheritance

1. Comte de Brienne and Loménie de Brienne, *Journal de l'Assemblée des Notables de 1787*, ed. P. Chevalier, Paris, 1960, 79.
2. Duc de Croÿ, *Journal, 1718–84*, ed. Vicomte de Grouchy and P. Cottin, Paris, 1906–07, 4 vols, III, 135, 144.

Chapter 2   The education of a king

1. F. Furet, *The French Revolution, 1770–1814* , trans. A. Nevill, Oxford, 1996, 28.
2. Furet, *French Revolution*, 30.
3. P. Girault de Coursac, *L'Education d'un roi: Louis XVI*, Paris, 1972, 210–11.
4. Girault de Coursac, *Education*, 209.
5. Bibliothèque Nationale, Rés. Geo. C 4349.
6. Girault de Coursac, *Education*, 44.

7. A. d'Arneth and M. Geffroy (eds), *Marie-Antoinette: Correspondance secrète entre Marie-Thérèse et le comte de Mercy-Argenteau*, 2nd ed., Paris, 1875, 3 vols, I, 32–3.
8. Arneth and Geffroy, *Correspondance*, I, 313–34.
9. Arneth and Geffroy, *Correspondance*, I, 335–6.
10. A. Von Arneth, *Marie-Antoinette, Joseph II und Leopold II, ihr Briefwechsel*, Vienna, 1866.
11. Girault de Coursac, *Education*, 285.
12. Arneth and Geffroy, *Correspondance*, I, 432.
13. Arneth and Geffroy, *Correspondance*, I, 441.
14. Arneth and Geffroy, *Correspondance*, I, 425.
15. Arneth and Geffroy, *Correspondance*, I, 189.
16. Arneth and Geffroy, *Correspondance*, II, 10.
17. Girault de Coursac, *Education*, 57.
18. Arneth and Geffroy, *Correspondance*, II, 137–8.
19. Arneth, *Marie-Antoinette, Joseph II und Leopold II*, 39.
20. Prince Burliabled, [alias Paul Jones], *La Vie de Louis XVI jusqu'au 24 août 1774*, London, 1774, 28–9.
21. Abbé Proyart, *Oeuvres complètes*, Paris, 1819, 6 vols, II, 99.
22. J. Hardman, *Louis XVI*, New Haven and London, 1993, 221.
23. Marquis de Castries, Archives de la Marine, Journal de Castries, MS 182/7964 1–2, I, fo. 110.
24. J. Hardman and M. Price (eds), *Louis XVI and the Comte de Vergennes: Correspondence, 1774–1787*, Oxford, 1998, 388, letter of 26 September 1786.
25. Arneth and Geffroy, *Correspondance*, I, 364.
26. Hardman, *Louis XVI*, 21.
27. Louis's diary is in the Archives Nationales, AE 1–4 dossier 1.
28. Proyart, *Oeuvres* II, 137.
29. Proyart, *Oeuvres* II, 137.
30. Sénac de Meilhan, *Du gouvernement, des moeurs et des conditions en France avant la Révolution, avec le caractère des principaux personnages du règne de Louis XVI*, London, 1795, 145.
31. Girault de Coursac, *Education*, 96.
32. *Hardman and Price, Louis XVI . . . Correspondence*, 89 n. 134.
33. *Hardman and Price, Louis XVI . . . Correspondence*, 263, the king to Charles III of Spain, 19 June 1778.
34. W. Smyth, *On the French Revolution*, London, 1840, 3 vols, I, 52.

Chapter 3   1774: a new monarch – and a new monarchy?

1. J.-L. Soulavie, *Historical and Political Memoirs of the Reign of Lewis XVI from his Marriage to his Death*, London, 1802, 6 vols, I, lii.
2. Soulavie, *Memoirs*, II, 151.
3. Soulavie, *Memoirs*, II, 35.
4. Soulavie, *Memoirs*, II, 40–1.
5. Soulavie, *Memoirs*, II, 42.

6. Soulavie, *Memoirs*, II, 37.
7. Soulavie, *Memoirs*, II, 26.
8. Soulavie, *Memoirs*, II, 7.
9. Soulavie, *Memoirs*, II, 7.
10. Soulavie, *Memoirs*, II, 9.
11. Soulavie, *Memoirs*, II, 13.
12. Soulavie, *Memoirs*, II, 144.
13. Sénac de Meilhan, *Du gouvernement, des moeurs et des conditions en France avant la Révolution, avec le caractère des principaux personnages du règne de Louis XVI*, London, 1795, 148.
14. Soulavie, *Memoirs*, II, 142.
15. The best treatment in this tradition is D. Echeverria, *The Maupeou Revolution*, Baton Rouge, 1985.
16. M. Antoine, *Louis XV*, Paris, 1989.
17. W. Doyle, 'The Parlements of France and the Breakdown of the Old Regime, 1771–1788', *French Historical Studies*, VI, 1970, 415–58.
18. P. Burley, 'Louis XVI and a New Monarchy', unpublished Ph.D. thesis, London University, 1981, 147.
19. Soulavie, *Memoirs*, II, 159.
20. Soulavie, *Memoirs*, II, 210.
21. Soulavie, *Memoirs*, II, 163–7.
22. Soulavie, *Memoirs*, II, 220.
23. Soulavie, *Memoirs*, II, 191.
24. Soulavie, *Memoirs*, II, 208.
25. Soulavie, *Memoirs*, II, 195.
26. Soulavie, *Memoirs*, II, 209.
27. J. Swann, *Politics and the Parlement of Paris under Louis XV, 1754–1774*, Cambridge, 1995, 352–68.
28. Swann, *Politics*, 368.
29. Lenoir papers, Bibliothèque Municipale d'Orléans, MS 1421, section 2, Religion.
30. Burley, 'Louis XVI', 112.
31. Burley, 'Louis XVI', 97, 105.
32. Abbé de Véri, *Journal, 1774–80*, ed. J. de Witte, Paris, 1928–30, 2 vols, I, 128.
33. J. Hardman, *Louis XVI*, New Haven and London, 1993, 223.
34. Sénac, *Du gouvernement*, 141.
35. Burley, 'Louis XVI', 300.
36. Véri, *Journal*, I, 202.
37. Burley, 'Louis XVI', 92.
38. Burley, 'Louis XVI', 114.
39. Burley, 'Louis XVI', 119–20.
40. Hardman, 'Louis XVI', 35.
41. *Journal Historique* for 8 November 1774, quoted in Echeverria, *Maupeou*, 32.
42. Cited in Burley, 'Louis XVI', 98.
43. Burley, *Louis XVI*, 353.
44. Soulavie, *Memoirs*, II, 19–20.
45. J. Hardman and M. Price (eds), *Louis XVI and the comte de Vergennes: Correspondence 1774–1787*, Oxford, 1998, 318.

46. M. Fogel, 'Le système d'infomation ritualizée de l'absolutisme française', 1982, 141–9.
47. Abbé Proyart, *Oeuvres complètes*, Paris, 1819, 6 vols, II, 204.
48. W. Shakespeare, *Antony and Cleopatra*, III. vi.

Chapter 4   Louis XVI and Turgot

1. J.-L. Soulavie, *Historical and Political Memoirs of the Reign of Lewis XVI from his Marriage to his Death*, London, 1802, 6 vols, II, 317.
2. P. Burley, 'Louis XVI and a New Monarchy', unpublished Ph.D. thesis, London University, 1981, 365.
3. Soulavie, *Memoirs*, II, 80.
4. J. Hardman, *Louis XVI*, New Haven and London, 1993, 44.
5. Soulavie, *Memoirs*, II, 275.
6. Frederick II to d'Alembert, 19 June and d'Alembert to Frederick, 17 May, cited in abbé Proyart, *Oeuvres complètes*, Paris, 1819, 6 vols, II, 45.
7. Cited in Burley, 'Louis XVI', 89–90.
8. Abbé de Véri, *Journal, 1774–80*, ed. J. de Witte, Paris, 1928–30, 2 vols, I, 419.
9. Abbé de Véri, MSS journal, cahier 109, Archives Départementales de la Drôme, Valence.
10. J.-L. Soulavie, *Mémoires historiques et politiques du règne de Louis XVI*, Paris, 1801, 6 vols, III, 142–3.
11. Burley, 'Louis XVI', 364.
12. Véri, *Journal*, I, 448.
13. These and Turgot's proposals are to be found in Soulavie, *Mémoires*, III, 139–54. I have translated the extracts from the French edition because the English version contains some inaccuracies. For a summary of the debate see H. Glagau, 'Turgots Sturz', *Historische Zeitschrift*, 37, 1906, 473–510.
14. Véri, *Journal*, I, 448.
15. See A. R. J. Turgot, *Oeuvres complètes*, 2nd ed., Paris, 1808, 8 vols, VIII, 434–504, for the text of the memorandum.

Chapter 5   Necker, 1776–1781: charlatan or saviour?

1. P. Burley, 'Louis XVI and a New Monarchy', unpublished Ph.D. thesis, London University, 1981, 289.
2. J.-L. Soulavie, *Historical and Political Memoirs of the Reign of Lewis XVI from his Marriage to his Death*, London, 1802, 6 vols, IV, 194.
3. J. Hardman, *Louis XVI*, New Haven and London, 1993, 58.
4. J. F. Bosher, *French Public Finances 1770–1795*, Cambridge, 1970; R. D. Harris, *Necker: Reform Statesman of the Ancien Régime*, Berkeley, CA, 1979.

5. Archives Nationales, K 163 no. 13.8.
6. Soulavie, *Memoirs*, IV, 34–5.
7. Abbé Proyart, *Oeuvres complètes*, Paris, 1819, 6 vols, II, 205.
8. Archives Parlementaires, I, 496–8.
9. Cited in Soulavie, *Memoirs*, IV, 176–7.
10. J. Egret, *Necker*, Paris, 1975, 128–9.
11. Sénac de Meilhan, *Du gouvernement, des moeurs et des conditions en France avant la Révolution, avec le caractère des principaux personnages du règne de Louis XVI*, London, 1795, 128.
12. Soulavie, *Memoirs*, IV, 17–18.
13. Soulavie, *Memoirs*, IV, 195.
14. J.-L. Soulavie, *Mémoires historiques et politiques du règne de Louis XVI*, Paris, 1801, 6 vols, II, 154.
15. Soulavie, *Memoirs*, IV, 252.
16. M. Price, 'The "Ministry of the Hundred Hours": A Reappraisal', *French History*, 4: 3, 1990, 318–39, 330, 337–8.
17. Soulavie, *Memoirs*, IV, 241–56.
18. Soulavie, *Memoirs*, IV, 261.
19. Soulavie, *Memoirs*, IV, 204.
20. Harris, *Necker*, 122.
21. J. Hardman and M. Price (eds), *Louis XVI and the comte de Vergennes: Correspondence, 1774–1787*, Oxford, 1998, 167.
22. Soulavie, *Memoirs*, IV, 202.
23. Lévis, duc de, *Portraits et souvenirs*, Paris, 1813, 12.
24. Burley, 'Louis XVI', 289.

Chapter 6   Foreign policy, 1774–1789

1. A. R. J. Turgot, *Oeuvres complètes*, 2nd ed., Paris, 1808, 8 vols, VIII, 476.
2. A. Sorel, *Europe and the French Revolution: The Political Traditions of the Old Regime*, trans. and ed. A. Cobban and J. W. Hunt, London, 1969, 244.
3. Sorel, *Europe*, 332.
4. J. N. Moreau, *Mes souvenirs*, ed. C. Hermelin, Paris, 1898–1901, 2 vols, I, 321.
5. J. Hardman and M. Price (eds), *Louis XVI and the comte de Vergennes: Correspondence, 1774–1787*, Oxford, 1988, 190–1.
6. Abbé Proyart, *Oeuvres complètes*, Paris, 1819, 6 vols, II, 160.
7. Hardman and Price, *Louis XVI . . . correspondence*, 256.
8. Hardman and Price, *Louis XVI . . . correspondence*, 190.
9. Hardman and Price, *Louis XVI . . . correspondence*, 237.
10. A. F. Bertrand de Molleville, *Mémoires particulières pour servir à l'histoire de la dernière année du règne de Louis XVI, roi de France*, London, 1797, 3 vols, I, 232–3.
11. Hardman and Price, *Louis XVI . . . correspondence*, 255, the king to Charles III of Spain.

12. J.-L. Soulavie, *Historical and Political Memoirs of the Reign of Lewis XVI from his Marriage to his Death*, London, 1802, 6 vols, III, 413.
13. All references to Louis's marginal comments are taken from J.-L. Soulavie, *Mémoires historiques et politiques du règne de Louis XVI*, Paris, 1801, 6 vols, III, 398–412.
14. Hardman and Price, *Louis XVI . . . correspondence*, 214.
15. Soulavie, *Memoirs*, III, 349–50.
16. Proyart, *Oeuvres*, III, 69.
17. Hardman and Price, *Louis XVI . . . correspondence*, 236–8.
18. J. Dull, *The French Navy and American Independence: A Study of Arms and Diplomacy, 1774–1787*, Princeton, NJ, 1975; C. H. Van Tyne, 'French Aid before the Alliance of 1778', *American Historical Review*, 31, 1925, 20–40.
19. P.-A. Caron de Beaumarchais, *Correspondance*, ed. B. Morton and D. Spinelli, Paris, 1969–78, 4 vols, III, 82.
20. J. F. Labourdette, *Vergennes*, Paris, 1990, 190–2.
21. Bertrand de Molleville, *Mémoires*, I, 232–3.
22. Hardman and Price, *Louis XVI . . . correspondence*, 63–5.
23. Hardman and Price, *Louis XVI . . . correspondence*, 69.
24. Hardman and Price, *Louis XVI . . . correspondence*, 252–3; H. Doniol, *Histoire de la participation de la France à l'établissement des Etats-Unis de l'Amérique*, Paris, 1886–89, 5 vols, II, 51.
25. Proyart, *Oeuvres*, II, 291.
26. T. C. W. Blanning, *The French Revolution: Class War or Culture Clash*, 2nd ed., Basingstoke, 1998, 26.

Chapter 7   1781–1787: personal rule?

1. Marquis de Castries, Archives de la Marine, Journal de Castries, MS 182/7964 1–2, I, fos. 91–3.
2. J.-L. Soulavie, *Historical and Political Memoirs of the Reign of Lewis XVI from his Marriage to his Death*, London, 1802, 6 vols, VI, 82.
3. Castries, Journal, I, fo. 92.
4. A. de Tocqueville, *Coup d'oeil sur le règne de Louis XVI*, Paris, 1850, 167, 185 n.
5. Soulavie, *Memoirs*, IV, 247.
6. M. Price, *Preserving the Monarchy: the comte de Vergennes, 1774–1787*, Cambridge, 1995, 111.
7. Price, *Vergennes*, 111.
8. B. Stone, *The Parlement of Paris, 1774–1789*, Chapel Hill, NC, 1981, 81.
9. De Tocqueville, *Louis XVI*, 203.
10. J. Michelet, *Histoire de la Révolution française*, ed. G. Walter, Paris, 1952, 2 vols, II, 57.
11. Michelet, *Révolution française*, II, 114.
12. De Tocqueville, *Louis XVI*, 188.

13. J. Hardman and M. Price (eds) *Louis XVI and the comte de Vergennes: Correspondence, 1774–1787*, Oxford, 1998, 376–7.
14. R. Darnton, *The Literary Underground of the Old Regime*, Cambridge, MA, 1982, 195, 201–2.

Chapter 8 Watershed

1. Abbé de Véri, MSS journal, cahier 122, Archives Départementales de la Drôme, Valence.
2. Comte de Brienne and Loménie de Brienne, *Journal de l'Assemblée des Notables de 1787*, ed. P. Chevalier, Paris, 1960, 80.
3. J.-L. Soulavie, *Historical and Political Memoirs of the Reign of Lewis XVI from his Marriage to his Death*, London, 1802, 6 vols, III, 146.
4. Brienne, *Journal*, 79.
5. J.-L. Soulavie, *Mémoires historiques et politiques du règne de Louis XVI*, Paris, 1801, 6 vols, III, 147.
6. J. Swann, *Politics and the Parlement of Paris under Louis XV, 1754–1774*, Cambridge, 1995, 368.
7. For a more detailed discussion of the breakdown in relations between crown and parlement, see J. Hardman, *French Politics, 1774–1789: From the Accession of Louis XVI to the Fall of the Bastille*, London and New York, 1995, 222–31.
8. J. Egret, *The French Pre-Revolution, 1787–1788*, trans. W. Camp, Chicago and London, 1977, 29.
9. J. F. X. Droz, *Histoire du règne de Louis XVI . . .*, Brussels, 1839, 167.
10. Brienne, *Journal*, 45.
11. Egret, *Pre-Revolution*, 29.
12. Marquis de Castries, Archives de la Marine, Journal de Castries, MS 182/7964 1–2, II, fo. 335.
13. Droz, *Louis XVI*, 179.
14. Archives Nationales, K 163 no. 8. 31.
15. Brienne, *Journal*, 59.
16. J. Hardman, *Louis XVI*, New Haven and London, 1993, 122.
17. Droz, *Louis XVI*, 182.
18. Brienne, *Journal*, 63.
19. Hardman, *Louis XVI*, 126.
20. Soulavie, *Memoirs*, VI, 188.
21. Soulavie, *Memoirs*, VI, 259.
22. Soulavie, *Memoirs*, VI, 246–7.
23. Egret, *Pre-Revolution*, 282 n. 71–2.
24. On this question see C. Lucas, 'Nobles, Bourgeois and the origins of the French Revolution', *Past and Present*, 60, 1973, 84–126.
25. J. Michelet, *Histoire de la Révolution française*, ed. G. Walter, Paris, 1952, 2 vols, I, 75.
26. Soulavie, *Mémoires*, 148–53.
27. C. A. de Calonne, *Lettre au roi*, London, 1789, 54.
28. Soulavie, *Memoirs*, VI, 267.

29. Quoted in W. Smyth, *On the French Revolution*, London, 1840, 3 vols, I, 152.
30. Soulavie, *Mémoires*, III, 144.
31. Soulavie, *Memoirs*, VI, 260.
32. Soulavie, *Memoirs*, VI, 260–3.
33. Soulavie, *Memoirs*, VI, 268.
34. Baron Acton, *Lectures on the French Revolution*, London, 1910, 44–45.
35. J. Michelet, *History of the French Revolution*, trans. C. Cocks, Chicago, 1967, 96.

Chapter 9   1789

1. J. Hardman, *Louis XVI*, New Haven and London, 1993, 142.
2. Baron Acton, *Lectures on the French Revolution*, London, 1910, 43–50.
3. Acton, *French Revolution*, 59.
4. *Recueil des documents relatifs aux Etats-Généraux de 1789*, ed. G. Lefebvre et al., Paris, 1953–70, 4 vols, I (1), 253.
5. Acton, *French Revolution*, 75.
6. J. Michelet, *History of the French Revolution*, trans. C. Cocks, Chicago, 1967, 113, 115.
7. J.-L. Soulavie, *Mémoires historiques et politiques du règne de Louis XVI*, Paris, 1801, 6 vols, III, 152.
8. Soulavie, *Mémoires*, III, 152.
9. P. and P. Girault de Coursac, *Enquête sur le procès du roi Louis XVI*, Paris, 1982, 177.
10. P. Caron, 'La tentative de contre-révolution de juin–juillet 1789', *Revue d'Histoire Moderne*, 8, 1906, 5–34, 649–78, 25–8.
11. E. Burke, *Reflections on the Revolution in France*, ed. L. G. Mitchel, Oxford, 1993, 83.
12. M. Price, 'The "Ministry of the Hundred Hours": A Reappraisal', *French History*, 4:3, 1990, 317–39.
13. Acton, *French Revolution*, 83–4.
14. Acton, *French Revolution*, 80.
15. J. Hardman, *Robespierre*, London and New York, 1999, 22.
16. J. N. Moreau, *Mes souvenirs*, ed. C. Hermelin, Paris, 1898–1901, 2 vols, II, 439–41.
17. J. Hardman, *The French Revolution Sourcebook*, London and New York, 1999, 136.
18. Hardman, *French Revolution*, 125, Louis XVI to Charles IV, 12 October 1789.
19. P. and P. Girault de Coursac, *Louis XVI, roi martyr?*, Paris, 1976, 8.
20. Girault de Coursac, *Enquête*, 178–84.
21. J. Necker, *Sur l'administration de M. Necker par lui-même*, Paris, 1791, 328.
22. Michelet, *French Revolution*, 250–1.
23. Acton, *French Revolution*, 137.
24. Acton, *French Revolution*, 140.

Chapter 10 Varennes

1. For all references to Louis XVI's 'declaration' see J. Hardman, *The French Revolution Sourcebook*, London and New York, 1999, 128–36.
2. J. Flammermont, *Négociations secrètes de Louis XVI et du baron de Breteuil avec la cour de Berlin (décembre 1791–juillet 1792)*, Paris, 1885, 8, 17.
3. P. and P. Girault de Coursac, *Enquête sur le procès du roi Louis XVI*, Paris, 1982, 255.
4. Archives Parlementaires, LIV, 513–14.
5. Girault de Coursac, *Enquête*, 216–17, 240–2.
6. Baron Acton, *Lectures on the French Revolution*, London, 1910, 178.
7. A. Sorel, *Europe et la Révolution française*, vol. II, *La Chute de la royauté*, Paris, 1908, 227.
8. Archives Parlementaires, LIV, 474–5.
9. Acton, *French Revolution*, 177.
10. Archives Parlementaires, LIV, 467, La Porte to the king, 20 April 1791.
11. P. and P. Girault de Coursac, *Sur la route de Varennes*, Paris, 1984, 228.
12. Sorel, *Europe*, 268–9.
13. Duc de Choiseul, *Relation du départ de Louis XVI le 20 juin 1791*, Paris, 1822, 34–5.
14. Théodore de Lameth, *Notes et souvenirs*, ed. E. Welvert, Paris, 1913, 224–5.
15. I. Dunlop, *Marie-Antoinette*, London, 1993, 246.
16. Girault de Coursac, *Varennes*, 229–30.
17. M. A. de Bacourt (ed.), *Correspondance entre le comte de Mirabeau et le comte de la Marck*, Paris, 1851, 3 vols, I, 167.
18. On Robespierre, see J. Hardman, *Robespierre*, London and New York, 1999.
19. Choiseul, *Relation*, 35.
20. J. Michelet, *History of the French Revolution*, trans. C. Cocks, Chicago, 1967, 580–95.
21. J. Hardman, *Louis XVI*, New Haven and London, 1993, 105.
22. J. W. Croker, *Essays on the Early Period of the French Revolution*, London, 1856, 146.
23. W. Shakespeare, *Antony and Cleopatra*, II. vii.
24. Michelet, *French Revolution*, 595.
25. Croker, *Essays*, 148.
26. J. Michelet, *Histoire de la Révolution française*, ed. G. Walter, Paris, 1952, 2 vols, I, 633.
27. Croker, *Essays*, 149–50.
28. Published in M. Mortimer-Ternaux, *Histoire de la Terreur, 1792–1794*, Paris, 1863, 8 vols, I, 353–71.
29. Girault de Coursac, *Varennes*, 87.
30. Girault de Coursac, *Varennes*, 87.
31. Acton, *French Revolution*, 194.
32. Michelet, *Révolution française*, I, 758.

Chapter 11   The fall of the monarchy

1. A. F. Bertrand de Molleville, *Mémoires particulières pour servir à l'histoire de la dernière année du règne de Louis XVI, roi de France*, London, 1797, 3 vols, I, 210.
2. J. Hardman, *The French Revolution Sourcebook*, London and New York, 1999, 145.
3. Baron R. M. Klinckwostrum, *Le Comte de Fersen et la cour de France*, Paris, 1878, 2 vols, I, 199.
4. J. Flammermont, *Négociations secrètes de Louis XVI et du baron de Breteuil avec la cour de Berlin (décembre 1791–juillet 1792)*, Paris, 1885.
5. J. Hardman, *Louis XVI*, New Haven and London, 1993, 208.
6. Comte d'Allonville, *Mémoires secrètes de 1770 à 1830*, Paris, 1838–45, 6 vols; *Louis XVI, Marie-Antoinette et Mme Elizabeth, lettres et documents inédits*, ed. Feuillet de Conches, Paris, 1864–69, 6 vols.
7. A. Sorel, *Europe et la Révolution française*, vol. II, *La Chute de la royauté*, Paris, 1908, 524.
8. T. C. W. Blanning, *The Origins of the French Revolutionary Wars*, London, 1986, 99.
9. Sorel, *Europe*, 331–2.
10. P. and P. Girault de Coursac, *Enquête sur le procès du roi Louis XVI*, Paris, 1982, 290.
11. There are no mistakes of gender in Louis's entire correspondence with Vergennes.
12. Sorel, *Europe*, 270.
13. Sorel, *Europe*, 436.
14. Hardman, *French Revolution*, 137–9; Sorel, *Europe*, 275.
15. Flammermont, *Négociations*, 9.
16. Blanning, *Origins*, 98.
17. J. Michelet, *Histoire de la Révolution française*, ed. G Walter, Paris, 1952, 2 vols, I, 897.
18. Girault de Coursac, *Enquête*, 291.
19. Flammermont, *Négociations*, 29–30.
20. Michelet, *Révolution française*, I, 881–2.
21. Blanning, *Origins*, 101.
22. Bigot de Sainte-Croix, *Histoire de la conspiration du 10 août 1792*, London, 1793, 88.
23. Bigot, *Conspiration*, 80, 88.
24. Bigot, *Conspiration*, 87; Hardman, *French Revolution*, 141.
25. Baron Acton, *Lectures on the French Revolution*, London, 1910, 224.
26. Girault de Coursac, *Enquête*, 309.
27. M. Reinhard, *10 août 1792: la chute de la royauté*, Paris, 1969.
28. J.-L. Soulavie, *Historical and Political Memoirs of the Reign of Lewis XVI from his Marriage to his Death*, London, 1802, 6 vols, VI, 401.
29. Reinhard, *Chute*, 301.
30. Sorel, *Europe*, 486–7; Quinet is cited on p. 487.

31. Michelet, *Révolution française*, I, 919–20.
32. Acton, *French Revolution*, 224.
33. Marie-Antoinette, *Lettres*, ed. M. La Rocheterie and marquis de Beaucourt, Paris, 1895–96, 2 vols, II, 415.
34. Sorel, *Europe*, 456.
35. Sorel, *Europe*, 475.
36. Soulavie, *Memoirs*, VI, 384, 392, 400.
37. Sorel, *Europe*, 513.
38. Bigot, *Conspiration*, 91.
39. Bigot, *Conspiration*, 55.
40. Michelet, *Révolution française*, I, 1000.
41. Bigot, *Conspiration*, 31.

Chapter 12   Trial and death

1. Duchesse de Tourzelle, *Mémoires*, ed. duc des Cars, Paris, 1904, 2 vols, II, 228.
2. Louis's will is published in P. and P. Girault de Coursac, *Louis XVI a la parole*, Paris, 1989, 315–18.
3. D. Jordan, *The King's Trial*, Berkeley, CA, and London, 1979, 95.
4. S. Dunn, *The Deaths of Louis XVI*, Princeton, NJ, 1994.
5. A. Soboul, ed., *Le Procès de Louis XVI*, Paris, 1966, 85.
6. Soboul, *Procès*, 84–5.
7. J. Michelet, *Histoire de la Révolution française*, ed. G Walter, Paris, 1952, 2 vols, II, 166–7.
8. J. Hardman, *Robespierre*, London and New York, 1999, 74.
9. Jordan, *King's Trial*, 101–2; Dunn, *Deaths*, 21–2; M. Walzer, *Regicide and Revolution*, Cambridge, 1974, 78.
10. Walzer, *Regicide and Revolution*, 77.
11. J. Hardman, *French Politics, 1774–1789: From the Accession of Louis XVI to the Fall of the Bastille*, London and New York, 1995, 106–7; B. M. Schapiro, *Revolutionary Justice in Paris, 1789–1790*, Cambridge, 1993, 163.
12. Walzer, *Regicide and Revolution*, 77.
13. P. and P. Girault de Coursac, *Enquête sur le pròces du roi Louis XVI*, Paris, 1982, 101–2.
14. Jordan, *King's Trial*, 113–14.
15. Cited in Jordan, *King's Trial*, 115.
16. J. Hardman, *Louis XVI*, New Haven and London, 1993, 226.
17. The record of Louis's appearance before the Convention is given in Archives Parlementaires, LV, 7–15.
18. Jordan, *King's Trial*, 114.
19. Jordan, *King's Trial*, 113.
20. Jordan, *King's Trial*, 111.
21. Hardman, *Louis XVI*, 222.
22. Walzer, *Regicide and Revolution*, 31.
23. Jordan, *King's Trial*, 137.
24. J. Jaurès, *Histoire socialiste de la Révolution française*, Paris, 1923, 6 vols, V, 276–7.

25. Jaurès, *Histoire socialiste*, V, 288–94.
26. J. Hardman, *The French Revolution Sourcebook*, London and New York, 1999, 112–13.
27. J.-L. Soulavie, *Historical and Political Memoirs of the Reign of Louis XVI from his Marriage to his Death*, London, 1802, 6 vols, II, 148.
28. Hardman, *Louis XVI*, 228.
29. Girault de Coursac, *Louis XVI a la parole*, 263–70.
30. F. Hue, *Dernières années du règne de Louis XVI*, 3rd ed., Paris, 1860, 430–1.
31. J.-B. Cléry, *Journal de ce qui s'est passé à la tour du Temple pendant la captivité de Louis XVI, roi de France*, London, 1798, 211–13.
32. Marquis de Beaucourt, *Captivité de Louis XVI*, Paris, 1892, 2 vols, I, 291.
33. Abbé Edgeworth, *Dernières heures de Louis XVI*, Paris, 1816, 217.
34. Edgeworth, *Dernières heures*, 225–7.
35. Beaucourt, *Captivité*, II, 172.
36. Walzer, *Regicide and Revolution*, 85.
37. Dunn, *Deaths*, 87 n. 87.
38. Michelet, *Révolution française*, II, 149.
39. P. and P. Girault de Coursac, *Louis XVI, roi martyr?*, Paris, 1976, 8.
40. Girault de Coursac, *Roi martyr*, 17.
41. Girault de Coursac, *Roi martyr*, 27.
42. Girault de Coursac, *Roi martyr*, 41.
43. Girault de Coursac, *Roi martyr*, 10.
44. Abbé Proyart, *Oeuvres complètes*, Paris, 1819, 6 vols, II, 378–9.
45. Michelet, *Révolution française*, II, 184–5.
46. Walzer, *Regicide and Revolution*, 11.
47. Dunn, *Deaths*, 43.
48. L. Trotsky, *History of the Russian Revolution*, trans. M. Eastman, London, 1967, 3 vols, I, 104.

Chapter 13 Three general perspectives and a conclusion

1. A. de Tocqueville, *The Ancien Régime and the French Revolution*, ed. H. Brogan, London, 1966, 141–2.
2. de Tocqueville, *Ancien Régime*, 133–4.
3. de Tocqueville, *Ancien Régime*, 194.
4. de Tocqueville, *Ancien Régime*, 166–7.
5. de Tocqueville, *Ancien Régime*, 130–1.
6. de Tocqueville, *Ancien Régime*, 187.
7. de Tocqueville, *Ancien Régime*, 206–7, 187.
8. de Tocqueville, *Ancien Régime*, 200.
9. de Tocqueville, *Ancien Régime*, 207.
10. Abbé Proyart, *Oeuvres complètes*, Paris, 1819, 6 vols, II, 10.
11. Proyart, *Oeuvres*, II, 192.
12. D. Van Kley, *The Religious Origins of the French Revolution*, New Haven and London, 1996.

13. Proyart, *Oeuvres*, II, 146.
14. Proyart, *Oeuvres*, II, 120.
15. Proyart, *Oeuvres*, II, 165.
16. Proyart, *Oeuvres*, III, 106.
17. Proyart, *Oeuvres*, II, 219, 213.
18. Proyart, *Oeuvres*, II, 161.
19. L. Trotsky, *History of the Russian Revolution*, Trans. M. Eastman, London, 1967, 3 vols, I, 101–8.
20. L. Laugier, *Turgot ou le mythe des réformes*, Paris, 1979, 204.
21. Extract from Véri's diary published by the duc de Castries in *Revue de Paris*, November 1953, 84–6.
22. Trotsky, *Russian Revolution*, I, 101.

Select bibliography

Primary sources

Adhémar, comtesse d' *Souvenirs sur Marie-Antoinette* . . ., Paris, 1836, 4 vols.

Allonville, comte d' *Mémoires secrètes de 1770 à 1830*, Paris, 1838–45, 6 vols.

Arneth, A. d' and Geffroy, M. (eds), *Marie-Antoinette: Correspondance secrète entre Marie-Thérèse et le comte de Mercy-Argenteau*, 2nd ed., Paris, 1875, 3 vols.

Arneth A. d', and Flammermont, J. (eds), *Correspondance secrète du comte de Mercy-Argenteau avec l'Empereur Joseph II et le prince de Kaunitz*, Paris, 1891, 2 vols.

Bachaumont, L. P. de *Mémoires secrètes pour servir à l'histoire de la République des Lettres*, London, 1777–89.

Bacourt, M.A. de (ed.) *Correspondance entre le Comte de Mirabeau et le comte de la Marck*, Paris, 1851, 3 vols.

Barentin, C. *Mémoire autographe sur les derniers conseils du roi Louis XVI*, ed. M. Champion, Paris, 1844.

Barentin, C. *Lettres et bulletins à Louis XVI*, ed. A. Aulard, Paris, 1915.

Beaumarchais, P.-A. Caron de *Correspondance*, ed. B. Morton and D. Spinelli, Paris, 1969–78, 4 vols.

Bertrand de Molleville, A. F. *Mémoires particulières pour servir à l'histoire de la dernière année du règne de Louis XVI, roi de France*, London, 1797, 3 vols.

Bigot de Sainte-Croix *Histoire de la conspiration du 10 août 1792*, London, 1793.

Bouillé, marquis de *Mémoires*, ed. S. A. Berville and J. F. Barrière, Paris, 1821.

Brienne, comte de and Brienne, Loménie de *Journal de l'Assemblée des Notables de 1787*, ed. P. Chevalier, Paris, 1960.

Burke, E. *Reflections on the Revolution in France*, ed. L. G. Mitchel, Oxford, 1993.

Burliabled, Prince [alias Paul Jones] *La Vie de Louis XVI jusqu'au 24 août 1774*, London, 1774.

Calonne, C. A. de *Réponse de M. de Calonne à l'écrit de M. Necker, publié en avril 1787*, London, 1788 (the appendix contains a letter of August 1786 from Calonne to the king concerning the Notables).

Calonne, C. A. de *Lettre au roi*, London, 1789.

Campan, J. L. H. *Mémoires sur la vie de Marie-Antoinette par Mme Campan*, Paris, 1849.

Choiseul, duc de *Relation du départ de Louis XVI le 20 juin 1791*, Paris, 1822.

Cléry, J.-B. *Journal de ce qui s'est passé à la tour du Temple pendant la captivité de Louis XVI, roi de France*, London, 1798.

Croÿ, duc de *Journal, 1718–1784*, ed. Vicomte de Grouchy and P. Cottin, Paris, 1906–7, 4 vols.

Edgeworth, abbé *Dernières heures de Louis XVI*, Paris, 1816.

Fersen, comte de *Journal*, ed. R. M. Klinckwostrom in *Le Comte de Fersen et la cour de France*, Paris, 1878, 2 vols.

Flammermont, J. (ed.) *Rapport … sur les correspondances des agents diplomatiques étrangères en France avant la Révolution*, Paris, 1896.

Glagau, H. *Reformversucke und Sturz des Absolutismus in Frankreich (1774–88)*, Munich, 1908 (an appendix contains letters between Calonne and the king on the subject of the Notables).

Hardman, J. *The French Revolution Sourcebook*, London and New York, 1999.

Hardman, J. and Price, M. (eds) *Louis XVI and the comte de Vergennes: Correspondence, 1774–1787*, Oxford, 1998.

Hue, F. *Dernières années du règne de Louis XVI*, 3rd ed., Paris, 1860.

Lameth, Théodore de *Notes et souvenirs*, ed. E. Welvert, Paris, 1913.

Lefebvre, G. et al (eds) *Recueil des documents relatifs aux Etats-Généraux de 1789*, Paris, 1953–70, 4 vols, I(1), 253.

Lévis, duc de *Portraits et souvenirs*, Paris, 1813.

Louis XVI *Refléxions sur mes entretiens avec M. le duc de la Vauguyon*, ed. E. Falloux, Paris, 1851.

Louis XVI a la parole ed. P. and P. Girault de Coursac, Paris, 1989.

Louis XVI, Marie-Antoinette et Mme Elizabeth, lettres et documents inédits ed. Feuillet de Conches, Paris, 1864–69, 6 vols.

Luynes, duc de *Mémoires du duc de Luynes sur la cour de Louis XV, 1735–58*, ed. L. Dussieux and E. Soulié, Paris, 1860–65, 17 vols.

Malouet, P.-V. *Mémoires*, Paris, 1874, 2 vols.

Marie-Antoinette *Lettres*, ed. M. La Rocheterie et marquis de Beaucourt, Paris, 1895–96, 2 vols.

Marie-Antoinette, Joseph II und Leopold II ed. A von Arneth, 2nd ed., Vienna, 1866.

Necker, J. *Sur l'administration de M. Necker par lui-même*, Paris, 1791.

Necker, J. *De la Révolution française*, Paris, 1797.

Proyart, abbé *Oeuvres complètes*, Paris, 1819, 6 vols.

Saint-Priest, comte de *Mémoires*, ed. baron de Barante, Paris, 1929.

Sénac de Meilhan *Du gouvernement, des moeurs et des conditions en France avant la Révolution, avec le caractère des principaux personnages du règne de Louis XVI*, London, 1795.

Soulavie, J.-L. *Mémoires historiques et politiques du règne de Louis XVI*, Paris, 1801, 6 vols.

Soulavie, J.-L. *Historical and Political Memoirs of the Reign of Lewis XVI from his Marriage to his Death*, London, 1802, 6 vols.

Tourzelle, duchesse de *Mémoires*, ed. duc des Cars, Paris, 1904, 2 vols.

Turgot, A. R. J. *Oeuvres complètes*, 2nd ed., Paris, 1808, 8 vols.

Véri, abbé de *Journal, 1774–80*, ed. J. de Witte, Paris, 1928–30, 2 vols.

Walpole, H. *Règne de Richard III, ou doutes historiques sur les crimes qui lui sont imputés*, trans. Louis XVI, ed. Roussel l'Epinal, Paris, 1800.

Secondary works

Acton, J. E. E. D.-A., Baron *Lectures on the French Revolution*, London, 1910.

Antoine, M. *Louis XV*, Paris, 1989.

Arnaud-Bouteloup, J. *Le Rôle politique de Marie-Antoinette*, Paris, 1924.

Baker, K. M. *Inventing the French Revolution*, Cambridge, 1990.
Beaucourt, marquis de *Captivité de Louis XVI*, Paris, 1892, 2 vols.
Blanc, L. *Histoire de la Révolution française*, Paris, 1847–63, 6 vols.
Blanning, T. C. W. *The Origins of the French Revolutionary Wars*, London, 1986.
Blanning, T. C. W. *The French Revolution: Class War or Culture Clash*, 2nd ed., Basingstoke, 1998.
Bosher, J. F. *French Public Finances 1770–1795*, Cambridge, 1970.
Browne, R. 'The Diamond Necklace Affair Revisited', *Renaissance and Modern Studies*, 33, 1989.
Burley, P. 'Louis XVI and a New Monarchy', unpublished Ph.D. thesis, London University, 1981.
Caron, P. '*La Tentative de contre-révolution de juin–juillet 1789*', *Revue d'Histoire moderne*, 8, 1906.
Censer, J. R. and Popkin, J. D. (eds) *Press and Politics in Pre-Revolutionary France*, Berkeley, CA, 1987.
Croker, J. W. *Essays on the Early Period of the French Revolution*, London, 1856.
Dakin, D. *Turgot and the Ancien Régime in France*, London, 1939.
Darnton, R. *The Literary Underground of the Old Regime*, Cambridge, MA, 1982.
Doniol, H. *Histoire de la participation de la France à l'établissement des Etats-Unis de l'Amérique*, Paris, 1886–89, 5 vols.
Doyle, W. 'The Parlements of France and the Breakdown of the Old Regime, 1771–1788', *French Historical Studies*, 6, 1970, 415–58.
Doyle, W. *The Parlement of Bordeaux and the End of the Old Regime, 1771–1790*, London, 1974.
Doyle, W. *The Origins of the French Revolution*, Oxford, 1980.
Droz, J. F. X. *Histoire du règne de Louis XVI . . .*, Brussels, 1839.
Dull, J. *The French Navy and American Independence: A Study of Arms and Diplomacy, 1774–1787*, Princeton, NJ, 1975.
Dunlop, I. *Marie-Antoinette*, London, 1993.
Dunn, S. *The Deaths of Louis XVI*, Princeton, NJ, 1994.
Echeverria, D. *The Maupeou Revolution*, Baton Rouge, LA, 1985.
Egret, J. *Louis XV et l'opposition parlementaire*, Paris, 1970.
Egret, J. *Necker*, Paris, 1975.

Egret, J. *The French Pre-Revolution, 1787–1788*, trans. W. D. Camp, Chicago and London, 1977.

Fay, B. *Louis XVI ou la fin d'un monde*, Paris, 1955.

Flammermont, J. *Négociations secrètes de Louis XVI et du baron de Breteuil avec la cour de Berlin (décembre 1791–juillet 1792)*, Paris, 1885.

Girault de Coursac, P. *L'Education d'un roi: Louis XVI*, Paris, 1972.

Girault de Coursac, P. and P. *Louis XVI, roi martyr?*, Paris, 1976.

Girault de Coursac, P. and P. *Enquête sur le procès du roi Louis XVI*, Paris, 1982.

Girault de Coursac, P. and P. *Sur la route de Varennes*, Paris, 1984.

Grosclaude, P. *Malesherbes*, Paris, 1961.

Hardman, J. *Louis XVI*, New Haven and London, 1993.

Hardman, J. *French Politics, 1774–1789: From the Accession of Louis XVI to the Fall of the Bastille*, London and New York, 1995.

Hardman, J. *Robespierre*, London and New York, 1999.

Harris, R. D. *Necker: Reform Statesman of the Ancien Régime*, Berkeley, CA, 1979.

Harris, R. D. *Necker in the Revolution of 1789*, London, 1986.

Jaurès, J. *Histoire socialiste de la Révolution française*, Paris, 1923, 6 vols.

Jordan, D. *The King's Trial*, Berkeley, CA, and London, 1979.

Klinckwostrom, R. M. *Le Comte de Fersen et la cour de France*, Paris, 1878, 2 vols.

Labourdette, J. F. *Vergennes*, Paris, 1990.

Laugier, L. *Turgot ou le mythe des réformes*, Paris, 1979.

Lever, E. *Louis XVI*, Paris, 1985.

Lucas, C. 'Nobles, Bourgeois and the Origins of the French Revolution', *Past and Present*, 60, 1973, 84–126.

Mansell, P. *The Court of France, 1789–1830*, Cambridge, 1988.

Michelet, J. *Histoire de la Révolution française*, ed. G. Walter, 1952, 2 vols.

Michelet, J. *History of the French Revolution*, trans. C. Cocks, Chicago, 1967.

Mortimer-Ternaux, M. *Histoire de la Terreur, 1792–1794*, Paris, 1863, 8 vols.

Price, M. 'The "Ministry of the Hundred Hours": A Reappraisal', *French History*, 4:3, 1990, 317–39.

Price, M. *Preserving the Monarchy: The comte de Vergennes, 1774–1787*, Cambridge, 1995.

Reinhard, M. *10 août 1792: la chute de la royauté*, Paris, 1969.

Schapiro, B. M. *Revolutionary Justice in Paris, 1789–1790*, Cambridge, 1993.

Scott, S. F. *The Response of the Royal Army to the French Revolution . . . 1787–93*, Oxford, 1973.

Soboul, A. (ed.) *Le Procès de Louis XVI*, Paris, 1966.

Sorel, A. *L'Europe et la Révolution française*, vol. II, *La Chute de la royauté*, Paris, 1908.

Sorel, A. *Europe and the French Revolution: The Political Traditions of the Old Regime*, trans. and ed. A. Cobban and J. W. Hunt, London, 1969.

Stone, B. *The Parlement of Paris, 1774–1789*, Chapel Hill, NC, 1981.

Swann, J. *Politics and the Parlement of Paris under Louis XV, 1754–1774*, Cambridge, 1995.

Tocqueville, A. de *Coup d'oeil sur le règne de Louis XVI*, Paris, 1850.

Tocqueville, A. de *The Ancien Régime and the French Revolution*, London, ed. H. Brogan, 1966.

Trotsky, L. *History of the Russian Revolution*, trans. M. Eastman, London, 1967, 3 vols.

Walzer, M. *Regicide and Revolution*, Cambridge, 1974.

Chronology

1754
Birth of the future Louis XVI to the dauphin Louis-Ferdinand, only son of Louis XV, and Marie-Josèphe of Saxony. He is christened Louis-Auguste and created duc de Berry.

1756
The 'diplomatic revolution' (treaty of alliance between France and its hereditary enemy Austria).

1757
Crushing French defeat at Rossbach makes the new alliance unpopular.

1758
Publication of Voltaire's *Candide*.

1761
Death of the dauphin's eldest son, the duc de Bourgogne, leaves Louis-Auguste the ultimate heir to the throne.

1762
Publication of Rousseau's *Du contrat social*.

1763
Humiliating Peace of Paris: France cedes Canada and control of India to England.

1765
Louis-Auguste becomes dauphin on the death of his father.

1766
Louis-Auguste begins his diary.

1767
Death of Louis-Auguste's mother.

1770
Marriage of Louis-Auguste to the archduchess Maria Antonia, daughter of the Empress Maria Theresa; dismissal of Choiseul; Maupeou's disciplinary edict against Parlement wins approval of the new dauphin.

1771
Maupeou remodels the *parlements*.

1774
Death of Louis XV from smallpox and accession of Louis-Auguste as Louis XVI; the new king recalls the comte de Maurepas who soon becomes unofficial prime minister. On Maurepas's advice Louis appoints Turgot finance minister and recalls the exiled Parlement. Turgot abolishes internal customs barriers to the circulation of corn.

1775
First shots fired in the struggle between England and its American colonies.
April–May
'Flour war' bloodily suppressed by Louis and Turgot.
June
Malesherbes appointed minister for the household (Interior).

1776
March
Turgot's six edicts commuting the *corvée*, abolishing Parisian craft guilds etc. registered in Parlement by *lit de justice*.
May
Louis authorizes the secret payment of 1,000,000 livres to the American colonists; dismissal of Turgot, the obstacle to naval rearmament, and resignation of Malesherbes.
July
Declaration of American independence.

October
Necker made director-general of the royal treasury.

1777
Necker becomes director-general of finances; American victory at Saratoga Springs.

1778
Bavarian succession dispute; France enters American war on side of colonists; birth of a daughter to Louis and Marie-Antoinette; Necker sets up a pilot provincial administration in Berry.

1779
France mediates in Austro-Prussian dispute over the Bavarian succession and avoids war on two fronts. Necker sets up a second assembly at Montauban.

1780
Necker freezes the amount raised by the *taille*: any increase has to be registered in the Parlement.

1781
February
Publication of Necker's *Compte rendu*, falsely suggesting that royal finances are in surplus, despite the war's having been financed by loans rather than taxes.
May
Resignation of Necker.
October
Decisive Franco-American victory at Yorktown; birth of a dauphin secures the succession and enhances Marie-Antoinette's authority.
November
Death of Maurepas; Louis leaves his office of *chef du conseil royal* vacant and begins his personal rule.

1782
French naval defeat at The Saints.

1783
January
Peace preliminaries signed with England; France makes modest gains which, however, met her war aims.

October
Credit crisis ruins the finance minister d'Ormesson's attempt to end tax-farming.
November
Panicked, Louis replaces d'Ormesson by Calonne.

1784
Louis purchases Saint-Cloud for Marie-Antoinette without consulting Calonne.

1784/85
France mediates the Austro-Dutch dispute over free navigation of the Scheldt; signature in November 1785 of the Treaty of Fontainebleau between France and Holland, England's traditional ally, marks the highpoint of Louis XVI's diplomacy.

1785
March
Queen gives birth to the duc de Normandie.
August
Arrest of Cardinal Rohan and start of the Diamond Necklace Affair.
December
Louis castigates the Parlement for criticizing Calonne's administration.

1786
May
Acquittal of Rohan by the Parlement.
August
Louis visits the enlarged port of Cherbourg, his brainchild; Calonne presents him with plans for the overhaul of the fiscal and administrative structure of the regime.
December
Louis, expecting resistance from the Parlement, announces the convocation of an Assembly of Notables to endorse Calonne's programme.

1787
February–May
Notables reject Louis's reform programme; he is forced to dismiss Calonne and appoint Brienne, who has acted as 'leader of

the Opposition' in the Notables. Traumatized, Louis eats and hunts more and becomes dependent on Marie-Antoinette.

September
Anglo-Prussian invasion of Holland. Brienne declines to defend France's ally because of the financial situation. Collapse of Louis XVI's diplomacy causes a further deterioration of the internal situation.

1788
8 May
Coup d'état against the Parlement leads to widespread disaffection, especially in Brittany and Dauphiné.

August
Convocation of Estates-General promised for 1789; Brienne replaced by Necker.

September
Recalled Parlement insists that Estates be summoned according to the forms of 1614.

December
Résultat du conseil grants double representation to Third Estate and many constitutional concessions, though Louis intends to retain the initiative in legislation.

1789
Elections to the Estates-General by near universal manhood suffrage.

February
Publication of Siéyès's *Qu'est-ce que le tiers-état?*

5 May
Louis opens the Estates at Versailles; conflict between the orders.

3 June
Death of the dauphin; duc de Normandie becomes dauphin.

17 June
Third Estate declares itself the National Assembly.

20 June
Tennis Court oath not to separate until the Assembly had given France a constitution.

23 June
Louis attempts to mediate conflict in a *séance royale*.

July
Armed rising in Paris culminates in storming of the Bastille; Louis visits Paris to endorse the Revolution. Organization of a citizens' militia (National Guard) throughout France.

July–August
Peasant disturbances.
4–11 August
Decrees abolishing feudal rights and personal and provincial privilege.
25 August
Declaration of Rights.
5–6 October
October Days, royal family forcibly brought to Paris and installed in the Tuileries.
November
Churchlands nationalized and issue of *assignats* decreed.
December
Property qualifications decreed for voters and deputies.

1790
Spread of Jacobin network.
June
Abolition of nobility.
June–October
Royal family allowed to stay at Saint-Cloud.
July
Civil Constitution of the Clergy.
August
Mutiny at Nancy crushed by Bouillé; Louis congratulates him and tells him to 'look after your popularity; it may be very useful to me and to the kingdom'.
September
Parlements abolished.
November
Decree to enforce the clerical oath.

1791
April
Aborted Saint-Cloud departure; death of Mirabeau; Pope condemns Civil Constitution.
20/21 June
Louis escapes from Paris with the hope of renegotiating the constitution from Montmédy. Stopped at Varennes, he is brought back to Paris and suspended from his functions.
July
Champ de Mars 'massacre' precedes slight revision of the constitution in king's favour.

September
Louis accepts new constitution; Constituent Assembly replaced by Legislative Assembly.
November
Decrees against *émigrés* and non-juring priests vetoed by king.
December
Girondins press for war against Austria to reveal Louis as a traitor.

1792
January
Louis secures the dispersal of *émigré* troop formations in Trier.
March
Louis appoints a Girondin ministry.
April
Declaration of war on Austria.
June
Louis vetoes decrees against non-juring priests and setting up an armed camp at Paris to intimidate him; dismissal of Girondin ministry and occupation of the Tuileries.
July
11 'Patrie en danger' declaration.
27 Sections declared in permanent session.
29 Robespierre calls for king's deposition.
August
1 Robespierre calls for election of National Convention.
10 Fall of the monarchy.
13 Royal family imprisoned in the Temple.
September
2 Fall of Verdun to Prussians.
2–6 Prison massacres at Paris.
20 Prussian defeat at Valmy.
21 Convention meets. Declaration of the Republic.
November
Victory at Jemappes and French occupation of Belgium; discovery of the 'armoire de fer' in the Tuileries.
December
Trial of Louis; king separated from his family.

1793
21 January
Execution of the king.

Index